You Got Maled!

"Volume 1"

The Survival Guide to
Laughing Your Way Through
The Crazy World of Online Dating,
and Beyond...

Unfortunately, based on a true story.

STORY & PHOTOS BY:

Robin Roth

ISBN: 979-8-9854012-5-7 (hardback)
　　　 979-8-9854012-6-4 (paperback)
　　　 979-8-9900604-1-8 (ebook)

IMPORTANT DISCLAIMER, WAIVER AND RELEASE OF RIGHTS

harmless the Book Originators, collectively and individually, each of their predecessors and their respective officers, directors, employees, agents, representatives, successors and assigns (hereinafter collectively referred to as the "Releasees") from all actions, claims, causes of action, suits, liabilities or obligations of any kind whatsoever in law or in equity, that now exist or may hereafter accrue based on matters now unknown as well as known, and matters unanticipated as well as anticipated, which the Reader and its heirs successors and assigns can, shall or may have against the Releasees, upon or by reason of any matter or thing set out in the Book occurring from the beginning of time up to the date of this Release.

Each Reader and each of its heirs, successors and assigns expressly waives the benefit of any statute or rule of law, which, if applied to this Release, would otherwise exclude from its binding effect any claim not known by ROBIN ROTH, such Reader on the date of reading any portion, or being informed by third parties, of any portion of this Book.

The Reader and each of its heirs, successors or assigns further agree not to bring, continue or maintain any claim or legal proceeding against the Releasees before any court, administrative agency, or other forum by reason of any matters hereby released.

Each Reader confirms that it (i) understands all aspects of this Disclaimer, Waiver and Release, (ii) has had sufficient time to review it (and with its attorney), (iii) voluntarily agrees to all the terms in this Disclaimer, Waiver and Release; and (iv) voluntarily agrees to be bound by all the terms of this Disclaimer, Waiver and Release.

This Disclaimer, Waiver and Release shall be binding upon the undersigned and its successors and assigns and shall inure to the benefit of each of the Releasees and their respective successors and assigns. This Release is made and entered into in the State of Nevada and shall be in all respects governed under the laws of said state.

THINK BEFORE YOU BUY.

If you don't accept this DISCLAIMER, WAIVER AND RELEASE IN ALL RESPECTS, THEN PLEASE DO NOT PURCHASE OR READ THIS BOOK.

All Fictional Characters: All Characters referenced in this Book are fictional and do not reference anyone living or deceased. Any similarity of any Character in this Book to any living or deceased Person is purely coincidental.

Dedication

I thank you, my beloved parents, for being the greatest mom & dad who ever lived. You far and away surpassed the parental bar of excellence. My remarkable, extraordinary parents, you remain a constant source of love, support, and my forever North. You are eternally missed, loved, and cradled in my heart, always. I'm so blessed to have had you as my parents!

And I praise you, my spectacular children, Jennifer, and Chloe, for your infinite love, encouragement, and inspiration. Thank you for your constant sarcastic rolling eyes of judgment, helpful tips on what it really is to be a cool mom, and above all, your humor. You girls make me see the comedy of life in every way possible and bring a wealth of true-life events to keep us laughing endlessly. I am grateful for your friendship, support, and your astonishing wisdom and spirituality. I am immensely proud of the women you have both become. I love you beyond love, and I could not conceivably cherish you more. My precious daughters, you are my world and the love and light in my life! You make me whole, and I thank you for letting me be your mommy. I also dedicate this book to your fantastical children: Hadley & Jacob, Devorah, Chaya, & Levi, and all their children and children's children to follow.

Love and appreciation to my treasured friends: Shara, Elizabeth, Lynn, Geri, Joyce, Barbara, Shino, Richie, Fred, Frances, Robin, Adonis, Roberto, Shaina, Rachel, Josh, Linda, Stephanie, Aimee, Fred, Michael, Debbie, Giuditta, Angela, Melinda, Beth, Janet, Corrine, Jill, David, Lucrezia, Jeffrey, Sandy, Glynnis, Claudia, Estella, Merril, Andrea, Roberto, and Giuliana. Thank you, my dear friends, for your never-ending love, incredible memories, and your immeasurable support. You've gifted my world with unimaginable balance, laughter, fun, and joy throughout our many years of friendship and the many trials and tribulations of life. I am grateful for the gift of your friendship today, tomorrow, and evermore!

Table of Contents

Dedication v

Introduction ix

1. I Believe 1

2. Entering into "The World of Crazy!".........................7

3. Getting Started 22

4. The Strutting Egomaniac 41

5. Back to the Drawing Board Beginning to Date 54

6. The Italian Guy from Napoli 64

7. The Nice Guys...95

8. More Crazy Dates!... 116

9. Staying the Course 134

10. More Nice Guys 142

11. Taking a Break from the Insanity!....................... 171

12. On Assignment in Rio 182

13. Don't Cry for Me Argentina................................ 200

14. Back Home in the Online Saddle 214

15. Hold Everything, Dammit!....................................228

16. About My True Love. "The One!" 257

17. Alas, the Guy with Extreme Idiosyncrasies.....................264

18. Dating is No Bed of Daisies 276

19. The Guy with Extreme Peculiarities 295

20. Bobble Drew Part 1 311

21. Bobble Drew Part 2 343

Wait, Hold On! There's More!...353

Epilogue...357

In Summation..357

About the Author 359

Introduction

And just like that, there it was. I, Mollie Sloan, a successful, well-known news reporter, was at last ready to fall in love. I'm speaking of the deep, passionate, sappy, all-consuming, unconditional, gag me with a stick, forever type of love. I mean, the way over the top, love. And proud of it!

On a beautiful, sunny spring morning, I decided that it was finally time to settle down and find *"The One."* You know, "The One!" "The One," who has you at, *"Where have you been all my life?"* Also known as the ultra-trite phrase… *"You had me at hello!"* You know? "The One" you dreamed about and searched for your entire life. Frequently known by the other trite phrase, *"You complete me!"* The love of your life you are supposed to be with as in, *"And they lived happily ever after."* The one you love so deeply, but understandably feel petrified introducing him to your crazy family! The one who will lovingly tell you when your mascara is dripping down your face, when your hair extensions are showing, or when you have something stuck in your teeth. The one who remains calm, even when the Internet goes down! This easy, uncomplicated, stress-free pursuit of finding "The One," would no doubt be easy-peasy! Like, ya know… a piece of cake. Positively, a piece of *wedding cake*, that is!

I confidently and optimistically predicted I would unequivocally be married by the end of the year. No problemo!

You see now, that's the funny thing about predictions. Unless you are an authentic soothsayer, with mystical powers for predicting future prophesies like Nostradamus, they will typically be *wrong*. However, I carelessly didn't predict *which year* I'd marry. Hate when that happens.

Fast forward to the end of that year and my mistakenly predicted wedding date. Shit, buggers, drats, and foiled again. I staggered to think, how was it even possible that I was still single? What a disappointing, horrible realization. This was supposed to be a piece of cake! Wasn't it? Hello? There's no cake! I don't even have a cupcake! Not even a cookie!

So, there I was searching and dating online for over half a year. In eight months (which felt like forever and a day) all I accomplished was arduously rummaging through a countless number of, *"Totally wrong men!"* No, no, really, please try to *feel* my painful despair. I went out with men who were the bottom feeders and pond scum of the male species. I went out with the "gross, mucous, and pus that grow on the slimy Candida Fungus" class of men. They were all, *"Beyond the Totally Wrong Men!"*

I am thoroughly positive that all of you out there reading this right now are shaking your heads from your own disastrous personal understanding and dating experiences. I also sense your validation of my unreliable soothsaying abilities that shockingly failed me so miserably.

To no avail or lack of intense motivation and outrageous efforts on my part, there was *NO,* enormous diamond ring on my finger! There was *NO,* "Say yes to the spectacular dress!" There were *NO,* debates or decisions to be made about the gorgeous wedding ceremony and its heavenly beachfront destination. I could not begin to fathom how there were *NO*, expensive save-the-dates and stunning wedding invitations. How was it feasible that there was *NO*, picking out exquisite, costly flowers? Why wasn't I tasting and selecting that outrageously overpriced eight-tier wedding cake, with fresh exotic flowers and Irish lace between each layer? Last, but not least, there was *NO*, planning or discussions over the extravagant honeymoon around the world, for which I hoped to lose 10 pounds to go on! I was trapped in the universe of *"No, No, and No!"* What a major conundrum! There wasn't even that *"knot"* I was supposed to tie. My universe and belief system were turned upside down. I never would have believed this could realistically happen. Holy shit and more shit!

To be honest, there wasn't a glimmer of anyone realistically completing me. Sadly, there wasn't even a hint of "You had me at hello." For that matter, there also wasn't the hope of saying, "Where have you been all my life?" I was miffed. I was flabbergasted. No correction. I was absolutely, clearly shocked, understandably pissed, and traumatized. This was an unexpected, desultory predicament to find myself in. Especially after eight months. Ha, little did I know then!

Seriously, what was going on here? How could this be my reality? In what dimension was this conceivably happening to me? I ask, confused. Where the hell are my damn wedding bells? Even more horrifying, I don't see or hear those damn bells, even from a far-off distance! Where are my ding-dong wedding bells? Dammit, surely, they should be ringing by now!

So then, why is it, when I *was not* ready to meet "The One" and settle down, I met the greatest, in every possible way, ideal men? You know, the perfect marriage material, guys. The ultimate winners from head to toe! The men I'd want my family and friends to meet! Although fearful that they might run off leaving skid marks because my clan is a tad *insane* and a little dysfunctional. Come on, there used to be a gaggle of these guys. For the life of me, I couldn't wrap my head around the gloomy, discouraging realization of "How on earth is this possible?" I begged the question, "Where did all the good ones go?" Perhaps begged is a little too harsh. I might have only implored the question. No, wait, hold on a minute. No, I did essentially beg! Out loud, in fact.

I cannot accept nor assume that "The good ones," all quietly disappeared to another galaxy or planet far, far away. I couldn't imagine all the wonderful, eligible men gathering in the middle of the night and then, suddenly, they all jumped into a menacing black hole. As in, "OK now guys, one, two, three, jump!" Oh, come on now...

I also can't consider that "All the great guys" simply got married? With this ring, I thee wed, ding-dong *wedding bells,* and all? (My Bells!) Did I miss the memo reporting there was an outbreak of pregnant women and the nice guys had to do the right thing and marry them? Did I miss the breaking news headline that a major war had broken out? And ironically, only single men were drafted and wanted to go off to war as married men? Hell, this can't be right I *proposed* with a red, white, & blue patriotic sigh.

By the way, where was the man that was supposed to do just that? *"Propose!"*

After enduring online dating past my failed projected wedding date, I wondered with a sense of urgency. "Am I the only one going through all of this insanity?" Really, am I alone here? Or dare I dread to imagine, *"Is this just a 'Me' thing?"* Must I find a gypsy to conjure up a forbidden love elixir, a magic spell, or a romance potion? Voilà and Poof!

As a journalist, I interviewed a myriad of women and men on the dating topic. Most were normal, others, after dating, leaned towards not so much. Thus, here are the 7 continuously asked questions that unite us all.

1. "Is all of this 'Batshit crazy' just happening to me?"
2. "Am I the only one experiencing all of these crazy, dramatic, and *way-out-there* people?"
3. "Are other women and men going through these ludicrous, outrageous incidents, too?"
4. "Is there actually someone even out there for me, or am I just wasting my time?"
5. "Will I ever find my soul mate, or will I simply be alone forever?"
6. "It's all too weird to deal with. Should I flat out and out, give up?"
7. "I wonder if I should just accept and settle for the *wrong one*?

Ultimately, after gathering all my scientific research, I wish to provide some answers to the entire community of frustrated and bewildered single women, men, and others everywhere. To the above questions, I answer for you profoundly and firmly...

1. No!
2. No!
3. Yes!
4. Most Likely and No!
5. Most Likely and No!!
6. No!
7. No!

Those 7 captivating questions were the impetus and the driving force, which motivated and inspired me to write this book. I wanted to bring reassurance, truth, and, most importantly, comic relief to each one of those questions and more. I felt it was my journalistic civic duty and moral imperative to do so.

For all the single people tirelessly searching for "The One," well then, I broadcast emphatically once and for all…

"You Are Not Alone!"

It was astounding to discover there was radically more than a scintilla of truth and clear evidence proving this fact! So, wipe away the puzzled, pained, perplexed expressions that woefully linger upon your faces. I will not obfuscate the truth in any way. Hence, know this fact… "We Are All Going Through It!" Therefore, I send my utmost compassion to all of you confused daters and assuredly state once again… *"No, nope, nada…* **You Are Not Alone!"** Go put a pin in that.

Gosh, can't you just hear that song in your ear right now? You will undoubtedly find yourself hearing many of Michael's iconic songs while dating. Like, "Thriller, Beat It, Bad, Leave Me Alone, Scream, Dangerous, and Smile," way more than you would ever want, need, or care to.

Clearly, we've all endured and suffered ridiculous dating dramas, both off and online. AKA: PTSDD. *("Post-Traumatic Stress Dating Disorder!")* Yes, I made this syndrome up. I had to for the sake of medical advancement. Let me tell ya, I did the legwork & earned the right to do so.

One of the most important pieces of guidance I can offer anyone that cares to know… "It's OK to be extremely selective!" Please hear me when I state, *"Don't Settle!"* Because if you do, and take my word, there is no mistaking the statistic, you will be back online, combing the dreaded dating sites once again in no time at all. That is… for sure, for sure!

I'm not a gambler. You see, if I put down my hard-earned dollars, the least I expect to get is a designer outfit, a pair of couture shoes with a lovely matching bag, and all of it on sale! Regrettably, all dating, in a sense, is gambling. But without the tables, slot machines, angry faces because you didn't anti-up quickly, the grandiose screams of winning and losing, or the fabulous fashion and great shoes. You'll no doubt be screaming, though! Like a lot! The debate is still out on whether dating or gambling has the greater odds of winning. Honestly, for me, it's a toss-up.

Nowadays, we are all enormously busy. In our fast-paced world, sadly, this avenue of dating is one of our best and yet worst options. No matter what, don't give up on your search for love with that special person you'll cherish, as they will hopefully cherish you. *"The One,"* is there waiting and most assuredly buried unpretentiously at the bottom of all the codswallop. I reiterate, the very bottom of the huge mountain of garbage.

Keep in mind, "Cynicism chases away optimism!" OK, for real, that quote is such rubbish. Go right ahead. Be cynical. Enjoy yourself and bask in it. Complain, bitch, and moan all you want to your friends. It could essentially help to vent, and you have nothing to lose. Surprisingly, it might add a whimsical touch to your agonizing dating torment.

By the way, *be yourself completely!* Your true love should know the real you from the very beginning. "The One" needs to find out all your good, your bad, your ugly, and everything in between. It's a friendlier way of saying, to discover your weird, strange, and eccentric qualities. You're special and your future mate should know it. As a matter of fact, he should sincerely love and adore all those things about you.

Because I know that you will absolutely wonder...
It's now necessary for me to Make This Important Disclosure.

"You Got Maled!" is not merely *based* on a true story. *It is* a true story. Most of this book is *non-fiction*, with true-life stories that happened in real-time. All the good stuff, and by that, I mean the *"Oh My God, crazy, outrageous, shocking, messed up, and are you fucking kidding me," stuff,* all transpired! Seventy-five percent (maybe more) of the events literally occurred and the rest, by my calculations, twenty-five percent, are pure fiction. That quick calculation came as a result of 9-years of college (counting grad school), endless student loans, and some occasional weed. But like Bill Clinton, "I never inhaled!" *Wink-wink.* There was lots of flowing alcohol, mostly tequila and cheap wine from a box, which for 3 years was bought with a fake ID. And let's not forget the billions of study hours (groan) and too numerous to count innocent frat parties. Whoo-Hoo! Well, they could have been innocent, you know? Hey, don't judge me!

As you continue to read, naturally they'll be many times you will understandably doubt that I am writing any probability or semblance of the truth. I imagine you will surely be thinking... "Yeah, right." "No Waaaaaay." And "Oh, of course. That must be the 25 percent fiction part!" Most definitively, those are positively the parts that for sure transpired. I, being a compassionate girl, changed all the characters' real names. I did so to protect, to be kind, and in rare cases, to shield the innocent. Moreover, my lawyer insisted on it!

It's a given you will go out with many of the same types of people I have written about. Hopefully, this will bring you much-needed comfort, while proving again that you are not alone. You'll unquestionably identify with and relate to my stories. I fear my demeanor towards several of these online men might be pejorative at times. To that, I say with an unashamed, sneering smirk, "Oh, frickin' well!" You must trust me when I justify in my defense, *"They totally, completely, and entirely had it coming!"*

Above all, and in a positive therapeutic way, the primary purpose of this book is to *"Make You Laugh!"* I felt it was vital to help you see the irony and with any luck, add some humor and comedy to the dramedy of it all. Trust me, you'll experience more drama than in any Broadway play!

My objective is to educate and bring you crucial knowledge, insight, and direction. I strived to share some informative, relevant, optimistic awareness and wisdom, which you can apply to your own dating experiences. All the while, I implore you to always keep your eyes wide open. I aspired to caution you about the probable and endless pitfalls hiding beneath the surface of online dating. Primarily, I was determined to focus on guiding all of you, seekers of love, in an amusing 'LMFAO' fashion. I can assure you that if you don't laugh your way across this journey, I guarantee you will go completely berserk, if not entirely mad.

Understand because I am a *reporter,* I will pretty much tell it like it is. I will not attempt to sugarcoat it for you in any way. If I don't shoot from the hip, how could I honestly guide you? If the sound of this worries, scares, or hurts your feelings in the least, then for sure, don't even attempt to go online. I am the *"SuperCaliFragilistic"* Mary Poppins, and the Good Witch reincarnated, compared to what you'll witness and endure out there amidst the forest of wolves, in the insane world of dating. This isn't a place for the innocent "Little Red Riding Hood" types. Accordingly, fill your basket of goodies with balls of courage, and I'm talking big ones!

I hope to inspire, motivate, encourage, cheer you on, hold your hand, help you troubleshoot, and keep an optimistic energy while offering fun, healthy laughter throughout. My educational tutorial about everything concerning on-and-offline dating, love, life, and my shoulder to cry on is well worth reading this book. For you men, it will provide an enlightening, instructional experience. You will benefit greatly by sticking with it until the last page. Fair warning though guys, you might find it offensive at times. You might even rip the pages out and throw them on the floor as you read, saying out loud, "Fuck this stupid book! This is total bullshit!" That's cool with me. But keep reading because you can learn a thing, or two, or more. Try to be open. After all, love is the prize, isn't it? But dude, if you really hate the book, don't throw it away! Go ahead and repurpose it. It is the perfect size to put under any table to keep it from wobbling!

I fancy and consider this novel to be my version of an "Oprah Winfrey, Master Class." I trust my stories will provide men, women, green and purple aliens alike, with comfort, giggles, and a sense of camaraderie during your dating adventures. "Adventures?" Huh, such a darling way of saying "Hell!" Gee, who knows, you might theoretically find online dating entertaining and fun. Or perchance, even like it. Wow, that idea scares me!

Sometimes, we must climb over an intimidating wall, or a *Twilight Zone Tower of Terror* to find love on the other side. We might have to travel to the ends of the earth in pursuit of love. I must emphasize, throughout your search, *Never Stop Being, "You!"* You're the only person in the world *like you*. Appreciate that you are unique and deserve all your romantic dreams to come true. Search for what you want and need, and for all the things that will make you happy.

This is about you! So don't let go of your desires. Stick to your guns. In the immortal words of the great Scott Stabile... "Don't worry if you're making waves simply by being yourself. The moon does it all the time!"

I hope my personal stories foster gobs of fortitude and enthusiastic, courageous boo-yah! Dating is a constant whirlwind and a tornado of tumultuous sagas. After one of these storms, remain cool, smile, wipe yourself off, brush your wind-blown hair, and ease on down the road!

Also, be aware when searching for love, you will enter a world of total uncertainty. Nevertheless, do go on and take that leap of uncertain faith! Ergo, strap on your sanity belt, for you should know that you're in for a daring climb and a wild and crazy ride. But after all, how bad could it be? Okay, sorry, that was indeed a daring, stupid, and foolish comment...

To those who have already ventured into this chilling and menacing world of online dating (or any form of dating, for that matter), hang in there. For I promise you, it gets so much worse! Yes, indeed, you just heard me giggling. Hopefully, you shall too. However, don't give up. Remember, you need to fight your way through the battles to reach the joys of victory. And you will!

To all the seekers of love out there who haven't yet begun the online dating circus and home of the courting clowns, I want you to jump into the crazy game with zeal and courage, pushing all boundaries fully armed and guns loaded. Hmm, the NRA would totally love that concept.

To those of you beginners out there who say, *"Ha-ha-Ha-ha-ha! Whatever?"* *To you clueless fools,* I fiercely respond, giggling again with, *"All righty then... I wish you Godspeed and stacks of it!"*

Here is the part where I tell you, if it doesn't work out, you can freak the hell out, all you want if it helps. Afterward, go throw on a tiara, and have a margarita, with a big bucket of popcorn, and oodles of chocolate. For real, that pretty much fixes just about everything. Temporarily, anyway.

One final thought. In the world of dating, you will undoubtedly come across many lovely people. It's perfectly fine to go have fun with them, even if they are not your someone special. On the contrary, I've also included in this book, many types of people who will, for sure, not be your forever person. The purpose of this is not only to make you laugh (I hope), but for you to learn why, who, how, and what to avoid in your search for "The One."

In conclusion, my main objective is to save you time, disappointment, and heartache. Embrace the fact your excitement and fervor will not go unnoticed.

Hey, in the illustrious, famous words of Obi-Wan Kenobi...
"Remember, the Force will be with you, always."

Fiddle-dee-dee. *One can always hope! Right?*

NOW… READ ON!

P.S. Well actually, it's more of a warning…

IF BAD LANGUAGE OFFENDS YOU, PUT THE BOOK DOWN! NOW! Right now, or you'll seriously NOT be ok continuing on.

CHAPTER 1

I Believe

AKA, CHILDHOOD DREAMS, CHILDISH DELUSIONS, A LOT OF AH-HA, & ALL SPRINKLED WITH WHATEVER!

Before getting into all my hilarious, insane, true dating stories, I must jump back in time before all the "*crazy*" began.

I believe in true love! As a matter of fact, I have imagined it since I was an innocent little girl. Being extremely naïve as a child, I faithfully and continuously believed in the concept of *never-ending true love*. I realize that, on topics of the heart, my childish head was somewhat up in the clouds. I mean way up there! But, hey, that's who I am to this very day and why I single-handedly define the phrase "*Hopeless Romantic.*"

You see, (disagreeing with the *Barbie Movie*) I was that little girl who sincerely trusted and firmly understood that "Barbie and Ken" were madly in love with all their little plastic hearts and souls. Historically, and for all eternity, they are the happiest couple in the entire toy world! I can still remember it now. When gossip went around my playgroup that Ken liked Midge and other synthetic girl dolls better, and the news leaked out that he was *cheating* on Barb... *Wow*, and there it was! That was the very first time I ever used the word *bullshit*. Whatever the hell, '*CHEATING*' was! This is a detail I recollect vividly. Since both of my brothers ratted me out to my parents and told on me with merriment. Aha, that happened. Regardless, that's a whole other book entirely, not to be conflated or confused with this one.

Next came the hateful and deceitful rumors. They went viral like weeds growing in a jungle, that Ken was, in fact, gay. I didn't care! So what? Whatever, whatever, whatever! *Ken was the greatest boy doll ever. No matter what the hell, 'GAY' meant!* It didn't matter to me, not one iota! So very "*tabloid-esque*," I thought to myself. I was a freethinker even back then. All I knew, without a question of a doubt, was my Barbie and Ken were absolutely, undeniably enveloped in "romantic, eternal doll love!" Ken belonged only to Barbie… "*Period!*"

And just like that, life happened and sorrowfully when I turned 12, *I got mine.* That was about the time my once-cherished Barbie and Ken went into a drawer, attic, goodwill, or whatever sadistic thing my tattletale brothers did with them. O-M-Gosh, just speculating about what became of my beloved Barbie & Ken makes me cringe sadly, even now. Big sigh!

Nevertheless, I nostalgically kept my Teddy Ruxpin, Sally Secrets, Furbies, Cabbage Patch Dolls, American Girl, and Care Bears even after my heartless male siblings fed them to the dog to chew off several body parts. They are both vicious doll abusers! There should be a "*Picking-on-your-sister's-dolls, jail,*" for these common, malicious, and hardened, toy criminal siblings. When my parents punished them for their "*doll abuse,*" I tried explaining to them on several occasions. "Dad, *time-out* never works with them. It only gives them extra opportunities to conspire and come up with even more creative, spiteful, and mischievous antics!" I was a child, so my parents never listened to my wisdom. Even though we are all grown up, I never forgave my brothers for their cruel actions. Or their insensitive doll abuse, and *Texas Chain Saw Massacre*, slaughterhouse, behaviors.

My brothers will never be exonerated. Mostly because they continually bring up the countless cruel doll stories, still laughing at them (and at me), during all the family and friends' gatherings. Indubitably rude and so very callous! Though I admit with trepidation, I do go a little Linda Blair in "The Exorcist," or Sissy Spacek in "Carrie," when the entire family laughs along with them. "Oh, how macho and badass you both are, muscling innocent dolls and toys. Pitiful, you guys think you are so dope!"

It's funny how we all seem to retreat to our immature behaviors when our family reunites at our parent's house. One time, Jeffrey, Satin's spawn, and the more, evil one of my wicked brothers, retold a doll saga at a family Thanksgiving celebration. He laughed, glaring at me maliciously, stating, "Geeze, come on Mollie. Grant us reciprocity, and we'll stop!"

I snapped back. "No way. Gee-whiz, you both talk a lot of smack for grown-up little boys who don't admit to having been juvenile Pulp Fiction bullies." That is typically when a family member chimed in...

"OK you guys, you need to agree upon a little détente. For Pete's sake, this happened, like what? Like 100 years ago? Now, the three of you grow up already! What do you want Mollie, a plague upon both their houses?" That's when everyone roared with laughter, to my humiliation.

I mean, seriously, one can't take the sting out of something so traumatic as brothers messing with your cherished dolls. Well, unless they were Chucky or Annabelle Dolls, and no one was stupid enough to mess with them! Moreover, I will never grow up because it's important to keep the child within. Thus, my "Barbie and Ken, forever in love story" clearly substantiates that I'm an unrealistic, starry-eyed romantic. I admit proudly and unquestionably, guilty as charged. And as for my *"I'm telling mom & dad, brothers,"* a tiny plague upon both their houses would suffice nicely.

I'm compelled to interject something else interconnected here. During those tender years of childhood when I was playing with my limbless, half-eaten dolls, much chatter and whispering had been going around the playground that our elders were having *SEX!* With my "Ken, belonging only to Barbie philosophy and blatant innocence," I was also convinced that neither my parents nor their gross, old, grody-to-the-max, stupid friends ever had *sex!* Like seriously? Like Ever! So totally Ick! This completely yucky, fabricated, chin-wagging conversation was utterly revolting, and I meant it! Nnn-Kkk! *Whatever the hell 'SEX' was!* Gross.

As I began to grow up, still trusting in fairytales, I visualized in my head thoroughly what *'He'* (My Ken) would look like, just as most young girls do. Through my naïve, rose-colored eyes, he was hot in every sense of the word. Although, I am almost certain I didn't use the word *"hot"* back then when I was a lass! My man would have Mediterranean blue eyes, one a deeper shade of blue than the other, and thick brown, silky straight hair. How I simply adore that one strand of hair that always falls down his forehead, even though it drives him crazy. It makes me giggle when he attempts to blow it upwards with his lips puckered. He stands anywhere from five feet ten inches to six feet tall. His physique resembles the guy on the cover of GQ Magazine. I love his perfect body because it is the perfect body for me. I don't particularly like overly muscular guys. Just buff enough to recognize that he hits the gym periodically.

Even as a grown woman, I still believe in the unconditional mushy-gushy, fairytale, storybook, magical kind of love. I timidly confess that I wholeheartedly believe in the romantic Hollywood Movie type of quixotic love, but, without all the bad acting! Like… "The Notebook," "Somewhere in Time," "P.S. I love you," "Under the Tuscan Sun," "Sleepless in Seattle," "Titanic," "Ghost," "Casablanca," and "An Affair to Remember," idealistic films with sensitive portrayals of profound love.

Unrealistic as it is, I believe as well in the *"And they lived happily ever after"* declaration of love. I profess I long for that *"Great to be in love feeling"* and the *"I'm floating on air"* relationship. I can't stop myself from wanting to live in the *"Once upon a time"* and the *"Happy and carefree storybook existence!"* But then again, doesn't every girl? Indeed, even better when it comes with a fanciful diamond ring and tiara!

Yeah, I'm pathetic, and believe me, I'm well aware of it. Yet, all of us girls, I imagine, deep down, dream of the fairytale. I suppose we all, to some degree, desire a euphoric, enchanting, "Look at me, I can fly, love!" That love, which makes our knees weak. Honestly, Peter Pan, Superman, Iron Man, Wonder Woman, Mary Poppins, and others are still flying high.

My entire life, I was convinced that all those well-known corny movie phrases existed through genuine love. I concluded that those tender words of love and romance were only made fun of or mocked by those people who were bitter, jealous, and, unfortunately, never found or had faith in everlasting, unadulterated love. Like the movie *Titanic*…

"I'm king of the world! Winning that ticket, Rose, was the best thing that ever happened to me, for it brought me to you. Promise me you'll survive. That you won't give up, no matter what happens, no matter how hopeless. Promise me now, Rose, and never let go of that promise."

"I'll never let go, Jack."

All right, clearly, this will tear you up. Except here's the thing, Rose… If you had only shared that wooden plank bobbing in the water with Jack, he wouldn't have died, Rose! Beyotch! Oh, and while we are on that subject, why, in God's name, did you throw that priceless, 'Heart of The Ocean' blue diamond into the water before you died? That was so wasteful, stupid, and jewelry abuse. Seriously Rose, didn't your mother teach you not to throw diamonds into the ocean? OMG, Girl. I can't even!

With that said, I trust entirely in the concept of soul mates. And now, at long last, I was motivated and oh so very ready to find, "my Ken." I was fully prepared to fall in love. I mean, to fall deep down into the blinding tunnel of love! This decision was not merely a movie fantasy, but my future reality. I believed to the depths of my soul that "*The One*," is waiting somewhere out there for me. I have been Juliet, waiting for my Romeo to appear, and now he was so close that I could feel him. All my life, I've been falling in love with him, and finally, "*The meeting of our hearts*" was approaching. Thus, I enthusiastically entered the mysterious odyssey of love and the world of… **Online Dating and Beyond!**

Although apprehensive, I was fired up and all in! I felt a thrilling excitement, with all the passion and eagerness of your very first date, first kiss, the first or last day of school, getting your braces off, meeting your first love, graduating anything, getting a driver's license, turning 21, and of course, your first *great* sexual experience. Which, by definition, means "*Without faking it!*" *I was ecstatic and confident as I set off on my journey to find my true love. I sensed an electrifying energy racing through my entire* being with an exuberant sensation of, yes! Yes, and more Yes!

CHAPTER 2

Entering into "The World of Crazy!"
The Freak Show...

THE MAN WHO 'LOVES' HIS DOG
'WITH A KNICK-KNACK PADDY WHACK GIVE THIS GIRL A BONE?'

Let's begin this tale. I guess, to be more accurate, this little wagging tail? Wait. Hold on a second. Before I can continue, I need to grab a bottle of Riesling to relive any part of this, this, Dramarama! To be candid, I'm not quite sure what to call it. It's rather more of a Dogarama tailspin story.

OK, I'm back. I got the wine. Now, let's do this. (Sip, sip, sip.) It's been said, "Always remember the universe has a way of leading you to where you are supposed to be at the moment you're supposed to be there." Still, *as lovely as all that sounds,* sometimes the universe gets it wrong!

I'm ready to start the "Aubry, without an E" episode. Sip, sip, sip.

THE AUBRY CHAPTER...

Ah, yes, I remember Aubry. He was able to charm me long before I could detect the magnitude of his majestic weirdness. Being a journalist, I have experienced these types of men first-hand. So, permit me to inform you, "Those Aubry guys are extra frightening because they can fool you quickly and easily." Due to their quiet, laid-back nature, they can accomplish this feat effortlessly. On the outside, their demeanor seems soft-spoken, low-key, and passive, so they appear quite innocent. They don't disclose or divulge very much about themselves. This leads you to believe, for a while at least, that they are normal and perhaps merely shy. You know the type. We all do...

"He was a quiet man."

"He was our neighbor. He kept to himself, really."

"We all just assumed he was an ordinary, normal, peaceful guy."

"Good heavens? I never imagined he could kill anybody!"

"The kind of quiet type like that. Only without the murder and killing parts." *Sip, Sip, Sip... Extra sip!*

We spoke for several months before I agreed to fly clear across the map for Atlanta, to meet him. I accepted his generous invitation of a prepaid plane ticket and all, despite the big, bright, red, fluttering flags I will soon warn you about. You see, I too, don't always practice what I preach. Mind you, this was way before I learned everything I know now. Irrespective, I suppose this makes me somewhat of a hypocrite. Yet, as a result, theoretically, it also makes me the best one to guide you through this process and protect you from the raging storms of online devastation. "You're so welcome." So, again I repeat, *trust all the flags!* For example, that huge, telltale, beaming, red flag Aubry revealed when he explained to me while weeping over the phone. "Mollie, I've never gotten over the torment and harm I suffered from my 2nd-grade teacher, Miss Lilly. She traumatized me, making fun of my artwork in front of the entire class. It was a big class of 27 kids! I'm left feeling devastated and mortified to this day. After she put me through that horrible ordeal, I couldn't trust sharing my feelings or emotions with any-one ever again. Miss Lilly broke me! BTW, she did this to me many times and lots of other terrible things, too. Realize, Mollie, it's a big deal that I'm even sharing this story with you."

"Flag… Flag… Flagity… Faaa-Lag!!!!!!!!" (And, Sip, Sip, Sip…) I thought to *myself*, "Are you kidding me? That's it? That's your big, harrowing childhood woe? Like, oh man, Boo-hoo! Get over it, pal! Snap out of it. (Slap-Slap-Slap!) That happened over a lifetime ago! I have thousands of those childhood sagas with teachers who were insensitive bitches. Tales of anguish and shame, making Miss Lilly come off looking like Snow White! Perhaps Aubry might have been more balanced if only his mother had added that necessary *"E"* in his name… *Aubr'E'y*. Just saying, that's a possible diagnosis there. Dr. Meredith Grey, Dr. Gregory House, and Dr. Max Goodwin I am certain, would concur with me on this analysis.

Anyhow, I left on my journey to Atlanta with immense hope and excitement, nonetheless. I sensed I knew him well enough to stay at his house, but in the guest room, of course. Be careful with this one, sister daters. I was lucky, and it was fine. But I strongly warn you to be careful about staying at a man's residence early on. If you do, have backup plans.

Aubry graciously picked me up at the airport. I dressed casu-ally, wearing my skinny jeans, a cute fitted pink silk shirt, with a fabulous leather jacket and boots. Despite not being all dolled up & glitzy, I could see by the enormous smile on his face that he was pleased right away. He looked like his photos, but a not-so-good-looking version of them. Truthfully, I wasn't very attracted to him. Still, he had a sweet little boyish innocence and an inviting look about him. Though I was somewhat disappointed, I wasn't neces-sarily turned off. Surprisingly, I found his engaging persona subtly endearing. I was further intrigued as I noticed he had an adorable, deep-set dimple on each cheek. Therefore, I figured, what the hell? I was in Atlanta and chose to go with the flow and behave peachy sweet. After all, I was in Georgia, the Peach State. Plus, I had an important meeting there at the *number 1* rated *C*able *N*ews *N*etwork I freelance for.

Arriving at his residence in Buckhead, I was quickly captivated by his stylish home and its strikingly smart, cozy, warm decor. "Aubry, without an E" was able to soften me quickly with an impressive spread of delectable, epicurean appetizers, and a rare fine bottle of Australian Shiraz from his notable wine collection. It was impressive how he artistically arranged these lovely food delicacies, just for my arrival. He made me feel welcomed and spoiled by all the time and planning he took to prepare for my visit. He's a regular little Susie Homemaker. He should absolutely try out for "The Great British Bake Off." Surely, they'd spell his name correctly with an "E" in the credits. My visit appeared, so far, so good!

We spent the night enjoying a lovely time getting to know one another, eating, and drinking the special Clare Valley Wine. The more I drank, the more handsome he became. We kissed for hours. Wow, this boy could kiss. His ultra-soft, thick lips and his mind-blowing kissing expertise alone were well worth the 4 ½ hour flight in the middle seat, with poking elbows on either side of me. (Hmm? Well, almost.) It appeared his sexual tenderness was pulling me right in, and I unexpectedly grew more attracted to him with each passionate kiss. Sweet! I haven't "only *just kissed* for hours" since Jr. High. Later that evening, Aubry serenaded me brilliantly, playing away on his prestigious Baby Grand Steinway Piano. With great adoration and a sucker for talent, I was bashfully dazzled and putty in his hands as he caressed the ebony and ivory keys. While he performed,

I mischievously wondered what other grand talents this man possessed. I was determined to get to the bottom of it. Literally!!

Our little meet-cute was working out very nicely, I assumed, smiling to myself. We stayed up all night innocently cuddling, kissing, and talking about every topic imaginable. He was smart, easy to be with, diverse, and intelligent. Well, despite his political views, which entirely conflicted with mine. Correction. They conflicted far more than entirely. Whatever, I let it go. Not certain when Aubry crashed early that morning, but I fell unconscious around 5:00 a.m. When I awoke around 11:00 a.m., Aubry without an "E" was already busy at work on the phones in the kitchen. As a coveted engineer specializing in metals, he was one of the lucky ones who worked from home. (Even before COVID-19.) At first, I thought that was very cool until I discovered precisely why he worked from home. He invited me into the kitchen, where he whipped up a divine continental breakfast, including a freshly ground brewed cappuccino, with hot skim milk and four Sweet'N Low packages. Remarkable, just the way I take it. I was impressed by how he remembered those crucial coffee details from our phone conversations. It's the little things that impress us girls. Don't get me wrong, guys. We basically want it all! We want everything! And delivered overnight. Seriously, even Amazon knows that!

Before I could enjoy the first sip of my heavenly and much-needed cappuccino, out of left field, this gigantic, ugly, white Standard Poodle with a stained black nose jumped up and crashed onto my lap. Rather, she attacked and lunged (like a football bump and run) crushing me like the former defensive tackle players, Alan Page, of the Chicago Bears or "Mean Joe Greene" of the Pittsburgh Steelers. It was startling and entirely unexpected. This big gross dog leaped up, and *Body Slam*" tackled me by surprise. I immediately called for a time-out, claiming a technical foul for unnecessary "**Ruff**-ness!" Replying with a startled *ouch* and a puzzled, angry look displayed across my face, and hot cappuccino spilled all over my favorite jeans, I questioned harshly. "Where the fuck did this ugly dog come from?" I eliminated the fuck and ugly sentiments for fear of hurting Aubry's feelings. Way too thoughtful and understanding if you ask me.

Taken aback, soaking wet, with first-degree burns and stained clothes, I wanted to scream, "Ewe, yuck, what a beastly, nasty animal!" But sweet little ole me, with my respect for the Golden Rule of "Do unto others," I didn't have the heart to say it out loud. Though if I had, this might have been called a personal foul and a penalty of my own by the ruff (Ref), putting the dog and me pushing back to the starting 1 yard line.

Please, don't even go judging me people because I'm not looking for another dogfight. Hell, you know what? Let me just be perfectly direct. That little horrible bitch is atrocious looking! And ya know what else? Over the years, I've learned that it's nothing more than a fallacy to believe that all babies and dogs are cute. I'm keeping it honest. Just saying!

After Aubry laughed himself silly (while I wasn't laughing at all) he proudly explained, "Mollie, this is my beautiful beloved child, Bessie."

Entirely confused and without skipping a beat, I sarcastically responded. "Gee, golly, gosh, I didn't know you had a daughter. Where is she?" For some extra fun, I added, "Who Let the Dog Out? Who, who, who, who? Ruff!" It went over his head like a bad quarterback pass.

"Oh, ha-ha," he laughed with embarrassment. "I don't have a daughter." He went on to clarify. "I was referring to my precious little angel girl, Bessie! I picked her up this morning. You see, I brought her to an exclusive doggie hotel yesterday just for the first night of our visit, so we might have our privacy." He went on to brag, "The hotel for dogs here in Buckhead is more lavish than The Pooch Hotel in Silicon Valley. Bessie just loves their luxurious suites and all the fun doggie activities."

Being the warmhearted, sentimental gal that I am, my initial thought was, "Ahhhh, okay, wow, scary. *And* I Really Don't Give a Shit!" I quickly softened, reconsidered that approach, and requested, "Towel, please?" I reflected that on some strange, bizarre level, his overly zealous caring for this ugly animal could somewhat, perhaps, be considered, quite endearing. Yeah, but of course, that sentiment didn't last very long!

His beloved, Bessie, was not only the most awful dog I had ever met, but moreover, the most badly behaved, unlikeable, annoying, nastiest, and sloppiest snarling dog in the world. His entire demeanor and whacky personality were quite appalling. To be honest, no one could like this dog.

Breaking News Flash...
I officially want to set the record straight. "I love 'ALL' dogs, including poodles. The keyword being love. *Except for Bessie!*"

Letting my emotions go for the moment, I attempted to enjoy the beautiful homemade breakfast Aubrey, *oops*, 'Aubry (without an 'E') prepared for my morning pleasure. While we sat together scarfing up delicious dark chocolate croissants, a colorful display of assorted fresh fruits, and the authentically British blueberry and cranberry scones, there was a sparkle of hope in both of our eyes. The "You never know," sparkle.

While gobbling down our breakfast, Aubry proposed, cradling my hands gently, "I'd like to invite you for a lovely dinner tonight.

Or if you prefer, we can see a fun movie with popcorn. How's that sound, Mollie?"

Inquiring with a puzzled head-tilt, "Great, but why not both?"

He chuckled boisterously. "Impossible. My word, I would never leave my little girl alone for more than two whole hours. Unfortunately, I can't bring her back to the hotel because all the suites have been booked."

I responded, tossing all caution to the wind, and sounding much like, Cruella De Vil. "And why not? Why can't your dog be left alone longer than two hours?" To which he angrily and defensively whispered.

"Shush! *SHHH*, quiet! I don't want her to hear us! I don't like Bessie being by herself and lonely for any longer than that amount of time. She gets depressed. Mollie, you'll just have to *learn*. That's the way it is!" At that very, *"Learned, and that's the way it is"* moment, I wondered how quickly I could pack, go to my business meeting, and catch a plane home.

Noticeably upset, Aubry quickly jumped up and fanatically prepared a fresh home-cooked meal for his daughter, Bessie. This encompassed pan-seared chicken, in lemon-butter sauce, served with half a mashed Hass avocado, low-fat cottage cheese, and all sprinkled together with garlic and freshly ground pepper. "Just the way Bessie likes it," he beamed proudly, like a mother hen. He might have flushed, as well. Then, I kid you not, he proceeded to sit down on the floor to hand-feed the dog, all the while caressing, kissing, and petting his cherished Bessie. Whaddya know? And I thought I was the one going to enjoy some heavy petting?

I didn't mean to be a tactless bitch, just a bitch! Please forgive me, but this was so downright eccentric. Talk about the tail wagging the dog!

Increasingly horny from Aubry's "failure to launch" the previous night, his excessive display of affection, and this eccentric feeding presentation were not sitting well with me. I'm sorry, that whole scene was just too peculiar. But wait, there's more! Wait for it… Wait for it…

After Bessie-Wessie finished her freshly-weshly, gourmet, 3-star Michelin-worthy meal, Aubry suggested that the three of us go out for a walk. Bewildered and thinking to myself, I replied, "The three of us? Are we meeting another person? Perchance one of your friends?"

"No, hon." He chanted in response. "You, me, and Bessie make 3."

"I see," I countered, glaring at Bessie. "My apologies, Doggett… Silly me. Okay, let's go." I only agreed to the outing because I desperately needed the fresh air, so as not to puke. (Time out… Sip, sip, sip.)

Nine blocks and an uphill climb later… The *dog* did what *dogs* do outside. Thenceforth and not a moment later, Aubry swiftly picked up the animal and announced, "Time to hold my girl." Explaining further and with a straight face, mind you. "My sweet Bessie likes to be carried after doing her corporate business on these long walks." He awkwardly laughed at his silly, poor attempt at humor.

And there it was, I puked. Yep, I did! I swear I did. Darn, what a waste of a great breakfast. I wish I could've blamed it on too much wine the night before. But no, it's all Bessie.

"Yo, Aubry, you might have to carry the both of us. Don't worry, I'll carry Bessie's corporate briefcase!"

He sneered and completely ignored me. I suppose I should be grateful that he at least handed me a tissue. It was unmistakably clear who the alpha dog was and who wore the collar and leash in this family.

Returning to Bessie-Wessies's '*Bark*ingham' palace, covered in puke and coffee-stained clothes, I had one coherent thought. With heartfelt sincerity in the key of C… "What the Fuckity-Fuck-Fuck?" (Note, your jaw must remain open for at least ten seconds after saying that third fuck.)

With that, I excused myself, brushed my teeth, showered, dressed, and went to do my own corporate business downtown at the network meeting. So grateful I had planned this in advance. I desperately wanted to do something sane and more rational than this, "Dog Day Afternoon," minus Al Pacino and his famous movie quotes. Delighted, because my meeting was successful, I decided to stay and give the guy another chance. I arrived back at Bessie's just in time to dress for "dinner and *no* movie!"

We shared a nice Bessie-Wessie-less, authentic Churrasco dinner at a wonderful Brazilian Restaurant. Surprisingly, we enjoyed a normal (code word here, being normal) lovely time alone together. That is, until an hour and a half, clocked by. Aubry ridiculously rushed and warned me about our 'Bessie time schedule.' I have no clue as to how I restrained myself, but I used every ounce of discipline to keep from bursting aloud, "Hey dog, I'm sorry to be dragging my tail, but stop hounding me!" Exercising the protocol of, "clocked time precision" we returned to the house better known as, "The Monarch of her majesty, Bessie." Princess Dog really should be wearing a crown. Or a tiara, at the very least!

Back at the doghouse, Aubry lit the pre-arranged logs inside the fireplace. I must say it made a gorgeous blazing fire. He then presented me with a plate of lavish, *Harry & David's,* pricey, gourmet mixed cookies & truffles. He paired that with a splendid glass of Italian Chianti wine. Hmm, this was becoming something resembling a romantic setting. This works!

Suddenly, to my dismay and remarkably crazy as it was, Aubry proceeded to sit down by Bessie. He placed his arm around her tenderly, while caressing her lovingly right in front of the enchanting, roaring fire. (*Reminder. True story!*) Sitting across from the loving couple by myself, alone, solo, and excluded, I stated with a lilt of mockery. "Gee, you two look so romantic and dreamy together. Just like a picture postcard. Awe!"

It appeared my blasé cynical approach, evidently went impossibly unnoticed. E-less, Aubry spoke enthusiastically, "Yes! Wow, that is such a great idea! Oh, please? It would be awesome if you'd take a few photos of us with your professional Nikon. I've always wanted expert pictures of my Bessie and me together." A-Ha, yep, that's precisely when my mouth dropped open, causing the delicious Harry & David's gourmet cookie to drop onto the floor. Damn, what a waste! That was like a five-dollar bite.

Stunned, I gasped, "You're joking, right? You're not serious?"

He responded confidently, picking up the wasted cookie. "No, actually. Not really? Not at all! Perhaps maybe later, we can do a photo shoot? Bessie has an adorable tiara we can put on. She loves wearing it."

Readers, I get it. And I know as you are reading this, you're calling me a liar. You are also assuming this is bullshit and that I'm making it all up. I only wish I were. It was evident not only was 'I' the underdog but also the loser who was stuck in the kennel. Let me tell you, *"Nobody puts Baby in a corner!"* I should have just played dead right then and there.

Tragically, at this moment in my life, I was so starved for affection that I unimaginably contemplated the ludicrous impulse of attempting to have sex with this emotionally challenged woof-man. I desperately wanted to question him purely for the fun of it. "So, Aubry, do you like doing it doggie style? I just assumed it's your favorite sexual position?" Ironically, I didn't have the guts to ask him because I was too afraid of what his answer would be. Agreeing to "just sleep" in his bed, I thought… let me just put all my *paws* on the table and see how the rest of this tail-tale goes.

Anyway, with sex in mind and just in case, I slipped into a sensual, purple-laced teddy. (It's my thing. Let it go.) Had I known about his *'prohound,'* oops, *'profound'* dog fetish, I would have thrown him a bone and worn my pink poodle skirt instead. (Saddle shoes and all.) Damn, a totally missed opportunity there. Showered, powdered, and all sexed-up, I slid under his very fine silk covers and sheets, made with approximately a billion-thread count. I was reluctant to allow my scorn to show its ugly head and inquire, "Did Bessie-Wessie demand these very expensive sheets?" Fortunately, my now cold-hearted tongue was saved by the music. Aubry walked into the room and quickly put on some John Legend. Pleased and hopeful, I wagged him to come over to me. Correction… waved! *I waved.* At last, we began passionately kissing. It was sexy, and deliciously intimate, which happily replaced all the 'dog-whistle' drama of the day. I quickened to his touch and intense kisses. In doggie terms, "I lapped it up!" Luckily, things were looking increasingly better.

Then, the anticlimax arrived 20 minutes later at the most amorous, sensual moment, mid-stream of our lust. Good-ole Bessie attacked the bed like a lioness, capturing her prey, and sat down between us. Shit, this Brunhilda of a dog ruined the moment, yet again. I yelped, "Come on, really, Aubry?" I couldn't wipe away my 'bitchy resting face' expression. I was proud of myself, as I had never been able to cop this look so perfectly before. Well then, Hot-Diggity-Dog for me. Holding that face, I forcefully commanded, *"Bessie, down girl. Play dead!"*

I'll tell you what! Those were fighting words to Aubry's ears,

ENTERING INTO "THE WORLD OF CRAZY!" | 19

and boy oh boy, did he ever 'leash' out! (Sorry, lash out.) He howled meanly, "Hey, Mollie, stop it! I mean it. That was so cruel. What's your problem? Don't upset Bessie! It's no biggie, she'll calm down. Hell, give her a sec!"

I must say, I didn't like his tone one bit. Man, it really is a dog-eat-dog world. Surely, he was taking the phrase, "Let sleeping dogs lie," to a whole new normal. To be honest, I regretted holding back my tongue from spewing out, "Mr. Aubry without an 'E,' I'm not your bitch and you're one sick puppy." Instead, I replied to his rudeness with, "Yo, don't bark at me!" With that, we both started laughing. Darn, I wish I had one of those silent dog whistles, to mess with this Grande dame of a dog. If I were a "Let's Make a Deal" fan, I'd have one in my pocket, ready to pucker up.

Since his beloved *dog*matic Bessie killed our romantic mood, we just watched a movie instead. This obnoxious pooch was a wrecking ball, but without the Miley Cyrus and the sexy. I wickedly thought that I'd love to feed the *dictatorial, Bessie the canine,* an entire box of Ex-Lax! But then, Aubry wouldn't have a poodle anymore. He'd have a "Shit-Tzu!"

To be clear, having a dog and an ugly one at that, glaring up at me with hatred, while insinuating with her non-puppy-dog eyes that she wished to massacre me to a pulp, and then bury me in the backyard with the rest of her bones, was not the ideal amorous situation. If her looks could kill, I would have been a dead dog and roadkill. Bess was literally a total *bitch.* The absurd thought a man didn't have my back over a dog didn't bode well for me. The fact this man was weird enough to choose a dog over sex with me was enough to make this girl run and fetch a plane.

The next day, that is exactly what I did. I had enough of his silly shenanigans. Doggone-it, this 'ménage à trois,' love triangle with a dog, was not what I was chasing after! (Sip, sip, sip.) Early the next morning, I left quickly, and I didn't even say goodbye. But I did, of course, grab a handful of Harry & David's gourmet cookies on my way out. Come on, I'm not stupid! I ran away as fast as I could, like a teenager, when his parents find his stash. As fast as a straight guy runs away when he finds out he has been flirting with a cross-dresser. I ran away as fast as a teenage girl flees when her father catches her running off with her gang-member boyfriend. A hoodlum, who's 15 years older, as they zip away on his motorcycle, smoking weed. Whatever, I was so out of there! When "Aubry without an E" realized I had gone (if he even did), I've often wondered if he ordered Bessie to retrieve me like a ball. "Go get her girl. Go, Fetch!" Yea, Bessie-Wessie, while you're at it, fetch my dignity too!

Guys should really walk around wearing big disclaimer signs. On Aubry's sign would be printed: "*No Sex in The Buckhead City,* because *I Am in Love with My Dog!*" I quickly learned that Aubry was clinically afflicted with the well-known syndrome, (which I also made up) "*I have no children. Therefore, my entire life is my Fur-kid, for she is my child.*" *Too bad, there are no meds for his canophilia or dog-mania disorder.* As for me, I could never accept the dogma realization that Bessie would always be his priority. Yikes, was this guy ever barking up the wrong girl? I couldn't get away fast enough from him and his little dog, too!

I should have known right away something was strange when he accidentally passed wind in front of me at breakfast and then completely owned up to it and excused himself. It was so abnormal. I just thought, dude, be a man and point to the dog. Blame the dog, as all real men do! Aubry's peculiar syndrome would never allow me to fall for him or even feel puppy love. I guess it's true "You can't teach an old dog new tricks!"

When I reached home after a long five-hour flight and a three-hour time change, I was dog-tired. Shit, I growled, what a dating fiasco this guy wound up to be. As it turned out, Aubry was for sure, for sure, not the *"Best in Show,"* and not at all, "my best-*laid* plan," either. As if things couldn't get worse, I woke up the following morning sick as a dog.

And so, ends the saga of the dog with two tales… tails…

The moral of this wagging long-tail, tale of woe is…
"You can love your dog, but you can't '*Love*' your dog!"
Hence… "I Got Maled!"

In Conclusion…

**Girls, "WITH A KNICK-KNACK PADDY WHACK…
BEWARE OF THE DOGS!"**

CHAPTER 3

Getting Started

"THE... TO DO, OR NOT TO DO'S," FOR WOMEN!

Before I resume sharing my outrageous, hard-to-believe online dating stories, I'd like to give important advice to those of you just starting out.

Ladies, this chapter is designed to help you get started so that you won't be flying blind. To begin my innocent and hopeful readers, you will have to decide which online dating sites you would like to join. Some of them are free, but I sincerely don't recommend any of these free sites. I find this is where most of the "*strange ones*" lurk and congregate. I can almost hear the eerie theme songs from the scary movies "Dead Silence," "Paranormal Activity," or "The Exorcist" playing in the background of my mind just thinking of them. Trust me, in the long run, it is best to stick to the ones you need to pay to join.

Keep in mind you get what you pay for, and very possibly not even then. Furthermore, I strongly recommend you join at least 3 online dating sites. This will offer you a much larger selection. The more people you can rummage through, the quicker you might find the love of your life.

WRITING YOUR PROFILE

The next step, I found to be the most tedious, and no doubt you will too! It will be necessary to write your profile, which feels like a lot of Yada, Yada, Yada. Yes, indeed, it gets monotonous. Thus, my guidance here is to "copy and paste" what you write on the first site and save it in a file for all the other sites. This way, you'll only have to create your profile once, which is much easier and a huge timesaver.

While writing your profile, here is where you should be, *"Mostly"* honest. I discovered it's beneficial to simply cut to the chase. Regardless, be clever, funny, imaginative, and, by George, be true to yourself. Or whatever your name might be if it isn't George!

I kept my profile real, yet bejeweled, with my unique personality, style, and flair. Follow my lead. Be alluring and bring something different to the table. It appears everyone writes the same boring, lackluster, unoriginal statements. (Here's a clue… Read what others write, and *don't!*) Be creative, interesting, and produce something captivating to entice or intrigue "The One" you're searching for. Don't get sappy or Miss/Mr. America-ish by writing declarations like *"I only want and live for world peace."* Unless that is, you literally work for UNICEF or the Peace Corps. Avoid comments like, *"My dream in life is to save the whales, the rainforest, and reverse global warming."* Ignore this if you are an environmental scientist. Besides, truthfully, no one really gives a shit!

In my summary, I told the truth, the whole truth, and nothing but the truth, so help me God. Well, other than my real age! I'm not telling you what you should do, but I lied by five years. Now, before you start judging and going all, Simon Cowell on me, please allow me to rationalize this very significant point. Hypothetically, guys who contact you will most definitely be older than you. Plus, these men have surely lied about their ages by 5 to 10 years, or more. I believe this philosophy of mine evens out the score and predictably will save you a lot of time. Still, do what's best for you! Though I warn you, be careful of the younger guys who are only looking for a free ride. Don't go there. It's a waste of time. Also, keep a lookout for the much older guys. I fondly call them "The Smithsonian Guys." The dinosaurs foolishly lie about their ages by 25-ish years or so!

Don't, I repeat, **don't** lie about your weight. Your man accepts and loves you just the way you are. If not, it's his loss. And, besides, that's the cliché line they tell us to believe in the notorious film, "Bridget Jones's Diary" and the Billy Joel song. Moreover, the jig will be up at *hello,* leaving you further disheartened, if you possibly liked the guy.

Also, don't worry about being too picky. You must look for what you want in a partner and no apologies necessary. FYI, here's what I have personally discovered. The short, ugly, fat, bald, poor, loser guys are also selfish, egotistical, jerks, and obnoxious creeps just as much as the good-looking, successful ones are. Henceforth, you might as well look for what you want, desire, and need from the get-go. Keep searching for what's important to you and what you believe will bring you ultimate happiness.

When You Begin Emailing Back and Forth…
"Don'ts!"

1. Don't reveal too much when texting. Keep your life and private information about "*your world*" in the vault. Don't tell these guys anything important about yourself until they become a

part of your life. And maybe not even then. They don't need to know anything personal in the delicate beginning stages. "Easy-peasy? No!" Honestly, this is much harder than it sounds. But regardless, heed my advice anyway. You can impress him later when you know he can be trusted. Be on the safe side. Remember, Shhhhh!

2. Women, save valuable time and let them do all the talking. Interview the heck out of them! Old school, Diane Sawyer, and Barbara Walters, them to death! Go ahead and tsunami-interrogate them with numerous questions. Though tempting, why should you tell them anything at all private about yourself? If you do, and they don't want to meet or date you (or you don't want to meet or date them) they will know far too much about you. This scenario leaves you vulnerable, empty-handed, and with a great deal of squandered precious time. Especially if they are lowlife, quirky con artists, or who knows... even stalkers. I don't mean to scare you. Well, maybe I do! Understand and be aware the Ted Bundy, Jeffrey Dahmer, and Charles Manson dangerous types of guys are still out there on the loose. I know you hate to hear it, but damn, "Your mother was right!" And doesn't that just suck, big time? I promise, revealing a lot of personal information can be dangerous and not a wise idea. This is basically good dating protocol and much safer to boot. Let the men do all the talking and just stifle. It's easier, safer, and smarter. Besides, I have witnessed firsthand as a reporter, interviewing people from all walks of life, "You learn faster and attain far more knowledge by listening rather than talking." Here's another informative jewel to comprehend. Men totally love it when women allow them to talk about themselves. Fabulous for their egos. Notice, most men

will go on and on, and find it a rather unique phenomenon that you even let him do so.

3. Don't and I mean don't give out your telephone number, address, website, or where you work. Do not even email the prospect until you get to know more about him and become certain you might like him. Stick to the dating site for all communications. I get it's a real pain and you'll want to proceed by going off the site. But unfortunately, it's the best, most secure way to correspond in the beginning. Warning, you *must not* go out with any man *you haven't spoken with on the phone!* Press, * 67 before dialing. Hearing his voice, listening to him speak, and catching what he has to say will enable you to weed out most of the crazy guys!

4. Don't insult your ex or exes. This includes your ex-mother-in-law. No matter how difficult it might be, no bashing. Regrettably, that tends to accomplish the opposite effect and makes *you* look like the bad guy. Men don't want to hear criticizing, whining, nagging, or any other negative behaviors you think are suitable to do. All that nit-picking stuff you can do after you snag um! "Huzzah!"

5. Don't complain. No man will handle this well. They are all missing the "listening to complaints" and the "empathy about girls' bitching" genes. You'll most likely never get a response or a second chance if you do. You might even notice a few random skid marks on your computer screen. Which I must tell you is not only a real bummer, but hard to get off. When I speak of complaining, this includes comments about your kids, family, friends, pets, boss, hair, nails, your shitty old computer, lousy

hair straightener, your rundown car, personal problems, credit card and student loan debts, taxes, jury duty, bills, your crappy cell that you recently dropped, broke, duct-taped, and have to wait 8 months until your contract is up to purchase another one, or any other problems or dramas. Don't complain! Keep it light, easy, and fun.

Remember, complaining is literally one of the primary reasons for having friends. Bitching, moaning, and kvetching over greasy fries, nachos, and to-die-for-desserts, all washed down with cocktails, is the very essence and foundation of solid lasting friendships. This is where to vent your grievances. Not to online men, or anywhere else, for that matter. Wait until he can handle it because sex with you is so fucking amazing! Limit it, even then.

6. Take notice, for this one is a biggie. Read between the lines and categorically *look for red flags.* I promise you, they are waving, beckoning, flapping, fluttering loudly, and rocking like a sailboat in the wind! Red flags are a warning, a girl's best fight-or-flight protection, and our greatest defense against future problems. These flags restore the balance to the universe of dating. Don't ignore the flags, regardless of how they wave. Do you hear me?

7. Don't lie to a guy about not having marriages, pets, or children. It will only catch up with you later when your toddler crawls on his lap suddenly with drool and snot from his nose dripping down the guy's leg. This also applies to your ex-husbands or pets drool, and stuffy nose dripping down his leg! An unpleasant situation for all.

8. *Don't* disclose *right away* any info concerning venereal diseases

you might have contracted. It is downright off-putting. If you do, he won't even meet you, or get the opportunity to get to know you. A clear warning, nevertheless, *"Don't lie about it if asked."* It will only be harder, to tell the truth later. Appreciate, though, it is imperative for both of you to *come clean* before any sexual relations. AKA, fooling around and hooking up. If he'd walk out when you tell him, he'll walk out even faster thereafter, since you concealed such pertinent information. Or worse, infecting him. He will never trust you again if you lie about this serious matter. If he cares about you, together you'll work out these sensitive issues.

9. Don't tell any guy your biological clock is ticking or that you want 5 children. Especially if it's true. This is the kind of shit you tell your mother, your sister, or your Great Aunt Bertha. Zip it for now! This revelation will send him fleeing quicker than a cat running through a dog pound. It'll set him sprinting off faster than the fastest man in the world, Usain Bolt, the Jamaican runner who won nine gold medals sprinting at the Olympics. Way too much info. There will be more warning directions later in the book.

10. Wait until the first date to tell a guy you lied about your age. This way, he can see how fabulous you look in person. It likely won't matter as much as it would be from judging your online photo. To be candid, all daters are justifiably wary and afraid that you don't look like your photos. They will surely think your pictures are deceitful if you admit your real age before meeting. Make sure your photos are honest and current. BTW, *he* should also come clean concerning *his* "age *lie*" and other lies, as well. Hey, tell him you're an erotic dancer or dominatrix woman

before coming clean. That'll soften the blow of lying about your age. Kidding!

11. This next point is critical. Be cautious and pay close attention to each guy you're texting or speaking with. The number of men you might correspond with can grow too large to keep up with. Take my word as gospel. It can get confusing trying to remember all the facts about each of the men you might be interested in. It's a big embarrassing faux pas if you accidentally mix them up. I know, because I have slipped up many times, maybe more. Awkward! I mean, it's not a helter-skelter situation, but clearly a possible low point! (Thank you, Beatles, for that comparison and intro into heavy metal music.) I suggest you make some notes and keep them where you can get to them quickly. Your cheat sheet should include... What each person looks like or a photo, their name, city, occupation, age, their sign if you care, or any other pertinent information about them. Such as their kids, divorces, political views, animals, hobbies, favorite foods, if they drink or smoke, music preferences, family, passions, education, religion, physical traits, etcetera. Trust me, all of this is imperative to keep up with.

12. Beware of the guys who write under their careers... "*Entrepreneur!*" That is pretty much code for "*Out of Work.*" Most of these so-called *entrepreneurs* are phonies and lie about everything they can to impress girls on their profiles. This may include houses, cars, travels, yachts, or airplanes you see them posing in front of. Be vigilant! They are, for the most part, full of shit, and more accurately... "*Entre**Manures**!*

13. Ladies, I'm not advocating that you play hard to get. I am

merely suggesting, "Don't be easy to get," either. Know your self-worth and who you are. Hold back a little and let the guy woo you. Let him earn you. If he hooks and catches you too quickly, he'll surely throw you back into the dating sea just as fast. My gosh, didn't your dad ever teach you the rules of basic fishing, 101?

14. This next piece of guidance took me over a year to figure out. Don't talk, write, or date only one guy at a time. You don't owe him anything, not even an explanation. If you only concentrate on one guy alone and it doesn't work out, you just wasted "beaucoup, dinky-dau time!" Clearly, I'm not implying by any means, that you have sex with more than one guy at a time, or at all! I am just recommending that you give yourself a chance to look at all the merchandise before choosing. You need to mull over all your choices before you decide. You surely don't try on just one pair of shoes before buying them? Shame on you if you do! And you don't purchase an expensive jacket without checking out other jackets first. Right? You don't buy perfume without spritzing yourself with a few of them. Correct? I know you believe you're a good person and feel awkward dating several men at the same time. Girl, trust me, it's really the right way to do it and the quickest path to success. Realize the online world is your dating oyster. Men come in different sizes, shapes, colors & values. I promise you're not the only one *he* is going out with, either. There are many good and bad pearls to choose from. So, my proposal is to date a whole string of them. It's the fastest way to find the one, "Who *WILL* propose!"

15. I genuinely don't mean to be politically incorrect here... All *the same*, when you first get up in the morning, *do not* go online

to search for men. First, have your morning coffee and a muffin, or whatever your breakfast ritual is. Some of these guys are not good-looking (I mean really, really, *not!*) and can genuinely freak you out before a comforting morning cup of Joe. Do you get what I'm saying? For real, it could be too much "Ewe" in the early morning hours. Just don't. I can't express enough the "Don't point!" What? Oh, come on. Trust me when I say you'll soon see what I mean! Some of these men are positively "Spooktacularly" scary looking or worse. Really worse. Take my word for it. Searching later in the day will be more whimsical, and far less "*Boo* and frightening!"

16. **Make sure to read all your texts before pressing send.** If you don't and are lucky, you will just appear ignorant. This is even more applicable and important if you are dictating a message into the phone. For it never seems to type what you said. If you are dictating, allow me to give you a few true examples of what I am referring to. I once dictated a nice text to a guy. "I really can't wait to speak with you!" But it came out stating, "I really can't wait to sleep with you!" I dictated to another guy, "*I just got paid.*" What it wrote was, "*I just got laid.*" Another time I dictated into the phone, saying, "I will get back to you next week. I am touring for my job all over the country and bouncing around so much, I'm starting to limp. LOL." What he received was, "I'll butt back into you next week. I am whoring for my job all over the country and banging in and out so much with my pimp. Lots of love."

Embarrassing much? The visual on this text was as nasty as a frat house bathroom on homecoming weekend! As one could imagine, correcting this situation was humiliating. My counsel here is… "Always, (and I mean always) *Read Before Pressing Send!"*

17. Be stealthy. You can and should block guys from knowing you were looking at their profiles. If you check them out and then decide you are not interested, they will know you looked at them and assume you are interested. Thus, they will undoubtedly write to you. In addition, you can block people from seeing when you are currently on the site. I strongly suggest you do this as well.

18. The number one most important thing I can convey to you is, **"Believe No One!"** I Repeat, *"No One!"* Many of these guys are mega liars. I don't just mean about their age. They lie about what they think, and what they do, that they are single when they are married (very common), and even use other men's photos who are more handsome than they are. Guys sometimes do this because they have no intentions of meeting you. They're only trying to con you into having phone sex. Hey, you married or taken men, "We are not all fools!" Later, you'll read it almost happened to me, too. Luckily, I didn't fall for it. Stay vigilant of tricksters and fakers.

Oh, but wait! There's more!

Be aware that some guys (and girls) lie about working when they are unemployed, deny diseases they've contracted, give B.S. reasons why they never got married, why their ex-partner and children left him, and so forth. There are countless crooked scam artists ready to rip you off and take advantage of you in a million different ways. Be cautious and alert!

For example, I communicated with a guy who said he was a

highly successful, sought-after pediatric plastic surgeon. Yeah, well, he was nothing more than an out-of-work, desperate, nobody actor. He posted photos of himself performing surgery, which turned out to be nothing more than a cheap Hollywood set. Probably fooled many women with this.

Do your homework! Make sure to check out all the men you become interested in, *meticulously*. Try searching them on Google, Zillow, or ZabaSearch. If necessary, hire a private detective if it looks like it might get serious, or if you have any doubts at all. Don't look at it as spying. You need to protect yourself and know with full assurance what you are getting yourself into. Understand, "You're not spying. *You are being smart.*" I'm not asking you to James Bond, Ethan Hunt, Dick Tracy, or even Jason Bourne them, to death. I am, however, suggesting you put on your Inspector Clouseau or Inspector Gadget's proactive thinking cap. Try to think of this as being shrewd, vigilant, and a major necessity. It will help you to avoid most of the "Oopsies," "Oh shit," and "Uh-Ohs" later!

I was online for quite a while before I realized how crucial this knowledge is regarding a person's safety and protection. Let's not beat around the bush here. You're human, vulnerable, and your body, heart, and finances are possible prey to this species of men. You've worked your whole life to become the person you are and earned what you have. Don't let someone scam it away. I dodged many dangerous relationship bullets, doing background checks, researching men online, and others I thought I liked! Follow my advice to the max. Check out every person you talk to or text that you think might be a good prospect. Apply this rule shortly after you meet. Don't waste time. You can be sure *"they are checking you out!"*

Just for fun... Here are some more "Safe Things," you can lie about
and disclose later after you meet a few times in person:

Your extensions, natural hair color, fake eyelashes, breast implants, liposuction, nose job, acrylic nails, Botox, fillers, and veneers. Lying about these things isn't a problem. It's personal chick stuff like gossiping, loving 50% off sales, stuffing bras, exaggerating, counting calories, flirting, changing purses, nail polish, and jewelry to match our outfits, overindulging on Amazon, binge-watching TV series, and denying suffering from PMS.

Your number of *"sexcapades"* is off-limits as well. It's *none* of his business at the beginning of dating and perhaps ever! You should avoid answering if he is rude enough to ask. If he continuously harasses you, then run. You don't need his uncouth, controlling, domineering attitude.

As far as lying about ailments or addictions to drugs, alcohol, sex, popcorn, mental illness, candy, bipolar disorder, depression, food, or hating your mother, etc.? Hmm? I believe you are on your own here with these decisions, ladies. Having been a stripper, a hooker, or a Madame at some point in your life? What can I say? You go, girl! Realize eventually, though, they'll find out. They always do. Personally, all the men (every one of them) I've emailed, talked to, or gone out with have falsely accused their exes of all the above, anyway. So, whatever? There is that!

Moreover, I am so sick of everyone writing in their profiles how they love long walks on the beach. It's unoriginal and outrageously cliché, even if it is true. The only thing accomplished with this activity is sand trickling all over everything, including your crack (I don't mean cocaine), and inside, everywhere else. I wrote I hated long walks on the beach in my profile, if for no other reason than to be different from others. Be original, unique, and use your imagination. You'll stand out, just by being you.

PUTTING UP YOUR PHOTOS!

Please, pretty, please people, remember "Your Photos Are THE Number ONE, Most Important Thing of All **in the online dating process!"**

All the dating sites will request that you put up your photos. This, without a doubt, is the most critical step of all. Therefore, I strongly encourage posting several *fantastic* pictures. Here are some very pertinent photo suggestions. "Listen up!"

1. When taking photos, pay attention to sporting different looks, striking many poses, and wearing several flattering outfits. A straight-on face shot displaying a sincere, sweet, warm smile always works. A relaxed, confident, happy attitude is essential too. Adding some adorable facial expressions in your shots can also make you appear fun-loving. I said *adorable*, not insane, stupid, or outlandishly weird. If you avoid putting up photos on your profile, no one will contact you! Dating candidates will assume you are, at best, a hideous-looking creature. So put um up!

2. Make sure all your photographs are *"Current,"* in focus, and close-up. Include a few full-body shots as well as headshots. *Up To Date* is key. Do not post any photos where you cannot easily be seen because you are too far off in the distance. Also, I suggest no sunglasses. Your eyes, tell your story. If you absolutely love the way you look in shades, then one photo is acceptable. The same goes for hats. Guys love hair, so don't hide yours.

3. You have many great photos? Fine, put them all up. If you only have 1 or 2 great ones, "Girl, *only put those up!*" If your photos

aren't lovely and eye-catching, you'll lose your chance, and he will *rush* off to the next girl. Note, you are *only as pretty,* as your *worst photo. So,* make them all count!

4. Dear Lord, "Do Not Post Selfies! Dammit!" Get someone to snap a few photos for you. A selfie totally suggests you are lonely and implies that you have no friends in your life. Girlfriend, come on now…

5. Don't post your prom or sorority photos! Well, unless you are presently in high school or college. They are awkward and make you appear stiff, anyway. Besides, those photos were probably taken when you had your period, were bloated, and exposed a few zits you were hoping to hide!

6. Don't post photos of your wedding, your kids, or guys you once dated. This is a big turn off. Good Lord, *why do I even have to tell you this crap?*

7. Don't display photos with your girlfriends, especially if they are prettier or have a better body than you. Huge mistake! Geeze, why would you even do this? They will probably choose your friend instead! Which would be a giant bummer for you and embarrassing for your friend! Just put-up photos of *"You,* and *You* alone!" Ugh, I can't even?

8. Don't include "Slut Barbie" photos. First of all, it is an insult to Barbie. Secondly, it pisses off, Ken, big time! You know what I'm talking about! Those naked, vulgar, way too much info, shots, or your sleazy lingerie and bathing suit poses, mysteriously slipping off. Honestly, these photos will only attract the wrong guys. Well, unless, however, you want that. Cause if so;

trust me, this will work out beautifully for you. Just be classy. Keep your clothes on and strike a sexy facial pose instead. Be the girl every guy wants. The girl he hopes to marry is the girl he can bring home to meet his family. Slut Barbie will only get to meet his bedroom and maybe his cat! But hey, who am I to judge a purely sexual, slutty fun night in bed?

9. Lastly, if you don't put a photo up, people will assume you are married.

Remember, communicate with and date many guys at one time. As bad as it sounds, if you put all your eggs in one basket, you'll waste a considerable amount of time. Plus, if it doesn't work out, a whole lot of wasted eggs! When the time comes that you really like someone, then, of course, back off the rest of the prospects. I squandered far too many hours, concentrating on one guy at a time. I guarantee that I'm sparing you plenty of misspent time, which will be unproductive in the end. If it's not working with a guy, here's your dating mantra, "Next, next, and next."

This is an Imperative and Gigantic Warning! So Pay Attention!

And don't even begin to roll your eyes at me about the Date-Rape drug. It is real! Never walk away from your drink on any date. Take it to the bathroom with you if you must. I remember one awful night in college. I went out with a guy, and mid-date, he slipped the notorious drug into my drink. It's only because my girlfriends had my back, that I didn't wind up raped by him, and without even knowing it. Thank God! Although, I did learn I had been seen at 6 frat houses that night and woke up looking like the Whore of Babylon. Allegedly. Ladies, pay attention and do be careful!

Lastly, I warn you, while shouting at the top of my voice! *"Don't lower your standards!"* Seriously, I mean it. Don't lower them for anyone. Stay standing tall and firm. Perhaps it would help to put on your highest heels for this? Pursue the love of your dreams. Believe in yourself. Search for the one who will make life happy. Obviously, most of the people out there won't be right for you! Like, *AT ALL!* So, then sprint away quickly. Break a heel running off, or even a nail if you must. But don't settle.

Caution! When you begin dating, there will be many times that you'll find yourself frustrated, disillusioned, disappointed, and totally wanting to give up. You might even think that you have no other choice. But don't! And no matter what, don't accept second best.

Have faith that you are exceptional and deserve a mate who is special, classy, kind, wise, extraordinary, fun, caring, affectionate, ethical, intelligent, gorgeous, with a great sense of humor and loving. Don't settle!

Obviously, you might be mocking me. But you'll soon discover what I am talking about and why I'm warning you in advance. I swear on Gucci, people, it's *"Menageddon"* out there! The world is coming to a dating apocalypse due to some of the men on these dating sites. Along the way, you'll come to realize most of the guys out there are not members of *Mensa International.* However, don't worry. There are some good ones.

Here's a little hint to make your online searching process more fun. Have an online dating party and celebrate with some entertaining friends. Hunting through guys together with a bunch of girls is a bevy of hysterical fun! You'll be shocked at how many synonyms you'll come up with for the words *"gross and ugly!"* Put out an abundance of carbs, such as fried chicken wings, tacos, pizza, fruit, BBQ chips, chocolate, sweets, and wine. You will laugh your asses off, making fun of all the weird-looking guys, being wickedly cruel, and behaving like total bitches without them ever knowing. Come on back off and enjoy. #Justhealthyfunshallowgirlstuff?

Nevertheless, I could've killed my friend Elizabeth. During one of my online party-night powwows, she hit favorite on the worst of the worst guys on the sites. It took forever to find a way to remove them and block their nonstop texting. One was a frightfully eccentric, pierced-everything, shirtless, muscle man. His eyes hid chilling, acrimonious secrets. Another guy looked like Father Time, only older, toothless, and sporting a gray beard to the floor. This elder looked so ancient, he was most probably a classmate of Shakespeare, Galilei, Nostradamus, or Da Vinci. *"Gross & ewe!"* Let me tell you, payback for my witty friend Elizabeth was a bitch!

Looking for good prospects online is pretty much like searching for Big Foot or the Loch Ness Monster. What's the silver lining and good news, you might ask? There are wonderful guys hidden deep within the dating sites. Sure, very deep, in fact. But keep the faith, have some fun, and don't stop searching. Make cosmopolitans and margaritas and chuckle the night away. Remember, *"Don't settle or lower your standards!"*

Again, please appreciate "You are definitely not alone!" We all go through it, and that includes the rich & famous. And while you are looking for "The One," love, laugh, stay happy, learn, grow, and do try to enjoy the journey as you search for your love. I say persist with attitude, a smile, and know you can overcome any obstacle blocking your way with success and determination. And, if that fails, go ahead and re-thread your needle with fervor and a double knot. Of course, Oreos and Twinkies can help here too. I'm offering amazing, sage-old wisdom and common sense!

I shall resume guiding you throughout the book. But for now, I will continue sharing some of my own experiences with several on and offline guys who I went out with. Experiences! How cute is that?

To accurately set the stage for the crazy world of online dating, I must tell you that it feels exactly like the film "Groundhog Day."

Now then, sharpen your ears and listen to my cautionary tales…

A heads up… I'm starting with the good ones!

ENJOY!

CHAPTER 4

The Strutting Egomaniac

YALE WENT TO YALE… AND THAT'S ALL YOU NEED TO KNOW

Yale allegedly went to Yale, and for all intents and purposes, that basically sums him up. Do I even need to go on? Ah, but yes! I absolutely must. I need to. I must! Let's eagerly begin with a modicum of delight, shall we?

I had been speaking with Yale, another online character, for just over a week. Coincidently, I previously had plans to be in New York City on an assignment the following week, anyway. I was scheduled to be there for several days, gathering preliminary investigative research, before interviewing the Governor of N. Y. for an important feature story.

Meeting Yale in Manhattan meant breaking my cardinal-dating rule… *"Knowing someone at least a few weeks before getting together."* Finding myself in a bit of a *"Should I get together with Yale"* dilemma, I thought, "Hosh-posh," what the heck? It couldn't hurt. Warning… If you start any first date with the phrase, *"Hosh-posh,"* you should know right away you are in trouble. "D'oh?"

At any rate, since I'd be in town, why not meet the guy for a nice early dinner in the city that never sleeps? About this saying, and just to be clear, it's a fallacy and not at all true. Vegas is the city that never sleeps!

A few days later, at the time and place we agreed upon, I sat there alone, waiting 38 minutes past our meeting time. This is typically a deal-breaker for me, which left me feeling foolish and agitated. Being late is fine if there was a genuine emergency, or if I had received the "I'm going to be a few minutes late" call. Finally, I spotted Yale in all his glory, strutting into the restaurant without a care whatsoever as to his tardiness.

I surmised in only two seconds that he was fundamentally an elitist snob. Hell, I could literally see his ego dripping down the back of his leg from where I was sitting in the rear of the restaurant. His peacock posture, his swagger, and superior aloofness made it evident I was literally now sitting on the corner of "Hello and Goodbye streets." His hubris conceit was blinding! And so there went my hopes for a calm, hassle-free evening.

By the time he sat down, I was finishing my first glass of red wine. He greeted me with a cocky, "Booyakasha! Well, now, just look at you!"

"Hello, I'm Mollie. Nice to meet you, Yale, and right back atcha!" I went on to question him, still agitated by his unpunctuality. "So, tell me Yale, is that a good or a bad... *look at you?*"

"No Luv, you are a total 'cutesicle.' You look good enough to eat."

I contradicted, "Sorry, Luv, hate to disappoint, but I'm not on the menu tonight." I hoped his vast pride allowed him to recognize my answer was an obvious zinger. His only response was a flippant, childish pout. Hoping to change the subject on this uncomfortable start, "May I ask you a question, Yale? Why did your parents name you Yale?"

"Ha-Ha-Ha-Ha... good question."

Come on, man, I thought to myself. Who says those words out loud, with a straight face? "Ha-Ha-Ha-Ha?" I chuckled internally, but then realized some of it had leaked out. Hitherto, I don't believe he caught on.

He proudly continued. "My mother always loved the whole Ivy League scene. However, she didn't care much for the name Harvard. Thus, she cleverly hypothesized that if she named me Yale, it would ensure my acceptance into the University one day. The funny thing is, she was right! I just love my mom! I always do what she asks, says, or wants."

I visualized on-the-spot, Yale rubbing his mommy's feet and asking, "Am I a good boy, Mommy? Am I?" Huh, Glory Be? What a perfect moment to have reacted with my very own, "Ha-Ha-Ha-Ha!" But, darn, I couldn't bring myself to do it, even though I felt his whole Ivy story was entirely pompous and pretentious on every showy level. Yet, knowing for sure this wasn't a love connection, I stayed with the notion of being courteous. I bounced back with a non-confrontational "That's cool."

Yale went on talking about himself, rarely stopping to take a breath, yet long enough for me to finish my second glass of wine. I was delighted when our server, Ben, cut him off abruptly to take our order. While placing my entrée, I noticed Yale pulling out a rare old-world silver pocket watch. Ironically, that jewel of an antique timepiece was my favorite thing thus far about this pedantic guy. Still, the night was young.

As soon as Ben walked away, Yale retorted anxiously, "So Mollie, where was I? What fabulous thing was I telling about my amazing self?"

Cringing inwardly, I reacted, "Ah, yes, you were talking about the pros and cons of alien abductions and how it affects animals running wild in Brazil, causing a global warming tsunami, in a molecular combustion!"

"Pardon? What?" He questioned, tilting his head. "Huh? Oh, I get it! You're teasing me, right? Ha-Ha-Ha-Ha-Ha, Ha-Ha-Ha-Ha-Ha."

Wow, swift on the uptake, and there he went again. But with six extra-added, "Ha's," this time around.

"Yale, I'm curious," I questioned bluntly. "You're American. You were born in Boston. So, then, why the phony British Madonna accent?"

"It's not phony at all! Dear journalist, I summered in London after my freshman year of college. I simply picked up the accent, and it stuck."

Trying to respond in a sweet innocent manner, "Yale, that was over fifteen years ago, and you were only there for what? Less than three months? It doesn't happen that way. Come on now, seriously?"

He interrupted with his consistent, self-important laughter. "But of course, it does, Honey-Hon-Hon! It happens that way all the time."

At that point, I swear, this "Honey-Hon-Hon" had no other choice here. None whatsoever. For good measure, I had to throw in an equally condescending, "Okay, whatever! Ha-Ha-Ha-Ha... Ha?"

His posture stiffened, eyes hardened, and his brow recoiled when I "Whatever'd" him, along with my mocking his affected Ha-Ha-Ha-Ha's!

"Guess what?" He ignored me and changed the subject entirely. "If you're looking for a captivating story, you need not look any further. You simply must write a piece about me. In fact, I insist! It's clear that I am an important, multi-talented person. Moreover, I'm a richly fascinating man."

I looked up at him with an ill-concealed aversion. Though I didn't respond, I wanted to say, "Yo, Ivy Man, #humblemuch? Lord,

I would sooner write a story on the aardvarks roaming over most of the southern two-thirds of the African continent!" Grrr! The pretentious, counterfeit, British-accented Yale was so uniquely beyond bogus and fake that I truly wanted to reach across the table and cheerfully smack him. His *"The world revolves around me"* comments would have knocked my socks off had I been wearing any. Rescued by the 3rd glass of wine, it suddenly dawned upon me that since being with the governor all day, I hadn't had a chance to eat. I was desperately in need of sustenance and so I stuffed my face with the tasty honey butter, garlic bread. It helped, but it wasn't nearly substantial enough to keep me awake while listening to him drone *on and on, on and on, 'And' on…* Big yawn!

It goes without saying Mr. University Yale was a grandiose stuck-up narcissist. His snob-o-meter registered as vast and cosmic as a galaxy floating past the outer limits. Whilst tirelessly and swiftly babbling on, he resembled the Energizer Bunny, only without the adorable little bunny-isms! He really sounded like an alien, hopped up on crystal meth.

Yale was ever so content basking in his conversation for one. He relished the glory of all his *"Me, Myself, and I"* topics. I, on the other hand, was showering in the hopes and glory of escaping far away from this self-important show-off and his "nonversation solo performance."

To be honest, though, this 34-year-old, Ivy-League graduate was seriously hottie-hot-adorable and drool-worthy. All 6 foot 3 of him had good reason to be confident and deserved a healthy portion of ego. That said, and despite his brashness, he was utterly nauseating. It was hard to distinguish if I was out with Mr. Semi-Honest Guy or Mr. Swoft Guy. It was challenging to discern any valid truth about him. Either way, I was in the thick of his personal, La-La-land! This guy was *so on his brand.*

Alas, Yale shifted topics to the always inevitable, sex and more sex, tête-à-tête conversation. Now, everything coming out of his crude mouth was sexual and just shy of vulgar. I thought, "I'm sorry, but that's way too much porn talk before I had a chance to eat today. Or *ever!*"

Just when I thought the date couldn't get any worse, Yale glared at me like a hungry fox with his tongue hanging out of his mouth, bobbing it from side to side, and grunting. "Are you my Happy Meal tonight?"

My facial expression in response had to be some flabbergasted version of an "Eeks-Icky-Ick-Barf," sneer. Unable to brush off his stupid comment, "Do I look like Little Red Riding Hood? Um, NO! And you're not going to be my Big Mac, either." Holy cow, when I agreed to meet this guy for dinner, I didn't realize I, was *going to be dinner!*

My steak and lobster arrived just in time to save the day or, in this case, the date. Or so I thought? And just like that, Yale reached under my skirt and grabbed my private girly space. Irate, with tumultuous fuming anger, I screamed at him with disdain, "Are you kidding me, Harvard?" While yelling, I accidentally spit out a beautiful piece of steak as well. Reaching for my purse, "I am sooooooo outta here!" (Reader, please make sure you read that with all the necessary, all-important O's, in sooooooo.)

He retorted defensively, "No, no, no. I'm sorry. Don't go. I can see how that might have been a smidge out of line."

"No Kidding? Ya, think?" Irate, catching my breath from shock, I yelled, "Do it again Harvard, and I'm gone. And try not to be you!"

Without skipping a beat, he went on disputing my Harvard slams. "Correction, little lady, my name is Yale. You got the wrong university!"

With my inside voice, I thought, WTF, you snooty Harvard, Yale, Cornell, Princeton, Ivy-League hobnobber, with your cavalier attitude! But out came a demanding, "La-di-da! You got the wrong girl and don't touch me again! I can't even begin to tell you just how *'Don't,'* I mean!"

I desperately wanted to escape this moronic man. Sadly, his pride would not allow him to notice how fiercely he upset me as he pressed on even harder with his arrogant self-importance. Oddly enough, he thought his next comment would impress me, pushing me over to his seedy edge.

"I own a 'classic six' on the Upper East Side, with a terrace over-looking a view of the park. I also drive a Model X Crossover Tesla."

I didn't care if he owned all of Manhattan and a Rolls Royce Sweptail. Trying to remain civil, I retorted unimpressed, "That's nice. Good for you. I'm sure your Ivy mom is very proud. Do save your breath, though, for your charms are entirely lost on me." But he couldn't shut up!

"Yes, but my charms are lucky charms!"

At that very leprechaun moment, I sat straight up in my chair and said, "Hocus-Pocus, where is my Crazy-Freak Fairy when I need her?" Not my most skillful misdirect, I'm guessing. This Ivy League brat might not use drugs (and I am only saying, might not) but he surely doesn't need to. Yale is flying high as a kite on his own self-image and amour propre. He's the epitome of the word *turnoff.* But fortunately, not enough to turn me off the sinfully amazing lobster that I was just about to devour.

That's when he leaned in, (not at all gently) grabbed my breast, and kissed my mouth filled with lobster. This was an unexpected bummer, not to mention a waste of the *perfect bite.* I slobbered out fuming, "OK, forget it, pal! Stop, and I frickin' mean it!" Where the hell is the 'Me Too Movement' when you need um? I'm a Masterdater, and this preppy suffers from a severe case of "*Restless Dick Syndrome!*" He was so smug and haughty that it had become impossible to get through the dinner. This date felt like a bad 10-act, high school play dragging on forever. Mortified, as people around us started to notice, I stupidly and foolishly decided to stay.

I waved down our server and meekly demanded, "Wine me, Ben, quickly." He walked away laughing and feeling my pain. The one saving grace, which kept running through my mind, was that I couldn't wait to get back to my besties to "inter-whine" and have a laugh-fest about this night. A guaranteed girls' night out of giggles. I was certain this fiasco would become funnier in a week or two. Or maybe, perhaps never! Every word he uttered and every gesture he created were so fastidiously calculated. What a pathetic poser. In addition, Yale had quite the *Matthew McConaughey* ego. Only without the talent, fame, money, or the Oscar to warrant it. I'm not kidding. I was literally waiting for him to take off his shirt in the middle of the restaurant at any moment. He was remarkably vain, sexually inappropriate, beyond conceited, and exasperating.

With no effort at all, I thought sipping my fourth glass of Shiraz (I had no other alternative, people, so don't you dare judge me), I should at least have a drop of fun tonight. Alone in my own little world, I childishly aped every obnoxious motion he made, which was infinite. Yale is the definition of a conceited man. So much so that he didn't even pick up on my silly antics. But how could he not notice? I behaved so visibly blatant, everyone around our table noticed. The jig was up. Even server Ben was laughing on the floor by this point. Damn, really disappointing, too.

On a positive "high-C note," I was certain by this time there was no possibility whatsoever of having to fake an orgasm. However, I was contemplating faking an emergency exit. I reconsidered since the steak and lobster were exceptionally delectable. Being a glutton for punishment, I hung in there. Still, if he said or did one more inappropriate, disrespectful thing, I was out the door as rapidly as a rock star after a concert.

And just because Yale was Yale, he bent over and whispered in my ear, "You're crazy about me! I mesmerize you. I charm you. I hypnotize you. I beguile you. You, my little journalist, want me badly! I can always tell. Let me help you out by giving you a memorable, euphoric, erotic night. You know you want it. You know you want me. Go on, admit it!"

Rather determined to make my point in a straight-up, nefariously deliberate, enraged manner, I continued with my retaliation. "As charming as you think all of that was, are you insane, downright demented, or on Google's most irrational list? Are you delusional, Mr. Princeton? I'm not mesmerized, nor hypnotized. I am especially not, 'Dickmatized,' with any of your actions this evening. And I venture to say any other evening in this lifetime or any other!" I hastened to add, "BTW, you should know that 'No One' has ever beguiled me. Like Ever!" I paired my statement with an unladylike hand gesture and an expression that implied, "true that!"

"Yeah, right," he slammed back harder than Andre Agassi could have aced a serve. Just then, with no scruples whatsoever, Yale groped me uncomfortably hard under my dress, yet again. "Nice, hot pussy, babe!"

And there it was! Mr. Yale, hottie, Mc-hot-hot, was way too hot for me. I was completely certain and would gamble to say that this Ivy punk is in dire need of a *Sexorcist*! Something shifted in me as if I was possessed, and I snapped. I couldn't be shit-faced enough to deal with this bastard any longer! With a cascade of anger, I yelled,

"Guess what, Ivy-creep? Push just came to shove and I choose shove, you nasty dickwad!"

I accept my reaction was historically lacking refinement and totally unsophisticated. Regardless, I had been violated! I was done and finished with him! As infuriated as I was, before storming out, I had the presence of mind to go to Ben, the splendid server, and ask him to please hurry and wrap up my dinner. What, people? No self-respecting girl would ever say *no* to a takeaway bag of obscenely gourmet steak and lobster. Besides, I was starving. I returned to the table, remained silent, tapped my nails, and ignored Yale. Impatiently waiting for my food, I thought, man this Ivy jerk really takes the cake. Amendment. He takes the whole damn bakery!

Anxiously waiting for Ben to return, Yale looked me in the eye and said (and I kid you not), "Do you want to sit on my cockpit? We can have a cockfight! Hey, I have a loaded gun between my legs for you to cock and shoot off all you want!" That was the precise moment Ben returned with my takeout, and just in time for my 'One-Woman-Show.'

I stood up and looked directly at Harvard Yard, squarely in his eyes, and declared for all to hear, "Princeton, you are a smug, insane, perverted, small-minded, strutting, egomaniac molester! More to the point, you are a pig-in-a-suit! And by the way, that's an insult to both Pigs and Suits!" Everyone in earshot range busted out laughing. Then, in a perfect British accent, far more convincing than his, "Your mother might have given you a class education, but she totally neglected to give you any class. In case she didn't admit to it, *you are not a good boy!* Fare thee well and bugger off you savage. This ship's sailing away to safe waters!"

Point, game, set, and match for the journalist. I waved goodbye to Ben, picked up my glass of savory wine, and *swilled a swig.*

I swaggered out, swinging my sinfully satisfying, savory, super, supper in a sack, with my self-pride safe and secure, strutting sweetly, smiling splendidly, self-importantly, and swashbuckling on out, all the way to the street. Wow, that was indeed a run-on sentence and a major attack on the letter, 'S!' I blame my poor grammar on the 4th glass of red, and not eating all day.

They say there's a lid for every pot. Sadly, Yale's pot overflowed with his bigheaded self-worth, which had flipped his lid way off into another dimension. Clearly why he couldn't shut up and put a lid on it?

I hailed a taxi and sat there feeling victorious and exonerated. Now 6:00 and still early, I was at last enjoying my steak and lobster in peace on the corner of "Thank God," and "I am so glad I got the hell outta there," Boulevards! With a sense of pride and still munching, I murmured out loud without caring one iota if the driver could hear me. "Well, now that didn't turn out to be a happily ever after Internet date!" Snickering happily, I popped another perfect bite into my ravenous mouth. When I looked up, I saw the driver smiling at me in the mirror as he drove.

Unexpectedly, at a red light, the taxi driver from India turned around to look at me in the back seat. He then commiserated and validated me with his heavy native accent. "Rough night? It was bound to happen! I take it this evening was not very ginchy for you?"

I giggled. "What does that mean? Is ginchy a word from India?"

"No, my dear. It's a combined word, derived from the words boss, groovy, bad, rad, cool, bitchin, and sick!" Hearing his answer made me laugh till tears ran down my face. I most definitely needed a laugh at that moment! It was extra funny with his cute, thick broken accent, and dialect.

I asked, "How do you even know that word?"

He clarified, "I have a 14-year-old daughter! She's a screenager!"

I replied, "Ah, yes, that word I know. She has an aptitude for the computer and the Internet!" I smiled at him over the partition and said, "Very Ginchy!" Together, we burst into joyful laughter.

"So, lady, are you a Twitterati?"

Still chuckling and eating, "No, a journalist!"

He laughed, correcting me, "No, no, no!"

"I know what you mean. I'm just kidding. I don't tweet often. Too busy! What's your name? What is your screenager, daughter's name?"

"My name is Aarav… it means peaceful, wisdom, and musical note. My daughter is Aanya… it means grace."

"Lovely! You are a very kind man. I am delighted to meet you."

"What is your name, lovely lady in the back seat of my taxi?

"My name is Mollie. It means… star of the sea!"

"Beautiful name. Just like you, beautiful Mollie. Worry not, my dear. Your true love is most surely out there looking for you! I feel it. Pray and meditate, 'Dhyana,' and he will find you soon."

"Thank you, dear Aarav, for your kind advice. You made my heart smile, and I will heed your words!"

Rewarding my gutsy exit tonight, I changed my plans and requested, "Dear Aarav from India, take me to Macy's Herald Square, please. I am looking for some much-needed shopping restoration."

He replied, laughing, "My daughter would ask to go there too. I believe she's what they call a shopaholic. Very well, Mollie, as you wish!"

I cracked my window open, for this very lovely man's taxi reeked of curry. I giggled inside, thinking this was both humorous and rather cliché. Arriving at my destination, I gave Aarav a huge tip. Mostly for his compassion and humor. I wished him a fond "Namaste" and fled.

I love this gargantuan Macy's store in Manhattan and luckily, there were three glorious hours left until closing. Frolicking around, I smirked, recalling yesterday when I put my Visa credit card up to my ear. I swear I heard the card panting out of breath. To my chagrin, I ignored my disciplined economic thoughts. Besides, I rationalized, there was a fabulous sale going on tonight. I was theoretically saving money! That's my self-serving denial, and I'm basking and luxuriating in it.

Now I ask you, readers, what have we learned here from this 100% true story? What is the conclusion to this Ivy Chapter? Perhaps it is, "Beware of the narcissistic boy who cried sex!" Embarrassingly, I was reminded that this is specifically why I never like to break my rule of knowing someone at least a few weeks before getting together. "Balls In My Face!" In addition, this will also be the last time I ever say, "Oh, Hosh-Posh," to my reasoning again.

Realizing I dodged another nasty dodger, I was immensely grateful to cross off another weirdo from the online list of candidates.

Although meeting with Yale-Harvard-Princeton wasn't a triumph, my business meeting with the governor, meeting Aarav, and my shopping spree at Macy's truly was! I'm talking two thumbs up, triumphant. No, it was even better than that. It was like two boobs up… after implants. (Which I don't have!) So, there's that…

May life always be filled with steak and lobster without Yale, great meetings, Macy's, Ginchy, Dhyana, and *Namaste*!

And let us say… Amen!

CHAPTER 5

Back to the Drawing Board
AKA...LESSONS
Beginning to Date

SIGNS AND ADVICE...
UGH, ZEEEESHHHH, AND BUYER BEWARE

WHEN STARTING TO DATE
Here Are A Few Important Warning Signs...
Things To Avoid and Red Flags to Look Out For:

1. Be mindful that the dating process is monotonous and tedious at best. You will start each rendezvous at ground zero with optimistic hope, faith, and promise. You'll have to explain (Take a big breath) who you are, what you do, what you enjoy, things about your family, your travels, your goals, dreams, and aspirations, what you love and hate, hobbies, political views (If that matters to you), your sign, past relationships, and so forth. Even though all these questions were probably answered either in your profiles or previously on the phone, both of you will invariably have forgotten the responses to these questions and need to ask again.

Unless, of course, you are a Virgo, and in that case, you would have anally documented all that info perfectly. Regardless, this is why I recommend taking notes. When answering emails, get to the point and make it short. Remember to let him do most of the speaking and writing. Men love this and find it refreshing. Most of the girls he has gone out with in the past (unless they were shrewd) never cared to ask him diverse questions about his life or persuaded him to share things about himself. Girls typically ask, *"What do you do for a living? What kind of car do you drive? Do you own your own house? Do you have a 401k?"* It's a good idea to refrain from asking men these types of questions right away, as it sets off the *"gold-digger alert button"* in their brains. Which is indeed understandable.

2. If he only calls or texts a couple of times a week or less, he is most probably not very excited about you. Pay attention. This is an enormous flag. Don't be waiting around the phone all day for him to call. Besides, don't you want someone who is going to be your best friend and looks forward to sharing with you? Huh? Well, don't you?

3. If he sprints away to answer his phone or smiles and lets it ring, then articulates to you, *"Yeah, it's only a business call. I'll get back to it later."* Or insists, *"Please do continue, it's nothing important."* Oh girl, snap! Recognize this is a gigantic sign. It's a massive flag showing he is dating others or is perhaps, dare I say, *married*? Understand, men *never* avoid business calls, especially at night. You can also assume you too will be the girl left on the ringing phone. The girl he doesn't pick up his cell for when he's on a date with another woman. This insinuates that *you are nothing important to him, either.* Don't be foolish letting your ego think otherwise!

4. Is he super-paranoid for you to see his phone? Does he sneak, hide, lock his phone, and take it with him to the bathroom? Well, my dear, you can be certain there is someone or something else going on. It's like a *"duh,"* sign. This is a big *waving red flag,* girlfriend. If he's a sneak, a liar, or a cheat in the very beginning, it'll only get worse down the road. I certainly don't think this is who you are looking for. Gosh, I sure as hell hope not!

5. If he's texting throughout the entire date and claims it's about the football score, he undoubtedly has another girl who doesn't know about you, on the other end of the phone! Mumbo-jumbo… A flag! FYI, a person who is constantly texting, is called an "informania." Besides, texting the entire time you are out with someone is altogether rude. Football or not, there's a flag on the field. Well, unless, of course, he's the head coach. But still, why is he out with you instead of coaching the team? So, he's cheating either way you throw, pass, fumble, or kick the ball around! But, if he *is* the head coach, then he totally more than likes you, playing hooky on a game or a practice for you. But what are the odds of that happening? Besides, do you really want to be with an unreliable, fickle football coach? That's clearly a technical foul, and so far out of bounds! You might want to intercept this guy at the very start of the game.

6. If he lacks excitement when he's with you (and he didn't do this in the beginning), that's a dismal sign. If when you are together, he doesn't want sex very often, but always used to want it all the time? Girl, *please!* Come on, you must know that's a flickering sign. A twinkling billboard sign, up in lights, proving he's getting it elsewhere. Or a possible herpes outbreak he doesn't want you to know about. In any case, a lose-lose situation, and

a flapping flag for you. I just hate a double dipper, don't you?

7. If he tells you he is, "*Oh, So Busy,* these days," and doesn't have time to see you regularly like he used to... Hey girl, can you not see that big flag? If you tap into your intuition (as you should) your ears will be ringing. This is your instinct telling you he's not, "*Oh, So Busy,*" for another girl. Don't you want a man who is excited to see you and can't wait to be with you? If so, you need to get *"Oh, so busy yourself"* and swiftly walk on...

8. If when you first started going out with a guy, he lavished you with adoring affection and attention, and now he currently seems bored, aloof, or distant... Seriously girlfriend, that is beyond a sign. This is a blatant red flag that he's no longer enchanted or enamored with you. No doubt, he found someone else that he's enchanted with. You better crank up your mojo or he's gone. If you ask me, *I say, let em go!* Most likely, it's not you at all. He's just a player and a scoundrel who wants to move on to another flavor. Rest assured; he'll be bored with the next girl soon enough. You'll need to decide if you should proceed with Mr. Disenchanted. If you do, use caution. Still, be honest and open. Tell him exactly how you feel!

9. If he starts putting down your life, your looks, your weight, your friends and family, your success, or lack of it... honey, wake up! That is a screaming sign. If he insults you regularly, he is evidently not confident in himself. This loser apparently has many issues of his own. He most assuredly is not capable of loving you or anyone else. Once this sort of behavior starts, it will continue. It's obvious he doesn't even like himself. And it is very likely Mr. insecure is getting ready to dump you. Don't

give him the chance. Dump him first! You deserve someone who worships you and adores everything you are. Don't be bullied from him or *anyone*. If you don't respect yourself, why would anyone else? Tell him to piss off!

10. If a man yells at you or is *violent in any form whatsoever*, I beg you to understand that this is way more and far past the parameters of a sign. I swear on a stack of Dior outfits, this is *abuse!* I'm warning you. It will not be a one-time thing! This is only the beginning. A nightmare will ensue, and it won't end well. So, "Run, Jane, Run!" Honestly, if I were you, I'd go find Dick & Spot and hang with them instead! "See Smart Jane, run!"

11. If a man is unkind, offensive, uncaring, aggressive, hurtful, obstinate, cruel, mean, or not a gentleman, Sweetie, that is more like a bevy of signs. *Don't cha think?* Girl, I hope you can see this without my having to tell you! Keep a watchful eye out, no matter how gorgeous or great you think he is in bed. You must want love, affection, and tenderness in your life. Find the guy who will revere, appreciate, support, and cherish you. And, of course, drive you crazy in bed, too. Even if you need to teach him how! Trust me, ya just may have to. News flash: *"All men are not great lovers!"*

12. Instead of enjoying the lengthy, fun, intimate, intriguingly wonderful conversations you shared in the beginning, he is now answering you in succinct brief responses? Honey, that's a bright rosy flag! If you used to experience hours of lovemaking and afterward luxuriated in each other's arms, and now you're having quickie unsatisfying sex, and then he sprints out the door? OK, that is a big, flashing warning flag. Girl, you are totally

scaring me if you can't spot these flags. Prepare yourself, for he is ready to skedaddle. I say, open the door wide, and announce loudly for all to hear, *"The player has left the building."* Then send him a thank-you card!

13. Without question, count on and be ready for Murphy's Law! When the day finally arrives for that special date with the guy you really like and feel excited about, you can fundamentally expect to get your worst period ever, retaining water, leaving you puffy, in pain, and having to deal with raging PMS. Thanks a lot, Murphy! Or, pathetically, you could also wake up very sick and need to cancel. Also, when you get up in the morning to brush your teeth, you discover a dreaded, colossal, aching zit that gets even worse when you try to pop it! Hell, this is not a sign or a flag. This is classic karma harassment and invasion of the human body. Dammit, Murphy! BTW, popping a zit before it's ready only tends to complicate matters. Funny, we all know this, yet we still attempt to pop it anyway.

14. What are my feelings about sex soon after meeting? Here's the thing. Don't! Just Don't! Not because of morals or ethics. I feel if a man gets what he wants so easily (and men always want sex), he'll move on and leave you before he even gets to know who you are. I assure you that if you wait, he will have the time and opportunity to respect and appreciate just how wonderful you are. Don't allow the wrong guy to see the "Ho" in you, or even the right guy to see your "Inner Ho" too quickly. At this delicate time, so early on, he doesn't deserve to experience you in this fashion. Make him earn the reward, which should come from knowing, caring, and even loving you. The sex, by the way, is so much better with genuine emotions behind it. If you wait,

you might develop a greater possibility of a long-term relationship. Give success a chance. Sleeping with men too soon might be part of your problem, which has resulted in you still being single. (Please, don't shoot the messenger.) Sex, just for the sake of having sex, is not love. It's simply a placebo of love. Recognize the disparity and grasp they are entirely 2 different things. To be blunt, this is what "sex buddies" are for and why they were invented. Not that I condone, support, or believe in them. Nor am I against the concept. Back off!

Here's a tip I endorse. Use your vibrator before going out on dates. It'll keep you from falling into the "sex too quickly trappings" because you are horny. If you apply number 13 above, Murphy's Law, the batteries will undoubtedly be dead. Keep extras handy. Damn you, Murphy!

15. Don't, I repeat, don't drink too much on a date with a new guy. This irresponsible, reckless, *"fun before puking"* behavior is only to be enjoyed with your girlfriends. While dating, you must be in control. Forget about that extra drink. Have some carbs like fries and a cheeseburger instead. Speaking of carbs, *never* ask a guy, "Does this outfit I'm wearing make me look fat?" That question is *only* to be asked of a trusted, great friend!

16. *"Don't ignore the flags and signs, No Matter What!"* If you sense something isn't right, then believe me, it isn't! Know your power. Listen to your inner voice. She's clever and smarter than you are. Signs and flags are *never wrong.* To ignore them might very well turn out to *be wrong!*

17. **A Crucial, Critical, Vital, Imperative, Warning!!!!**
    If, and when, you have sex with anyone... "Wear A Condom!"

Even two if necessary! *Girrrl,* I'm telling you, cover that thing up!!! It is a hazardous world out there, filled with all types of people who lie about everything. Which also includes their sexually transmitted diseases. Who the hell knows, they might even be unaware that they are carrying one. **Remember, the pill or other similar birth control methods do not protect you from STDs!!!! For real!** I don't care how perfect, good-looking, rich, successful, clean-cut, or honorable a guy appears to be. The mere fact that he seems to be so fricking perfect is what offers him endless opportunities for unprotected sex, and typically the one who'll contract a disease. He will then pass it on to other naïve women based on this same, '*he's so perfect,*' misguided logic. I suggest before rushing into sex with a guy, both of you should get tested for a variety of STDs. Sure, it's a pain in the ass and embarrassing. Regardless, I plead with you to obey my warning! It could save your life or even some painful hassles in the future.

No matter what, don't take any unnecessary chances or risks concerning your health. Do you hear me, Samantha? Just teasing all of you, Samantha's out there. Just thought I'd scare you straight! But I really meant to say, Jessica. Still joking, Jessica! I am, however, not joking when I say an unprotected orgasm, no matter how magnificent it might be, is not worth the gamble! I get that most men (and some women), don't like the way most protection choices feel. Whatever, heed my words. "**HIV, AIDS, herpes, syphilis, chlamydia, HPV, gonorrhea**, and all the rest will feel a *whole hell of a lot worse than wearing a condom!*"

Moving on, I recently had an interesting thought after receiving countless, offensively vulgar, *red-flag* online messages from rather uncouth men. I'm preparing you for them, so you won't be caught off-guard. At some point in your search, you will also struggle with these naughty messages and come to agree with me about the following idea.

How cool would it be if there was a special hole in our computers enabling us to squirt pepper spray at these contemptible men in response to all their offensive and disgusting sexually inappropriate emails and texts? I feel as though I sometimes need to wear a Hazmat Suit to stay safe and protected from these filthy texts. Just a passing notion you will come to understand. There is a chapter later, which fully demonstrates these vile, horribly inappropriate emails. Unfortunately, you too will receive many of your own. For the life of me, I don't understand what the hell is wrong with these wicked men. I mean, did someone drop a house on their sisters? Like, "What in tarnation?" What permits these twisted, deviant perverts to be out there roaming about freely? "What in tarnation," (pronounced, whut nn ternay-shun) is a southern, nicer way of saying, "What the fuck?" Anyhow, if you do go online, and I shudder to say, in today's fast-paced world, you might find it necessary. Please understand you'll innocently be entering "The Twilight Zone," or AKA, the peculiar, freaky dating zone!

Anakin Skywalker, with all his memorable wisdom, once said, "Fear is the path to the dark side." My personal views and wisdom say, "Online dating is the dark side!" The upside? You never know for certain what's going to happen! You might get lucky, meet the love of your life, and have some great fun along the dark side's bumpy road of terror.

All kidding aside, there really are some awesomazing people out there, if you know what to look for and what to avoid.

Defining the art of love and dating can sometimes be an ideological, intimate, and personal concept. So just go out there, have fun, enjoy, and define it for yourself.

Above all, keep the faith, stay positive, and remain hopeful. That includes both you Samantha, and Jessica! Lord knows you will need it!

A Final Thought

If a man tells you he never wants to get married, and (or) he doesn't ever want to have children, take him at his word. Believe him the first time. Trust me when I say, "Don't attempt to snag him deceitfully." Entrapping anyone unfairly never works out in the end. Continue your search to find Mr. Right, instead. Honesty is the right road to travel on.

Gee, with all the advice I'm offering, I guarantee I'm gifting you pearls of wisdom, rare gems, and diamonds here, people! I'm not a sage, a love guru, or Socrates. I'm merely a journalist. But I know of what I speak! *Especially about Pearls, Rare Gems, and Diamonds!*

CHAPTER 6

The Italian Guy from Napoli

AKA, THE BEST SEX OF MY LIFE????
OFFICIALLY KNOWN AS... I HAD IT COMING'!

Like a grown-up, mature woman, I take full responsibility for my actions in this specific online dating portion of the program. I asked for it, I got it, and I also surmise to say I'll never forget nor regret it. This was the most radical, spontaneous, and romantic experience I had ever known. Not to mention, with this endeavor, I exceeded my winning record for the most irresponsible, impulsive, and reckless behavior to date. That's specifically why I cherish, "The Italian from Napoli Caper." Interesting, I'm proud of this venture despite all the frustrating and 'WTF' situations that go along with this story. In my defense, this guy could sell the ocean a cup of water.

His name was Valerio, a mega, smokin hot, molto-bello, bangin' sexy Italian hunk of a man. We met on an Italian online dating site. That alone should have set off the alarm bells and my *first flashing red flag.*

Since I speak Italian fluently, I figured, why the hell not? Rather perplexed by his profile photos, I naturally thought, how could any man look this picture-perfect in real life? And, if he is truly this *studtacular,* how could he still be single, and in Italy, no less? Irrespective, I was all in.

We wrote back and forth, asking an infinite number of questions of one another until we were better acquainted. After all the endless cross-examinations and interrogations were completed, we began to FaceTime, (a very long distance) on the phone. WhatsApp and Messenger, people. It's free! I found everything about this alluring man to be overwhelmingly suggestive, from his Italian accent to his velvety, seductive voice. He was exquisitely irresistible and dashing, causing me to feel aroused, ecstatic, and hoping to experience his savoir-faire in person. I believed I had hit the online dating jackpot and was a very fortunate, lucky girl. Allegedly!?

I must stop here for a moment to reveal that I am more than a bit disturbed with myself for using the antiquated word '*dashing,*' *above.* I don't even think my grandmother used this word. That's up there with "swell, fella, and too-da-loo!" Please accept my sincere, mortified apology for my old-world slip of the tongue. Hopefully, it won't happen again. Dashing? Did I just say dashing? Eek, I clearly said dashing! Ugh!

Amending my vocabulary, Valerio was seriously hot! We shared the most delightful conversations. And in case you are wondering... yes, of course! After an appropriate amount of time, (Or not. Truthfully, it was the 3rd call), we randomly had a little sexual fun-tastic on the phone. Fortunately, Valerio never became disrespectful or crossed over that fine line into cheeky or vulgar during our several sexy tête-à-têtes. I saved all the decadently exciting, vulgar, sexually immoral, and nasty behavior for when we met! Aha, there you go, reader. I see you judging me! You would've crossed the puritanical line too if you saw him. Besides, "A girl's gotta get her groove on!" I confess, I impishly enjoyed embarrassing him by asking lots of personal, provocative questions about sex. I saw him blushing all the way from Italy. Which naturally only turned me on more.

We shared a harmonious rapport, making it quite comfortable for us to talk to one another. We felt safe enough to discuss the most intimate topics and trusted we spoke in complete confidence. One night when I felt extra daring, I wanted to know if he did or didn't like hair, *down yonder*, on a woman's body. You know what I mean, "To hair or not to hair?" I was curious because I heard Europeans have very different views on this issue. When I sensed the time was right, I tiptoed in and presented my question to Valerio. He emphatically replied, "*NO* hair, bella, amore mio!" Good to know, I thought. And thus, it is written and tucked away.

After four months of FaceTime, and speaking on the phone, I contemplated flying off to Italy to worship him in person. I mean, how can anyone blame me after hearing Valerio say things to me such as… "Mi sono infatuato di Te!" (*"I'm infatuated with you!"*) "Ti voglio baciare." (*"I want to kiss you."*) "Sono pazzo / pazza di Te!" (*"I'm crazy about you."*) "Mi abbagliare." (*"You dazzle me."*) "Giorno e notte, io sogno solo a te." (*"Day and night, I only dream of you."*) "Tu mi hai stregato con la tua magia." (*"You have bewitched me with your magic."*) "Sono incantato e incantato da te." (*"I am charmed and enchanted by you."*) "Nei tuoi occhi c'è il cielo." (*"Heaven is in your eyes."*) And "Quando sento la tua voce la distanza." (*"When I hear your voice, the distance disappears."*)

Come on! No woman could defy such extraordinary romance! Yes, indeed, it was Casanova overkill. I'm not a total blonde! Of course, I realized possibly, feasibly, and imaginably, Valerio was completely *full of shit!* After all, I wasn't born yesterday. Though I have to say, they were fantastic lines. Seriously, I gotta give the guy credit. How could any girl resist. It was hot and impossible not to fall for it. Especially spoken with his heavy Italian accent. Any normal girl would melt with this guy. If nothing else, Valerio deserved recognition and appreciation. For it takes a lot of superb fakery, for a liar to appear this honest. No matter what the truth, kudos to him! Meanwhile, I was going to get to his bottom. I mean, I intended to get to the bottom of the truth, that is. Or with some luck, both!

Naturally, I recognized Valerio ultimately was not "The One." Nonetheless, he was definitively the one for right now. Plus, I urgently needed a fling. What else could I do? Was there any other choice here? Even so, I was struggling with my innermost logical feelings of, "I would be crazy, stupid, reckless, foolish, insane, plus reaching epic proportions of madness to fly 6,107 miles to Italy (another country), for a man I had never even met! The mere notion was irrational, to the max."

The very instant I heard myself say those words out loud, I laughed and swiftly ran to book my flight. This excellent decision was negligently careless, rash, and precisely why I wickedly opted to go! It was a supremely delicious, undeniably silly, impulsive choice, and a bad idea. *God, Aren't Those the Best!!!!* I highly advocate everyone doing more than a few of these devilish choices in your life. After all we only live once. Though personally, I don't agree with this, *one life* philosophy at all!

My Italian and I spoke only one time after I told him of my plans to come to Italy. Looking down at his *studnormous* photos on my laptop, I crumbled like a cookie. Valerio's gorgeous appearance effortlessly fanned the flames of my aching desire for him. I was smitten to my core. Oh, shit, *"smitten?"* Good Lord, that's right up there with *dashing*, isn't it? I can't begin to minimize my shame here. What, in the vocabulary, world is happening to me? Anyway, this Victorian-tongued lady was going to Italy.

I spent days buying the sexiest lingerie with the hopes of driving my Italian stud-muffin towards the amatory city of Lust-ville. No prim, proper, goody-goody, puritanical morals hiding deep within me were heading off to Europe. Nope, this was going to be an absolute *sexscape*.

Ciao, Italy! One week and a crucial Brazilian wax later, I was on a plane headed for Rome to meet this stunning gentleman from Napoli.

The tediously long flight seemed an eternity with my anticipation bursting at an all-time high. I was going out of my mind with excitement during the entire flight. Knowing it would be a long journey, flying so many hours, I realized I needed to be comfortable. Nevertheless, I still wanted to arrive impossibly stunning, simple, and yet classic the first time he laid eyes on me. Accordingly, I wore a fitted Versace black sweater, showing just a hint of the girls', my favorite perfectly skin-tight yet comfy Armani Jeans, set off with an adorable Gucci belt, and a pair of very high, trendy Manolo red heels, and of course, sexy red lipstick to match.

At last, the plane landed in Italy. Like I always say, "There is no place like Rome and *in an Italian's arms!*" Suddenly, and equal to an *on-air, broadcasting cue*, my heart started pounding because Valerio was to pick me up at the Rome Fiumicino, Airport. After retrieving my luggage, I walked through the security doors shaking, as I searched for my Italian. Nervous and anxious, my legs went weak. I could feel my heart racing way too fast for it to be considered healthy. O-M-Gosh, and just like that, there he was. The instant I saw him waiting outside of security (although far off in the distance), he took my breath away. (Eventually, though, I'll want that back!) All things measured, it appeared Valerio, in all his glory, takes the gold medal for the "Gorgeous Man" category in any Olympics.

He was far more exquisite than his photos presented him to be, which is exceptionally rare for online dating. From what I could see, he wore a body-hugging, baby blue collared Italian designer shirt, and very snug jeans. So tight, he must have literally painted them on. Even from a distance, it was visibly noticeable he had achieved six-pack abs and was positively circumcised. Since many Europeans aren't, I was pleasantly relieved. To be honest, it was good to know in advance, as to avoid the *"UM, OH MY"* gasps. Sorry to be insensitive to the uncut guys out there. But personally, uncircumcised penises look like a Shar-Pei dog, a pig in a blanket hors d'oeuvre, or a penis wearing a turtleneck. To the contrary, I suppose if I ever needed a skin graft, these uncut guys would come in rather handy. Since there is "no end" to my point, I'll cut it off right now!

While I didn't sleep a wink during the flight due to my excessive enthusiasm, I somehow miraculously looked fresh and rested. I was pleased I had taken the time to reapply my makeup on the plane and quite thrilled my hair stayed so perfect. As I approached closer to Valerio, it was as if this moment became frozen in time. What I was feeling for him was undeniably a *sinful sexual desire at first sight*. I wanted to order a side of him, 'al dente,' with Alfredo Crema Salsa, E Rapidamente. By the looks of Valerio, it appeared my jet had landed in Utopia, Italy. My first vision of his classic Italian good looks imprinted forever in my mind. However, not to be confused with imprinting, in the film "Twilight."

Valerio is 32 years old, 6 feet, fabulously ripped, with a flawless body. He resembled a Roman idol, the Greek Adonis, or a Phoenician Demi-god of beauty. There he stood with his evocative statuesque posture, happily smiling at me as I ran towards him. His chocolate-brown eyes, magnificent golden olive skin, and his thick head of silky black hair, (with the slightest hint of premature salt to his pepper) gave me goosebumps. I wanted to run my fingers through it at once. But that would be so wrong, profoundly aggressive, and too much too soon, even for me! Damn...

Exuding pure delight, now seeing him before me in the flesh, I couldn't help but notice his signature trait of deep-set dimples. They were so sexy. I childishly wanted to jump into them. Instead, I jumped into his awaiting open arms, hugged him tightly, and immediately ran my fingers through his hair. Sometimes I can just be so tacky. No discipline, No self-control, No restraint, and No class... I just loved that about me! I'm glad I did it and would do it again. Mr. Napoli flirtatiously laughed and then ran his fingers through my hair. *Touché*! I loved his carefree style and poised confidence. I giggled, as I spoke in Italian, "Valerio, `e così bello conoscerti, finalmente." ("*Valerio, it is so nice to meet you, finally.*")

To which he answered, "Così meraviglioso conoscerti troppo bella ragazza, Sei stupendo!" ("*So wonderful to meet you too, beautiful Mollie. You are gorgeous.*") He pulled me close to his chest and passionately kissed me. We were undeniably off to a bewitching start. Even exhausted, I instantly perked up, looking at this fierce, savage, brutally awesome, yummy man. The meticulously fine Italian was a steamy double cup of arousing espresso. Clearly, I needed to drink a big goblet of him, instantly!

We drove 3 glorious hours from Rome to Napoli, conversing solely in Italiano. I loved speaking this beautiful, romantic language. Strange, and as out of character as it was, I shockingly liked how perilously fast Valerio was driving. I noticed everyone else was driving dangerously fast, too. Which in Italy is typically faster than a speeding bullet. Studying him as he drove, I couldn't get past how gorgeous he was. I tried not to appear obvious and strained to look at him from the corner of my eyes. He was justifiably the holy grail of handsome. I just couldn't understand how he could still be single. Not a moment passed by before he brought to my attention that I wasn't fooling him in the least. Responding with a crooked smile, "Bella, why so much are you staring at me?"

I replied timidly. "No, oh no, I'm not! I'm a, just, you know, trying to, um, avoid the wind blowing in my eyes?" We both laughed. I was so busted. Regardless, I continued to stare. With the top down on his Alfa Romeo convertible, our hair blew wildly in the wind as he sped along to Napoli. It was a splendid sunny day with clear blue skies and a slight nip in the air. We chatted while listening to American music and the Italian singers, Vasco Rossi and Marco Mengoni. Valerio's soft hands and long fingers were caressing my legs and holding my hands throughout the drive. Quivering, I thought of far better places his hands could be caressing me right now. Ooh-la-la!

Life surely doesn't get any better than this, I thought, gushing like a teenager. I grinned, thinking, how fortunate could a girl get? He noticed my smile, as he did everything, and quizzed, "Why to smile you, love?"

"Oh, Valerio, I'm just so happy to be here with you at last!"

"Bella, I too, happy am!" I was melting inside from the sensuous smell of his cologne and his erotic beautiful... *"Everything!"* I tried desperately to keep my cool. Yet, I don't believe I did a great job of it at all. Yep, shamefully, not so much! His magnificently chiseled face, superhero physique, and fashion-model hair gave me a horny twinge. This was not only noticeable, but he drove me senseless. It was surreal, being here in Italy, with a perfect stranger. Perfect in every sense of the word. He was powerfully touching my heart without even trying. And I loved it.

By the time we arrived, less than three hours later, I was all brushed up on my Italian and ready to speak with ultimate confidence. Although Mr. Italian invited me to stay with him at his house, I am no fool and wisely came prepared. I took assignments to write feature stories on five-Star hotels in Napoli, Sorrento, Ischia, Capri, Firenze, Toscana, and Roma on my way back. I wanted my independence, plus a "Plan B" just in case this imprudent lover's escapade didn't work out as designed. We arrived at my posh hotel, the exclusive Excelsior, and checked in. It is quite a privilege and outrageous good fortune getting to write feature stories about spectacular hotels such as these. Gosh, how I loved my job.

The refined bellman escorted us to my room. The second he left after placing my overweight luggage into the extravagant suite, Valerio threw me somewhat uncomfortably too hard, yet controlling and kinky, onto the bed. Disconcertingly so, I liked it. Without wasting a moment, he jumped on top of me. His aggression was devastatingly arousing, in a very XXX porn-film, maneuver-ish approach. The man was astonishingly sexy. How delicious to feel the weight of his dreamy, hard body on top of mine.

"Bella, Mollie," he moaned in Italian, "*Non potevo aspettare Un altro secondo di essere dentro di Te e una parte di Te. Ho sognato questo momento per così tanto tempo.*" ("Beautiful Mollie, I simply can't wait another second to be inside of you, to feel myself inside of you, and to be a part of you. I have been dreaming of this moment for such a long time.")

Valerio grabbed my hair firmly, pulled me towards him, and pressed his thick, luscious lips onto mine. He forcefully clutched the button on my jeans to rip them off. But instead, he literally tore the button off. My jeans button, which was never to be found again.

I was desperately excited. My endless anticipation of this moment was enormous, and my desire for him was boundless.

"Bello," I pleaded, "Feed Me. Please feed me, Valerio!"

He impatiently groaned, "Sto provando il mio Bellissimo angelo!" ("I am trying to, my beautiful angel!")

"No, no. Baby no. Listen to me," I begged. (Nessun, nessun, bambino mi asolta,") "I haven't slept nor eaten in over seventy-two hours. You need to feed me. I need something to eat so I don't faint on you."

I must interject. If there is anything in life, an Italian from Italy comprehends like no other culture, it's food and eating. With a huge, hard, pulsating penis, ready with desire, erupting under his zipper, he looked at me with a mischievous grin. In his funny English, "Problem no, love my. Go, let's quickly, Rapido!" I assumed he meant, No problem, my love.

With that, we jumped up and walked along the Mediterranean water's edge towards one of the charming Trattorias down the strada. I hoped none of the worshipers from the elite world of fashion noticed my now inappropriate button-less jeans. In Valerio fashion, he noticed and laughed when I tried to hide the fact. "No problema bella! I also, off, will my button rip. Will comfortable make you it feel more." Trust me, this sounded far more amorous in his broken English/Italian accent. Though he tried to speak English, I suggested we speak Italian for the rest of the trip.

Valerio was calming, relaxing to be with, and it goes without saying, abundantly easy to look at. I sensed I was humiliating myself with my adoring, silly, girlish glances. Guess what, I didn't care anymore. This whole situation I currently found myself in was nothing short of a real-life Harlequin romance novel. Plus, I knew the sweet, innocent pages would soon turn onto the steamy, passionate, hot, and erotic pages. I adored the essence and spirit of this long-awaited affair that was about to unfold. I was impassioned with slutty, prurient, unholy thoughts. Gosh, I loved that too! I imagine it's my *whoremoans!* I pinched myself, petrified I'd awaken back in America, only to discover it was all but a fantasy. Except it was real. I was here with Valerio, who was effortlessly making my heart smile.

How awesome to be dining together at this enchanting seaside trattoria. It was genuine ecstasy, feeling the cool, soothing breeze on my face while sitting across the table from Valerio at long last. This would undoubtedly be a magical memory to treasure. All I could think of, as we spoke in Italian over my Spaghetti Con Vongole and Vino Chianti Classico, was the many mischievous carnal things I was going to do to this man, endlessly, for hours. I don't know what he had hidden under his clothes, but I knew I wanted it and every part of him. I was the diva Eve, and I was positively going to take a bite of his crisp, delicious apple, and all his other forbidden fruits! Unable to wait another second, I leaned in, put my hand on his penis, and sensuously rubbed it until I found the Genie I was looking for. He turned red as the wine. No one cared. It's Italy!

I didn't know if it was the many months of waiting, the delightful, exhilarating drive from Rome, the vino, the divine pasta, or sitting outside under a cool, star-filled Neapolitan sky that made this night so irresistibly bewitching. Gazing into Valerio's eyes, I could see a clear reflection of the full moon shining on them. Then, it dawned on me for the first time all day. I realized this luminous, *sexy-as-fuck man* looked exactly like Brad Pitt in the film, "Meet Joe Black," except for the color of his hair. Though, I wasn't sure yet which Joe he was. Joe the sweet guy, or Mr. Death, Joe?

The whole affair was a provocative aphrodisiac, making me wild with concupiscent *sexpectations.* Perhaps it was simply my overabundance of pent-up desires and sexual longing for him that made me enormously enraptured. Just being next to him, his touch, and his smell were making me disconcertingly wet. I felt wickedly playful and hypnotized thinking about the "Fifty-One Shades of Valerio!" Feeling splendidly horny, I was hoping to experience his very last shade before returning to America. I was fervidly the prisoner of his alluring, sensuous seduction. Recognizing I was caught up in *Dreamland*, I quickly pushed myself to return from my lust-filled thoughts, back to my throbbing body in the restaurant. Valerio and I were now devouring every dolce bite of my favorite Italian desserts, the reverse "Bongo-Bongo and Tartufo di Pizzo." It was extra sweet as my hand deliciously enjoyed being down his designer couture pants.

Abruptly, my heart skipped a beat, as I knew within an hour, I would share slow, tender, sweet, passionate sex with this exquisite man. His already hard, throbbing penis would soon penetrate deep inside me. The long-awaited anticipation of this romance had been driving me fucking, delirious for months and it was promptly going to happen for real. My yearning for him had no logical or earthly limitations. Oct. 23rd would be a euphoric night I knew I would never forget, for he would bring me to dizzying heights of ecstasy. My imagination would soon cease, and reality would begin! Paradise was about to open its doors. I sensed I could safely say with appreciation, "Thank you online dating!" Ouch. Yeah, that hurt!

After enjoying Valerio's eye-candy good looks, some rest, delectable food, and his flirtatious sexy stares, I was rejuvenated. We happily strolled back to the hotel, arm in arm like 2 children on Christmas Eve. However, our gift to unwrap was happily far less pious or innocent.

FYI, in Italy, people don't walk at night. They stroll! Our stroll back to my suite seemed like an eternity. Judging by the obvious gazes from everyone in the lobby upon our entering, we were fooling no one with our casual, blasé demeanor. Perhaps I was just being self-conscious? Though it appeared, the entire crowd was giving us the *"thumbs up, have at it you two," accompanied with their chuckling wink-wink,* glares.

We ran into the elevator, and I quickly pressed the 15th floor. All the while, I was pressing up against his fantastic, bulging, hard-on. At that moment, as the elevator was closing, a very famous *'A-list' American actress* quickly snuck in before the doors closed. I couldn't help noticing she was relentlessly staring at us. Suffice it to say, I wasn't interested in her at all. I couldn't care less about her ogling Hollywood eyes upon us, as my Italian grabbed my ass and planted an impassioned kiss on my lips.

The young film star (who currently had a blockbuster movie out), giggled while trying desperately to be invisible. I was dying, for the elevator seemed to move in slow motion, climbing up to my floor. I ached to have this man inside of me at once. I craved and hungered for his strong, impeccable naked body on top of mine. I longed to enjoy his large, hard penis thrusting inside of me. I needed to be completely taken sexually by him. I was his submissive, willing to be controlled and erotically savaged by him. I fantasized about this moment for what seemed like a lifetime. The elevator reached the tenth floor. As the starlet walked away, she turned back to us, giggled with jealous wonder, unable to ignore Valerio's huge dick (which now displayed a wet spot on his pants), and chuckled, "Wow, have fun, you guys!" We laughed, but I thought to myself, Oh, I will! And by the way, eat your heart out, A-list actress!

After we stormed into the room, Valerio threw me up against the wall, kissing me madly, just like in the movies. No doubt, like in one of the elevator actress's movies. I always alleged this only happened in BS, unrealistic Hollywood movies. Nope, it's real. "Mamma Mia!" I pleaded, "Wait, Valerio! Wait a second! Please, open the bottle of Champagne, go sit on the balcony, and kindly wait a rapido ten minutes till I return." After traveling 24 hours, I needed to take a quick shower, perfume up, powder up, and put on a seductively badass outfit. The instant I returned to the room feeling sexy and enticing, I begged in Italian, ("Portami Valerio… prendere adesso. Inserisci me e Io sarò quello che mai è necessario che Io sia.") "Take me Valerio… take me now. Enter me, and I will be whatever you need me to be." Hours of mind-blowing sex had arrived at last.

And just like that, Valerio tore off my $250 brand new Victoria's Secret, sexy, red-laced courtesan tunic, garter belt, and thong without even noticing them. (A disappointing bummer.) He did some weird version of foreplay, and entered me forcefully, rapidly, and awkwardly, like a clumsy armature. I could only think, "WTF? Ouch. What the fuckity, fuck, fuck?"

And there he went, Bam-Bam, Bam-Bam, Bam-Bam, and Wham-Bam! Baffled, I thought, was that just practice sex? I didn't even get the customary "Thank you, ma'am," for *bad fucks* sake. I was confused and screamed at him at the top of my inside voice. "Are you kidding me? That was your shining moment we had been waiting for? Talk about *short Cummings!*" There was no legit sensual foreplay, no kissing, no romance, no tenderness, no passion or pizzazz, no finesse, and no sensitivity or style whatsoever. The only thing I got was a whole lot of unfamiliar "sexual No's!" Even worse (if you can imagine that) there was *No Orgasm for Me!!!!* Not one. Hell, there wasn't even enough time or desire to fake one.

My imagination and torrid dreams for this exciting romantic rendezvous were crushed. I repeated, *"Ouch"* and *"seriously,"* over a thousand times in my mind. Rightfully so, I was left feeling upset, bewildered, cheated, and thinking, "What the terrible fuck just happened here?" I didn't get it. Ironically, it appeared the joke was on me, Miss Hollywood movie star. I was the one eating my heart out! I waited for what seemed an era for the greatest sexual adventure of my life. Then, for about five-ish minutes (most likely less), Bam-Bam, Bam-Bam, Bam-Bam, and Bam, and Ouch, Ouch, Ouch, and Ouch. And then, the worst sex imaginable was over? I mean seriously, Italiano, *Valerio?* That was just *One Really Bad Shade of you.* What happened to the other fifty good ones? The only mind-blowing thing happening in this lovely hotel bed tonight was my "What The Fuck & Are You Kidding Me?" reactions. It was impossible to believe, and not among the ka-zillion scenarios I had constantly played over and over in my head for months. I flew 6,107 miles for this disappointing, unimaginable, bad sex? Hmm, "bad sex?" That's an oxymoron if I ever heard one! Totally disillusioned, I didn't know whether to laugh, cry, run away, or just return home over this horrific *Sexperience.*

Rather than indulge in a meltdown, I rebooted and refreshed my mind. I took a deep breath and calmly thought about it logically. Listening to my inside voice, (still screaming in my head) all I could think was, *"But he's Italian! What the fuck?"* Extra disheartening, there was no snuggling, afterglow, or tenderness. Valerio gave me a brisk goodnight kiss and left shortly after his tragic excuse for making love. His awkward skedaddle seconds afterward, with his head bent down, showed how mortified he was by his sexual performance. (If one could even call it that.)

Suddenly, like a news flash, I understood. Oh, I am so stupid. The poor guy must have been nervous as hell. After all, he did disclose he hadn't had sex since his divorce over a year ago. *If that were at all true. Just sayin'. So, I* compassionately did the rational big-girl thing. I let it go and *pretended it didn't happen.* Like that

THE ITALIAN GUY FROM NAPOLI | 79

foolish drunken night in college, when I decided to give myself bangs. With a match! Or, when interviewing Britney Spears, I called her Lady Gaga. Oops! So, I'll delete this unfortunate sexual faux pas from my consciousness, pretending it didn't happen. In more scientific terms, *Denial!* After all, tomorrow is another day. Surely, this was only a rare, isolated incident, and he was too humiliated to discuss it. But then, why did he think licking and sucking my nose, ears, and eyes, then biting my toes and knees for 20 seconds was foreplay? *Hurtful!* Whatever, I erased my negative thoughts, dropped this fruitless, sexless encounter, and fell into a much-needed, deep sleep.

At 6:30 in the morning, the exciting hustle and bustle sounds of the Neapolitan city coming to life awakened me. I felt refreshed, energized, and content to forget all about the previous night. Enjoying a cappuccino, a basket filled with muffins, bread, fresh berries & assorted cheeses from room service made everything better. I took pleasure in a divine breakfast while sitting outside on the veranda with its colorful stunning flowers. The lovely sunrise, perfect weather, and the Mediterranean Sea left me feeling peaceful, revitalized, and oddly enough, excited to see my Adonis again.

Valerio arrived at 8:00 A.M. on his shiny blue Vespa motorcycle. After exchanging a good morning hug and kiss, the sexually handicapped man (oblivious about last night), said, "Buongiorno, mio bello. Jump on!"

"Good morning, Valerio!" I went on to explain, "Oh, no honey, but thank you, anyway. Even though your Vespa is insanely cool and all, there is no way I would conceivably ride around Napoli on it. Your awesome invite is outrageously dangerous and completely out of the question."

He smiled back at me, ("No bella Problema. Vi Do IL mio casco.

Sarete al sicuro?") "No problem, beautiful. I will give you my helmet to use. You will be safe... Yes?"

"No, babe, you don't understand. No capisco. This is unsafe and I am afraid. Molto paura!" He gently, (radically unlike the night before), put his helmet on my head, strapped it on, picked me up, and placed me on his Vespa. He skillfully jumped back on, put my arms around his impeccably cut abs (what a waste), and took off in a flash. Guessing by the previous night, it appeared this man performs everything in a flash. I screamed at the top of my lungs, ("Ho Paura. Ho paura. Lento lento, arresto, Valerio.") "I'm Afraid! I'm afraid, slow, slow, shut down, slow down, Valerio!"

It was strange how I went from yelling at him to stop, while cars came within a tenth of an inch from my legs, to laughing and shouting, "Faster, go faster!" ("Rapido, rapido.") It was rather electrifying, zipping through the vibrant city streets, clinging tightly to Valerio all day. It was all so very Italian and stimulating in every way, *but one*. He took me through all the sights of his amazing city. Around 1:00, we stopped for lunch to enjoy the world-famous, yummy Neapolitan Pizza, and eggplant Parmigiano with mozzarella, like no place else on earth. A burst of flavorful memories excited my taste buds. The foods and sauces in this part of Italy are extraordinary, particularly the celebrated mozzarella.

Valerio gave me a complete tour of Naples to see the many wonders that his ancient corner of the world offers. It was all very old-world, movie romantic. We visited Castel Nouvo, Naples National Archeological Museum, and the Spaccanapoli, Naples' Historic Main Street. We witnessed many of the iconic sights on the Gulf of Naples, including Mount Vesuvius, and window-shopped the renowned stores along Via Chiaia, which begins at the foot of Via Toledo, one block from the end at Piazza Plebiscito. Late afternoon, we had the fortunate surprise to hear some talented opera students sing at the Teatro di San Carlo. It is a well-known fact, "The Opera is to Italy, what the ballet is to Russia."

We stopped around 4:30 for an afternoon espresso, a glass of vino, and a gelato cone with chocolate-covered cookies. Shamefully, I couldn't help observing Valerio as he slowly and suggestively licked the side of his cone that was dripping Nutella chocolate gelato down his wrist. His lips and tongue were masterfully provocative. Oh, how I wanted his tongue to do the same exact slow, gentle movement, precisely the same tantalizing way to me this very second. Or at least later! (Hint, Hint!) He caught me staring at his third long lick, and smiled down at me bashfully, like a little boy. Valerio knew exactly what I was thinking, too. I found myself so turned on all day that I could hardly wait for him to be inside me again. I was certain (I hoped) our lovemaking would be fantastic this time. At about 6:45, he dropped me off at the hotel, providing me ample time for a little siesta, a shower, and to leisurely change into something alluring.

Later that evening around 9:00, I met Valerio for dinner at an elegant restaurant, just as the majestic, bright red sun was magnificently setting over the sea. I enjoy dining outside in Italy, especially in the fall. The renowned, awe-inspiring Italian sunsets are impressively memorable.

I modestly admit I looked as gorgeous and sexy as I wanted to be in a little black, strapless, open-back dress, with pearls hanging down my backside. (A tip from Princess Diana.) Valerio's eyes transfixed on me while flashing one of his charming, splendid smiles. He spoke in Italian, "Bella, I cannot take my eyes off you and your incredible beauty. You are gorgeous, Mollie. I am the luckiest man in the world to be here with you."

I wanted to respond by saying, "Yeah, then prove it to me *gently* tonight." Of course, it would have completely ruined the moment. That's when I recognized it's rather difficult to master sarcasm in Italian.

The added touch of gifted guitarists singing and strumming away as they strolled about, topped off the glorious ambiance. Italians certainly know their romance. It was all enormously enchanting and provided that dreamy setting we ladies crave. Men, if there are any of you, still reading, (and wow, thank you!) this is all part of foreplay for us girls. We need our foreplay. Women don't just want to get it over with. Women who are into sexual activities need the whole canoodling thing. BTW, foreplay starts long before entering the boudoir. Hence, why it was such a turn on the way Valerio was watching me affectionately all evening. Our dinner included two bottles of Chianti Classico, the most succulent plates of Frutti di Mare over linguini, Osso Bucco braised with a red wine broth and served with risotto, vegetables, fried artichoke, followed by a salad, and fresh fruit. Delizioso. My Neapolitan fed me and licked my fingers when he splashed sauce on them. He alternated kissing me, holding my hand, and rubbing my legs all evening. I was in heaven. I never wanted it to end.

Relaxing and exchanging loving words and hugs, we drank the last of the remarkable Italian red wine from the local vineyards. This impressive cuisine was a foodie's orgy and, dare I say, far more satisfying than my forgettable non-orgy incident the previous night. Then it hit me! He's *not* a mind reader. I had to help this hunk of a man with some sweet prodding, gentle guidance, and encourage-ment. Like the quote in the movie, My Big Fat Greek Wedding, *"The man is the head. But the woman is the neck. And she can turn the head any way she wants!"*

Returning from my calculating thoughts, I saw Valerio gazing at me with lustful desire. We sipped cappuccinos and gobbled the delicious dolce. After the yummy tiramisu & cannoli, the Maître D' came over with 2 complimentary glasses of Sambuca. When he left, I seized the moment.

I delicately explained in complete detail, with hopeful sex in my eyes, exactly what I required. I artfully elucidated to Valerio (in Italian) what I wanted, needed, and must have tonight! I sensibly held back the "I mean it, dammit" part! "Bello," I said, *"Tonight we must make love my way… slowly, gently, tenderly, sensually, passionately, intimately, and erotically mind-altering."* Let me just tell you, that's a lot of adjectives to remember how to say in Italian.

He listened intently and beamed brightly while enjoying his glass of Sambuca and responded, *"No problem, bella. Whatever you like, I do for you, my gorgeous love. Don't worry, I make crazy fuck-love all over you!"* Then he affectionately kissed my forehead, making me quiver.

Yes, I do believe he's got it! He picked up the licorice-tasting liqueur and proposed a toast. "To fuck-sex-love tonight, your way, Mollie. Slowly, gently, tenderly, sensually, intimately, and erotically mind-altering!" Yes! I thought, ah-hah, yes! I'm going to have great sex tonight. So very, yea! I hope, I hoped, I hope-a? This was encouraging. Hearing the sultry way he said it in Italian, with his thick accent, almost gave me a major *sexgasim*. Yea, eat your heart out, elevator movie-star actress girl!

Following a relaxing stroll back to the hotel, Valerio burst open the door to my suite. For this sexual experience of mind-blowing multiple orgasms, I took the time to throw on a scandalously erotic, white-laced Chanel Bustier, ruffled lace undies, and white fury strappy heels. I added a few spritzes of Angel perfume and powdered some eatable honey dust on my freshly waxed privates. Eagerly parading my sexy self to the bed, I slid under the covers next to this handsome man, smelling his sweet aroma immediately. I noticed he lit a candle, poured 2 glasses of wine, and turned on romantic Italian music. All righty then, bravo! Fantastico! Incredibile!

He looked into my eyes sweetly and smiled. "Bella, you're so very exquisite. You make me so hard. You make me cum so strong."

Without allowing me to reply, he grabbed me affectionately. I was trembling with excitement, for this was the rapture I waited for. Allowing the tender moment to last but a second, Valerio savagely (and not the good kind of savagely) tore apart my brand-new lace lingerie. He ripped it off me ferociously and scrutinized my naked body. Hmm, I thought. That was way too fast to warrant the high price I paid for it. I didn't care anymore. But I for sure better cum at least 10 times. Whatever. Just make crazy-fuck love all over me as you promised! Gosh, my inside voice was exhausted!

The next thing I knew and before I could even get into a comfortable position… "Bam-Bam, Bam-Bam, Bam-Bam, and Bam! Ouch, Ouch, Ouch, and Ouch! And there it was. Déjà-Fucking-Vu!

A million thoughts ran through my mind, and none of them were good. Such as… "Oh, come on! No fucking way! Seriously? Excuse me? I mean? Like? What? Really? NNN-nothing? Do you really think any woman would enjoy what you just did here? How can such an elegant, charismatic man not have a clue how to make love? *How could an Italian man, born, raised, and living in Italy, not know how to fuck?* How could this be? It's theoretically impossible." I was completely freaked out, frustrated, and clueless. This wasn't an out-of-body experience… this was more like an *"out of vagina experience!"* Clearly, this was a perfect example of, *"Dé-Jà-bad-fuck-Ouch-Vu!"* I don't want to Do-Si-Do, this painful *tango* dance of his, ever again! To be frank (and I don't even like Frank, let alone pretending to be him) I was livid. More accurately outraged, like a hit-and-run accident. It felt like my freshly waxed vagina was broken. No joke! For real, I might require a vagina plastic surgeon.

So, there you have it... Valerio came, and I faked it! I had to. This was the only logical way to stop the painful, horrendous, bad sex from continuing. How did he not know how to do this? It wasn't even like bondage sex. Even that might have been *somewhat* of a kinky perk! This was just plain terrible sex, any which way you look at it. I was morbidly disenchanted. I had such great *"sexpectations"* with Valerio. And, what a waste of a perfectly good, circumcised penis! In disbelief and at a loss for words, I tried to be fair, making more excuses for him. Surely, he is aware this was the worst sex ever. I mean, how could he not? Wow, it was no surprise he was divorced! For this type of lovemaking alone, was grounds for it! I couldn't help but question, "How the hell did his ex-wife deal with it?" I was only too happy the Italian, bad lover ran off soon afterward. Ha, Italian bad lover? How is that possible? Relieved he was gone, I popped open the complimentary bottle of wine and chocolate-dipped strawberries. I peacefully soaked my sorrows and broken vagina in a hot whirlpool bubble bath. Aaaahhhh! For now, I needed serious vagina recovery time.

In the morning, Valerio picked me up on his Vespa. "Bonjourno!"

I promptly questioned, "Where is your Alfa Romeo?"

To which he replied excitedly. "This will be far more fun, my love. I wanted to surprise you and take you down the Amalfi Coast to Positano on my bike. I promise this will be the best fun ever!"

"Yeah, maybe lots of fun before we die, going over a cliff!" What the hell, I mused. Anything would be more fun and far less agonizing than the painful, horrendous sex of the past 2 nights. I giggled, thinking both these scenarios could bring disastrous endings and excruciating *'outcums.'*

The Amalfi Coast is one of the most beautiful and impressive coastal drives in the world, but equally dangerous and terrifying. I was petrified traveling through it the last time. What made it worse was riding in a huge tour bus with screaming old people. I insisted with my common sense, "Seriously, Valerio, we are going to die!" Laughter was his only response. Sure, after having sex with him, I suppose pain is his thing. Despite all my rowdy protests, his mind was set on taking his Vespa down this hazardous escapade. The way I looked at it, if I was going to die, I couldn't think of a cooler way to go than on the back of a Vespa, holding on to a gorgeous hunk, traveling through the most stunning, impressive coastline in the world. Truthfully, no one had to know he sucked in bed!

Swiftly biking our way alongside the panoramic views of the glistening blue sea, overlooking the awe-inspiring cliffs, I couldn't decide which was more breathtaking, the Amalfi Coast or Valerio?

When we arrived alive, Valerio led me through the enchanting Positano Village. It is beloved by the most elite, and of course, the rich and famous. Naturally, celebs and stars love it here and frequent it often. I should mention, in the film "Under the Tuscan Sun," this is the city Marcello (the Italian stallion), whom Diane Lane meets in Rome, takes her to. He lived in Positano. Luckily for her, Marcello was sexually brilliant and a masterful *sexpert* in bed! My God, I'm so jealous.

This small, picturesque region in Campania, Italy, is crowded with wonderful quaint shops, marvelous restaurants, and splendid coastal views. This unique, intimate town is perched on the face of a hill. It's unimaginably beautiful. Following our long walk-about, we dined at a restaurant positioned right on the beach. We indulged in an impressive lunch with a wonderful bottle of Italian wine from the province. Bravo!

Throughout the day, he was loving and affectionate. I must say, he most certainly mastered the art of gallantry *outside* the bedroom. In my mind, I repeatedly thought, how could this conceivably be the same man from the past two sexually inept, depressing nights? How could he be the Bam-Bam Man who broke 'my girly zone?' Mid bite into my gamberetto spaghetti aglio e olio, Valerio winked at me and burst into a naughty grin. Proud as a peacock he boasted with conviction in *English*. *"Sex-fuck so great, fantastic, night last, yes?"* Oh, dear God. Ya think? Hell, he really doesn't have a clue. I thought I'd choke on my pasta and need the Heimlich maneuver. Without opening my lips, "Um, huh? Ah-ha?" Then I added the old girlish *"Giggle-giggle"* standby. Like a Michelangelo statue, I sat there frozen. I should've said, "I don't understand the question." I just couldn't tell him what I really thought. Especially now, discovering that he believes he is Mr. Super Sex Fuck? This was a most bizarre situation. How could he not know? His poor ex-wife must have lied and faked her ass off with every sexual encounter. What a kind, compassionate woman! Nevertheless, I must hand it to him. It's not easy being this oblivious.

On the terrifying motorbike ride back to Napoli, I had my arms wrapped tightly around his perfect waist, holding on for dear life. He caressed my hands as we sang American and Italian songs. Sadly, I came to the realization this was the most intimate, gentle, physical affection I was going to receive from this clueless man who left me scoreless.

On the bright side, the drive to and from Positano was splendidly amazing. I experienced an extraordinary, liberating sensation.

Zipping along the twisting perilous coast on his blue bike, the wind blowing us along with my arms firmly draped around Valerio was a remarkable, rare memory to cherish. And as fate would have it, we lived. Indeed, it turned out to be one of the most unforgettable days of my life. Although he was entirely wrong about the sex being great, he was right about this beautiful day, including the Vespa ride. It was undeniably the best fun ever!

We met back at the hotel for dinner, since I had to include the restaurant in my feature story. Valerio looked celebrity striking and I was proud to be with him. At least until the sex part later. It was sweet how he looked adoringly at me all evening. Despite his astonishing good looks, I had all but given up any hope for grand passion on night 3. The whole sex thing was seriously disappointing and unacceptable, to say the least. Other than that tiny little sex detail, Valerio was the perfect guy. He was elegant, lavishly romantic, fun, and easy to be with. How he failed so miserably in the *crazy, fuck-love* department was a mystery to me? During dinner, Mr. 'super-bad sex' was endearing and charming, the way he flattered and complimented me. "Mollie, you look so sexy and gorgeous dressed all in white." I wore a stunning Givenchy ultra-short, strapless dress, cleavage, and all, with OMG Versace purple pumps. My outfit was totally glam.

Regrettably, after day 3, a compliment was not number one on my sex wish list. Fireworks and orgasms were what I was seeking after flying 6,107 miles. Faking it was really getting old, and not something I ever enjoy doing. I was not even good at it. Like at all! So, tell me, how could Valerio or any man be so easily fooled? Men, go watch the movie (and again, if you've already seen it), "When Harry Met Sally." I so get that Meg Ryan's faking-it-scene was spot on. But come on? How can you men, Harry, or Bam-Bam for that matter, not see through all the overdone, theatrical bullshit of girls faking it? It's embarrassingly obvious. Guys, be advised. The more she screams, it's very likely the more she's faking it.

Returning to the hotel suite, *the front line and battlefield of pain,* AKA, The *Dungeon of Agony,* I mustered up some *mild hopes* for sexual success. I'm a dreamer and a romantic. What can I say? Still, I didn't bother changing into another one of my new XXX-rated outfits. There was no point and luckily the price tags were still attached, so I could return them. I grabbed Valerio and whispered into his ear in Italian. "Please, make *sweet, gentle, gentle, gentle, slow, passionate, Gentle love to me.*"

He replied, "No problem, il mio amore! I make sweet, slow, deep, gentle fuck all over you! I can because I'm the best fuck-lover in the entire world. Bella, I know what you like, what you need, and what you want!"

Just two minutes on the bed, and there it was, "Déjà-Bam-Bam-bad-Fucking-Vu!" I had no choice. I just gave in like a cheap hooker without the pay and braced myself for the inevitable. And once upon a here we go again, Bam-Bam, Bam-Bam, Bam-Bam, and Ouch, Ouch, Ouch, Ouch. And oops, he did it again! Valerio's kisses were quick and hard. "Gentle baby," I murmured. "Slow, slow," I begged. All I could think was, man, screw me badly once, shame on you! Screw me badly three times, shame, shame, shame on me! I kept hearing (And BTW, this should be sung, not read.) *"Ding-dong, the Vagina's Dead!"* If this isn't the real meaning of a *Screw-Up,* then I don't know what the fuck is!

Valerio was equivalent to the tender and affectionate "Sex-Jekyll by day" and the rough and aggressive "Sex-Hyde by night." Good God, dude, how can you be a *straight, Italian man* and not know how to fuck a woman properly? It's unprecedented and goes against every law of nature. Just my luck to have ended up with the only sexually challenged Italian man in the whole world who ever lived! I accidentally mumbled out loud a big, huge groan. Oops, I hoped he didn't hear me. But I think I might have a dislocated vagina. For real and I think I heard it snap! My vagina was black and blue. Black and Blue, People! How does that even happen? More to the point, why should that ever happen? Meanwhile, he hurt me further, squeezing my breasts painfully hard. So forceful it felt like a mammogram machine crushing down on my boobs, only without being asked for my insurance card and co-pay. Wounded, I exerted an enormous, excruciating moan without caring if he heard me. OH-M-G, I had to LOL when he spontaneously yelled, "Yes, I'm cumming too, bella bambina!!!"

As exasperated as I was, I could have huffed and puffed and blown his ass down! I wanted to kick him right in his antipasto! I was at my sexual breaking point and wanted to go, "Pow, Pow, Pow!" But, thinking rationally, that evidently would have been illegal. Not to mention an international scandal. Rather pernicious of me, but so what? I was justifiably cranky! I was in Italy, so where the hell was the Italian mob and my Godfather when you need um? Then I mused, O-M-GOD, Andrew Lloyd Webber! Valerio is the real-life Phantom of the Vagina! And there it was, the sting in the tale. Literally. The unexpected miscalculation of the Valerio affair was rather a strange and sad reality to be faced with.

Ultimately, fate rubbed my nose in it, and there was no sexual nirvana with Bam-Bam as I had enthusiastically expected. Alas, the reality is, Valerio, the stud-muffin from Napoli, will sadly and forever be known to me as *"The absolute worst sex of my life!"* He shall be added to the historical legends of the greatest sexual bummers of all time. That totally should be a song. I pondered, how in the world this journey didn't end in a victory orgasm dance was beyond me. I will eternally find it unfathomable how a man who looks and acts like Valerio, as romantic and charming as Ryan Gosling in, The Notebook, never learned how to make love and give mind-blowing sexual pleasure to a woman! This proves once again you can't tell a book *or a man* by its cover. I can, however, tell you one thing. "Shame, disgrace, and dishonor upon his Italian father, who failed him so miserably. This *kind of father neglect* is a crime." Hey, dads of sons out there, let this be a "*fucking lesson*" for you. See what I did there?

This Italian online guy damaged, shattered, and visibly traumatized my broken, black, and blue vagina. No, honestly, I mean it. It was broken. I think it might have even entered a dark vagina depression. It's a true ailment. Google it! Still, looking at this in a positive light, "the colação de grau" was, I finally learned how to fake it! I never perfected this art form previously, and I accomplished it perfectly in just a few Italian days.

"Yes, just like that. Don't stop! Yes, faster. You're so big and hard. Oh god! And then, the loud faking it, finale screams!" (And scene!) I'm so proud of myself. There's my silver lining. I'm such a positive person.

Valerio and I met the following morning for breakfast. To save myself, and what was left of my despondent kitty, it was necessary for me to out-and-out lie to him. It happens? I had to break away from this non-orgasmic, anticlimactic, no-climax romance, and immediately. I explained to him I had an updated hotel feature-story deadline, and my editor needed me to move on to the other hotels at once. That lie was one big, enormous *fauxpology*! I gently explained to him in a sad voice to soften the blow...

"So sorry, il mio amore! I feel so awful about this. But duty calls!"

"Mio Bella, Mollie, please stay. Please, I don't want you to leave!"

"Oh, mio Bello, nor do I! But I must go!" He looked so sad and forlorn, holding my hand, and constantly kissing me at breakfast.

Later that morning, Valerio cried while we hugged and kissed each other goodbye at the Molo Beverello Port. Before I jumped on the Alilauro Hydrofoil Ferry to Capri, I performed my (award-worthy) dramatic farewell scene, pretending to be as emotionally sad as he was. I was downright in awe of myself, how I skillfully pushed out a sweet little fake tear matching his. I did a lot of acting with Valerio. So much so that I even thought of going back home and applying for my SAG /AFTRA Union Card. Hell, I'll apply for an Actors' Equity Association card, too!

With one last kiss, I cried, "Ciao, mi amour. Arrivederci, Valerio."

He answered in Italian for all to hear, lighting a cigarette. *"Ciao, my love. I had the time of my life.* **You're the Love and the Very Best Sex-Fuck of My Life**. *I want to come to America soon to be with you! I adore you, my beautiful lover! You are my destino. (Destiny) Arrivederci!!!!!"*

After the applause and bravos from the crowd of people on the pier died down, I looked at Valerio dumbfounded. All I could do was shrug and grin. Throughout my theatrical performance, I was thinking, "Are you fucking with me right now?" The only come-back I could think of in response to his delusional send-off boasting about, "The very best sex fuck of my life" (Actually, I would like that put on my tombstone!) was another final hug and a sweet kiss on his lips. A gentle, tender, slow, soft one!

As the hydrofoil sailed away for Capri, I searched for a comfort-able position to ease my sexual injury. I waved goodbye, smiling with my polished, *'faking it, sad, and teary-eyed expression.'* Executing perfect, sympathetic acting skills (as the movie script would have directed, while sentimental music played in the background), I blew Bam-Bam loving kisses, "Ciao, Valerio! Arrivederci!" Seriously, this scene alone would have earned me an Oscar! "PHEW," I exhaled a long sigh of relief!

The happy ending to my story is I had a great time for 2 weeks in Ischia, Sorrento, Amalfi, Toscana, and Firenze. I have many close Italian friends. So, this offered me the opportunity to visit them at the hotels that I was to write about. Italy, without question, is my favorite place on earth.

On the plane home, I contemplated my mind-boggling Valerio saga. Since the sex was horrific and I didn't have a single orgasm, I justified this affair wouldn't count as sex. Thus, it will not add a ring to my *sex number.* Hey people, it's *my* number and *my* rules!

The Italian encounter turned out to be a disappointing charade. It's a bit ironic because this little tryst had so much potential and promise. I compare it to a bad romantic comedy, only without all the romance, great sex, or the comedy. The Valerio, "Mr. worst-sex-ever, caper" was heartbreaking on so many levels, leaving me in the unprecedented frustrating state of horny-dom. Not a good way to leave a girl.

After traveling a very long, uncomfortable 26 hours back to the States, I was thrilled to be back home. I burst through my front door, poured a glass of vino, and followed my six-horny rules of protocol.

1. Take a long, hot, relaxing shower.
2. Turn off the lights.
3. Reach into the bedside drawer.
4. Get under the covers so dead relatives and other dead people won't see what you are doing and think badly of you.
5. Turn on my vibrator to Max!
6. Enjoy! "Yes, just like that. Don't stop! Oh, yes. Harder. Yes, go faster. You're so big and hard. Oh god, don't stop!"

What? It was broken! Shit, my loyal, faithful "Vi" was inoperative. I just cannot seem to catch a sexual break. "What a Buzz Kill." Indeed.

My thoughts about lack of sex, and you can take it as gospel… "Sex is like oxygen, it's not important unless you are not getting any."

I still chuckle and think of Bam-Bam affectionately every time I wear my button-less jeans. Sentimentally, I never did sew another button back on them. I still wear them because they have history, and the memories are just too damn good.

And by the way, my vagina healed up nicely…

Oh, PS: I neglected to tell you that when Valerio saw my freshly waxed, (now recovered) vagina, he said in amazement.

"I have never seen a grown woman with no hair down there."

"Gosh, Valerio, you said you didn't like hair down under."

He responded laughing, "Oh, my love, I thought you meant hair on your legs and underarms."

He was categorically exquisite, but evidently, the "IQ and Sex Fairies" never knocked on his door! This gorgeous, *dashing* minuteman continues to contact me. Every now and again, I take his call. Our lovely time together will forever be cherished, as a beautiful, Italian, *worst lover ever*, romance!

My fond memories of Valerio, the Bam-Bam man, make me smile painfully, to this very day…

Bam-Bam-Bam… Damn! I Got Maled!

CHAPTER 7

The Nice Guys...

BUT, YEAH, NO, ALL THE SAME!

THE WONDERFUL SHORT, NICE GUY

I wholeheartedly and sincerely want to be "thoughtful, sensitive, delicate, and not cruel in any way while describing the wonderful *short* guy."

I discovered straightaway the *short, nice* guy was more patient, kind, exceedingly complimentary, sweet-tempered, non-argumentative, or confrontational. I hypothesized this might be because the *short* guys try harder than the tall guys, perhaps to compensate. Just a theory...

Devin wrote me the number one loveliest email I received throughout the past few years I had been wrestling online.

I liked him right away from his very first communication. He wrote in his profile that he was 5′ 6″. I, myself, stand 5′ 7″. So, no big deal there, I initially thought. Yet, even so, I became suspicious scrolling through his photos. Since 5′ 6″ did not seem possible, as he was not much taller than the photo I saw of him, standing alongside the height of his 4′ 3″ Ferrari.

Whatever! We agreed to meet in Boston, where he lived, and the timing was ideal. I had to be in Cambridge for a feature story anyway, to report on the Freedom Trail and the prestigious higher education in "America's College Town." (Also nicknamed "Beantown.") I always take pleasure when visiting Boston in the fall for its beautiful picturesque "changing of the leaves." I had the good fortune to frolic around in the colorful foliage and meet Devin as well. It was a perfectly timed project.

From what I was able to ascertain, Devin was 29 years old, sweet, creative, successful, and generous. Regrettably, looks-wise, he was totally unappealing to me. Trying not to be a *"Shallow Hal,"* I wanted to get past his looks and height, or lack thereof. He seemed genuinely awesome, and the type of man I should be with. Therefore, I was going to give it the old Boston College try! Taking it a step further, I went *"out on a limb,"* preparing myself to be the best, open-minded me that I could be for Dev.

By the way, who literally goes out and hangs from a tree limb, especially for no apparent reason? Who made up this phrase anyway and who exactly does this? When does this essentially happen? And if so, does this help the situation? All of this hanging? Anyhow, I would try not to let his vertically challenged physicality bother me. I would not be insensitive or cruel like the mean girls in high school were. (And still are.) I'd give him a chance, be compassionate and put things in proper perspective. His height should not be a factor. I shall *stunt* my attitude and stand *tall* on the moral *high* ground. Ok, sorry, a possible little 'Oopsie' there. Regardless, you can be assured I was absolutely going to wear my 6-inch heels when we met on that moral ground. Despite his height. Come on, let's be honest here. After true love, the most important thing is footwear!

Wanting to dress casually, we met up at the famous Legal Seafood Restaurant for dinner. Reality ensued. Feeling duped, I gasped to see that Devin was not even close to being 5′ 6″. Realistically, he was maybe 5′ 4″. Meanwhile, I couldn't help but notice he had 5-inch lifts built into his *little* shoes. Whoa, the man was shorter than 5′! I felt like a tall *glamazon or a giant beanstalk* next to him. Seems I was the awkward giraffe in the room. The fact that I *'Eiffel Towered'* him was unsettling. Worse yet, the idea that I had to bend down to hug him hello was alarming. *In short: little* feet, *little* hands, and Umm… *little* bulge? Wait. Huh? Is he wearing *Guyliner?*

Judging by my cruel inner thoughts, I realized I was slipping right off the limb. I had to get back up onto that tree limb and start hanging immediately. It was vital to return to the moral *high* ground and be the best me I could be. *Shortly* after and mid-thought, the 6′ 5″ server (his height being something I would never have noticed before) with his "Pahked thah cah, in Hahvahd Yahd," Bostonian accent, asked to take our dinner order. As this was one of the most famous seafood restaurants in Boston, I was tempted to order the tender *little baby clams.* But how could I? That would be so wrong and way off the limb. A tall order of colossal *jumbo shrimp* and a huge piece of their famous berry *shortcake* for dessert would only have made matters worse… I'm guessing?

We enjoyed a lovely banter, devouring some of Boston's mouth-watering seafood, excluding the *shrimp*, but including the lobster. To be fair, Devon was such a good, decent guy. I quickly discovered he was also friendly and easy to hang with, *even without the limb!* We dodged all the *small* talk and shared deep intellectual conversations. We learned that even our hopes and dreams reflected our simpatico spirits. As we spoke about life, he stated with conviction, "I always look up to the future." Forgive me, but where else could he look, but up? I'd have said it aloud, but it surely would've gone over his head. Slipping! I was slipping!

Before the ice cream and Lattes, Devin excused himself to go to the *little* boys' room. When he left, I couldn't help but notice his jacket label, *"Saks Fifth Avenue Children's Department."* Oh, sweet lord. Taking a *short* cleansing breath, I wish I could *unsee* that. When Dev returned to the table, *I was clinging ever so tightly onto my limb. Clinging with all my might. My fingernails were burrowing & digging into the damn tree trunk. In fact, sap was oozing out all over the place, ruining my gel manicure.*

Sadly, he kissed my hand gently without having to bend down, even though I was sitting. "I'm so sorry to have left you alone waiting for me, my dear." Geez, the *little Saks Fifth Avenue lad* was so well-mannered and classy. Devin sat across from me, gazing, and doting adoringly. But it was creepy how he stared at me with a jocund expression, enthusiastically beaming upon his face. As he looked at me with great affection, it took all the discipline I had (which, believe me, was very little), to restrain my sarcastic remarks. I held back my tongue from asking, *"Are you originally from Munchkinland, a yellow brick road away from OZ? Did you go to see The Wizard with The Tin Man, The Straw Man, and The Cowardly Lion to ask for some more inches? You know!* "If I only had some height!" And that was the very moment I realized that I was truly a despicable person!

Plop! Splat! Crash! Yep, I heard it all, the deafening plop, the wet splat, and the loud crash! I sensed there wasn't any part of my body left hanging onto my limb. In fact, I fell smack down hard right out of the tree and smashed onto the ground. I mean, I was now entirely covered in sap! I might just as well have hacked off that frickin' limb with a buzz saw! I suppose, I just out and out blew my "wanting to be wholeheartedly, and most sincerely thoughtful, sensitive, delicate, and not cruel in any way, while describing the wonderful short guy." Alas, I determined I didn't get that 'be a *bigger person, gene.'* Still, I'm sure my jeans were bigger than his! Gosh, that was mean. I'm disgraceful and entirely ashamed of myself. But, come on, funny is funny! Though I so wanted to, I didn't really come out and say any of this to him! That should count for something. Right?

Mercifully, I was saved, for he spoke first while looking up at me… Like, really, *UP!* "Mollie, I want you to know you are the most amazing woman I have ever met. You are a total outlier. Could you even be more fascinating? I had a feeling from all our phone conversations we were kindred souls. I confirm, now seeing you in person, that I know with total certainty we will be together forever." Right there, saturated and drenched in sap, I wanted to kill myself! I needed a shower. Wait, there's more! "Mollie, if I asked you to marry me right now, would you say yes?"

Uh-Oh? Manic, panic! It was a Dr. Phil moment, and I don't even like Phil! Besides, he's not a real doc. Shit! I didn't see this coming. I was not at all prepared for it. Struggling for dear life, like the paparazzi struggles to get the latest celeb money shot, I tried desperately to crawl back up onto any part of that sap-bleeding limb. Mind you, no matter how tall he wasn't, and in all fairness to me, *this is a question a girl should never have to answer on a first date!* Little did he know inside my tall, private thoughts, I responded to his question with "Yikes, WTF, um? Hell no, and a gigantic Nuh-Uh!" Sitting there before him frantic and unable to speak, I *midgeted.* Oops, I mean, fidgeted! I anxiously recognized he was clearly still waiting for an answer. I had no clue whatsoever how to kindly respond to his question, remain on my limb, and stay on that damn moral high ground. Surely, I didn't want to be *short* with him. Shit, I did it again.

OK… Stop the presses! I think I need to play, "Want to be a Millionaire!" I not only needed to use a lifeline, but I needed all of them. And I'm talking immediately. I needed to phone a friend. I needed to ask the audience wherever the hell they were. I needed a 50/50, and I most definitely needed to change his ridiculous question! Wait a minute. Hold on! Relieved, I contemplated… I can also just walk away and keep the money. "Aha, yes," I screamed pompously… "I choose that one. The Zip-a-Dee-Doo-Dah, keep the money one!" Whew, now that was a close call! Freaked out, I realized the nice, cray-cray, *short* guy sitting across from me was still waiting for an answer. Regis, Meredith, Chris Harrison? Dammit, where the hell is the darn game-show host when you need em?

Clueless, I looked at Devin sitting, with his feet unable to reach the floor, and clumsily blurted out, "You want the *short* answer?" *Sh, to-the, it. Shit.* Anguish, shame, and oh, no! Tell me I didn't just say that with my outside voice. Yeah, but I did. I really did. It's official. I am the worst person in the entire world! I am confident the "Short Lives Matter" people will soon present me with an engraved golden trophy, stating just that for my mantle. Sigh, and a huge, piercing, short moan. I thought of hiding under the table, but first, I hesitantly scanned his kind face for a reaction.

He giggled! Devin giggled his very secure *little* man giggles and replied, "Lovely, Mollie, you surely did just give me the *short* end of the stick!" My God? This wonderful, *petite* man saved me from *me*. With that, we shared contagious laughter. Phew, what a humiliating narrow escape!

This is a little man to love. Sadly, for him, I'm not the woman to love this little man. I didn't even have the guts to give him the short end-of-the-limb that I strongly wrestled and fought to go out on. I really suck.

In my plea for vindication, the reason I can't be with Dev is not that he is *pint-sized, infinitesimal, Bostonian shrimplike, itsy-bitsy-teeny-weeny, puny, miniature, diminutive, small, and a mini-him.* It's not just because I find Devin somewhat unattractive. Or that he is the perfect model for the legendary store's children's department that I don't want to be with him. Ok, maybe, fine, perhaps it is a *tiny, wee bit* of all the above.

However, the truth, and the long and *short* of it. I am looking for *"The One,"* and this *little man* is not my Romeo. Life is *short*, as well. Thus, I must continue my "true love search." Devin is not the one, no matter how big or *small*, how many trees I cling to, or how many limbs I go out on! He is just not "The One!" Being with him was too tall an order. I could not live the rest of my life covered in sticky tree sap. Perhaps I am a waste of blood and oxygen. I am ghastly and the writing is on the wall!

This brings up another thought. When the writing is on the wall, where is the wall to see the writing? What wall? I have never seen writing on the wall. I've seen lots of graffiti, but not so much writing. Just a reporter's observation. The reality is plain and simple. I just couldn't be with Devin, his *shortcomings*, and his *little* bulge, too. No matter how nice he was, I suppose Devin just fell way *short* of my expectations!

In the immortal words of Princess Leia and Anakin Skywalker. "Aren't you a little *short* for a Stormtrooper?" To quote the feared Jedi hunter and antagonist General Grievous, "You're *shorter* than I expected."

In conclusion, *Fuggedaboutit.* And you know what else? I'm going to chop down that whole damn tree, limb by limb!

So that… is my *Short* Story! And a Sticky and Sappy **Next**…

THE FOXYMORON, NICE GUY

The "Foxymoron guy" is the oxymoron guy. It's a word I made up for Kevin. This guy was brilliant and stupid all at the same time. To put it diplomatically, *he was not a man of great wisdom.* Kevin was brilliantly gorgeous and so much fun, but a total idiot! These foxymoron guys run rampant, and because they are so handsome, we let it go and look the other way. Far yonder the other way. Still, I promise, just like me, you won't be able to stay here very long either. Because of the things they say and do, it will make you go "handsome-blind" quickly. I'd say hunky guy Kev had lost his marbles. But honestly, he never had many to lose in the first place.

With the foxymoron guys, when you scratch the surface of their intelligence, you hit rock bottom. Among, Kevin's typical sentences were, "What do you mean?" "I don't understand!" "What should I do?" "I don't get it?" The foxymorons' overall remarks include "What," "Hmm," "Nuh-uh," and of course, the always present, "Huh?" He is classically a "Dee's, Dem, and Dose," kind of guy. No matter how great he was to look at (and boy, was he ever), I couldn't linger very long with Kev. Because if I did, I would've had to gag him for all the stupid, senseless, foolish things that came out of his mouth *all the time!* I had to bolt, or I might have become a nasty woman. Kevin and the other "Foxymoron" guys are the world's *"illiterattie"* (illiterate people). Puzzling, how many pieces were missing from his box? Still, he was amazingly gorgeous and happy-go-lucky. I will absolutely give him that. A fiddle-dee-dee, and a Da-da-Da-dumb, **Next...**

THE WIDOWED PODIATRIST, NICE GUY

Michael was a thirty-five-year-old Podiatrist.

He seemed to be the perfect man, with his two feet planted firmly on the ground. Or so I thought at first.

Being an obsessive, shoe-lover kind of girl, I found his occupation most intriguing and particularly thought it might be quite beneficial one day. I had some sizable high-heeled hopes for this online doc. From his photos, he appeared to be a rather normal, (Don't they all?) distinguished, almost handsome, with the double perk of looking huggable and cozy. Judging by our first phone conversation, Michael was successful, highly educated, and possessed a great sense of humor. Caution: first appearances are not always what they appear to be. His family comes from Germany, and he's the first generation born in America. It was fortunate for him to have been given a good-ole American name, instead of something German like Klaus, Hanz, Vedasmitin, Shmatinshmotin, or Shnizelbogin.

Disappointingly, our second phone conversation was filled entirely with talk about bunions, corns, ingrown toenails, warts, athlete's foot, arch pain, infections, blisters, (Ick) calluses, and sweaty smelly feet (Barf). Oh, and yes, how could I forget plantar fasciitis? By the end of this call, I couldn't eat for two days. In fact, I was going to throw in the gross foot towel altogether *and tiptoe far* away from him. Instead, I took a step back with my lovely feet, which didn't have any of those vomit-worthy foot conditions and decided to at least let Michael get his foot in my door.

In truth, he appeared to be flawless, until our second chat, that is. Still, I wasn't going to slam my foot down on him yet! So, I let him slide and get away with all the revolting foot talk. Deplorably, though, it never stopped. It only got worse, more disgusting, and sickening. He just kept putting his foot in his mouth. Doctor Michael continued to describe his patients' foot problems in repulsive detail. He clearly didn't think he had to toe the line on these icky conversations. The good news was I lost three and a half pounds that week speaking with him.

Even though I presented him with endless hints, he never picked up on the fact that, with these highly unromantic conversations, he was shooting himself in the foot! This guy was turning me off and continued putting the shoe on the other foot, losing his footing, the likelihood of a relationship, or at the very least, possibly playing footsies with me. The following night, before going out with some friends to avoid gagging just thinking about those plantar fasciitis conversations, I adorned my feet in a pair of my favorite Stuart Weitzman, 'and all that jazz,' snazzy heels.

We spoke only a few times when the second red flag appeared, through my mist of hope. Michael had lost his wife Donna two years ago, leaving him with three children to bring up by himself. It was obvious Donna and Michael had shared a great love story. There was no doubt he was still grieving and too much in love with her to fall head-over-heels in love with me, or anybody else for that matter. While it was impossible for anyone to bridge his 1000-foot divide, I ignored the signs, kept positive, and took their love as a sign that he understood how to love and be loved.

By the fourth call, Bada Bing-Bada Boom! And there it was, the storm of lost hope, and my glass slipper came crashing down. In this conversation, Michael spoke non-stop about his beloved Donna. It was a relentless deluge of praise about Donna this, and Donna that, Donna was perfect, etcetera, etcetera, and so on! I realized I couldn't compete with the greatest ghost-love of all time. Well, at least since the movie "Ghost" with Patrick and Demi. I never asked, but I am quite certain Michael and Donna shared their very own barefoot sexual pottery scene. I didn't need Dorothy's "little dog Toto" to pull back the Wizard's curtain to discover that I nor any other woman could ever follow in Donna's perfect footsteps.

I didn't mind having these conversations with him because I felt he desperately needed someone to talk to about her. Still, they went on inappropriately. This man was evidently not ready or available to date, for he had one foot in the grave himself. With Michael still pining over his dead wife, there could be no future for us. The fact he was still carrying a glowing torch for Donna left us starting off on the wrong foot, and it was impossible to find our balance. To be blunt, he never had the chance to put his best foot forward with me. I didn't need to stay at the dance any further as Michael was, at this time in his life, dancing with two left feet and stepping on my toes. Painfully so! He was 360 feet from a touchdown.

Finally, the other *shoe dropped*. The good Dr. told me I should never, not ever wear high heels. "They're harmful, damaging, and can cause Haglund's deformity." He was seriously stepping on *my Achilles' heels, big time now*. With that, I kicked up my extra tall high heels and ran one pedicured foot in front of the other, and a step in the right direction. Good Lord, with a "No Heels" remark like that, the guy didn't have a leg or a foot to stand on!

Poor guy, as we never met, he never had the opportunity to sweep me off my feet. I happily moved on, footloose and fancy-free. Michael simply needed to find another Cinderella who would fit into the ghostly glass slipper! Clearly, a romance or a relationship with Michael would not be an easy *"Feat"* whether in heels or not!

Never, not ever, wear high heels? Dream on and God forbid! Michael will be remembered as a **Footnote** in my life*! I ran* away, as fast as my high-heeled running shoes could take me towards **Next**...

THE STUNNING, ITALIAN, NICE GUY ON THE PLANE...
A Plane and Turbulent, Airborne Romance...

OK, you know what? Online, offline, or in between lines... It doesn't seem to really matter because there is always something. There is always a gotcha, a situation, an agenda, a drama, a scheme, an excuse, a lie, or a story to be told. A simple little reminder. I know it's hard to believe, but all these stories are true-life events. They really happened!

I was on my way to Italy with as many outfits in my luggage as Lady Gaga or Beyoncé packs for a world tour. After my plane arrived in Rome, I was to catch another 3-and-a-half-hour flight to Jerusalem. I had several important interviews concerning high-security intelligence stories for a Cable News Network. This is the kind of news reporting I live for. So, there I was, minding my own serious high-security business, flying United Airlines from New York to Rome. I didn't know it then, but I was about to experience a fortunate, serendipitous situation. Or so I thought at the time.

Unfortunately, bumped from 1st class, with a 10-hour flight ahead of me, I was anxious about the possibility of losing my reserved window seat. I would no doubt be moved and get stuck in the middle of the plane, next to a huge snoring passenger, a crying baby, or the person with the deadly disgusting cough. When the door to the plane closed, I was ecstatic, for I realized I had hit the travel jackpot! The seat next to me was empty, an unexpected, rare gift, particularly when flying internationally. The configuration of the plane had four seats in the middle and two seats on each side, and I had them both! Overjoyed to have the extra room and privacy, this good fortune ensured some much-needed sleep. I was beside myself. Literally.

As soon as the plane took off, it was *wine o'clock*, and I ordered a glass to help me fall asleep. It was imperative that I slept so I could hit the ground running. Knowing it was a huge honor to even be put on this assignment, I intended to do a stellar job. I pulled out my travel pillow and blanket, my Beats headphones, slipped on my fluffy pink socks, and then searched for a cozy position. As if there was one to be found sitting in coach on a plane.

One hour into the flight, I felt peaceful and serene after polishing off two little baby airplane bottles of cheap-tasting wine. After finishing some last-minute work, reviewing vital questions, and adding some final notes in preparation for my interviews, I was unusually satisfied and ready to crash. Oopsie, being on a plane, perhaps let's go with doze off. Feeling well prepared, I reclined my seat back the one lavish inch that it offers.

That's when I noticed behind me and to my left, the most exquisite, stunning man I had *ever* laid eyes on in my entire life. And when does that ever happen on a plane? Yummy, hot, and sexy were my only rational thoughts. Merely gazing at him gave me a twinge. He looked like he just walked off a book cover of any steamy romance novel. I could not stop gawking at this urban man with his long, silky, straight, blonde hair, perfect olive complexion, royally ripped bod, and vivid blue eyes that were now staring right back at me. Oh, shit! I just got caught with my eyes in the cookie jar. Mortified, I thought, wait, was he checking me out or someone else? Just before jumping into my own personal, dark abyss of humiliation, I detected he wasn't looking at me at all. I was now sweating like a whore in church or a priest in a strip club. Then I realized, oh wow? Indeed, he was staring directly at me, nonstop like our flight to Rome. Well, now, it appeared we were both busted in that cookie jar. Holy cow, I was trapped in a seductive Taylor Swift song, like, "Sparks Fly." I became so self-conscious I found myself posing like a teenage girl taking selfies. Worse yet, I was ultra-posing, as in

Derek Zoolander, posing! I could feel this beautiful, chiseled man's exquisite eyes, glistening with secrets, continuously bearing down on me for hours. Although flirty fun at first, I eventually became frazzled, leaving me feeling awkward and a tinge insecure. I was surprised and annoyed by my coquettish behavior. Who was this woman I became? I hardly recognized her. How was it achievable for anyone, including this magnificent man, to turn me into such a pile of mush? The perverted, erotic thoughts running through my head could only be described as Satan's minions at work. And even worse, I liked it!

By now, I was foolishly Snapchat, Facebook, and Instagram-style posing. I was focusing on the perfect angle and flashing him those sexy, notorious, fish-gape pouty lips. Hating myself further, I reached up to turn on the overhead light, striving to achieve that flattering, perfect lighting. And if this wasn't pathetic enough, I twisted on both air vents to cue the Hollywood wind effect. I felt like model Kendall Jenner, *hamming it up* for a fashion photo shoot. I had no shame, as I artistically posed my hands, feet, face, and head. Even my butt was perfectly arched as if I were on a movie set, and the director shouted, "Ready? Places everybody, sexy butt arch, and action!" This was blatantly ridiculous, pitiful, and enormously exhausting, to say the least. I was angry with myself, knowing full well I should be sleeping, and not acting as if I were Julia Roberts or Angelina in a spy flick. I couldn't believe Mollie Sloan, a distinguished and successful news reporter on a serious, high-security intelligence mission, was being this showy and pretentious. Was all this play-acting for his visual pleasure, or just for my ego? Either way, it was ridiculous all the same. You see, this is exactly what happens when a woman isn't getting any! Sigmund Freud knew about this Female Hysteria disorder years ago. In all fairness, this dude was fucking *sextacular,* and his eyes remained fixated on me. Again, when does this happen on a plane? So, color me intrigued, for his attention raised my self-esteem higher than this plane was flying. The entire flight, we were flirting and secretly seducing one another. Most of the time, I tried to pretend I didn't notice him. Yeah, who did I think I was fooling? Surely not him! At least I attempted the art of faking *being aloof.*

Ultimately, I withheld my urgent need to go to the ladies' room long enough. I was relieved to hang in a smelly tiny bathroom, simply to take a break from his relentless ogling and my infinite posing, faking, and bad-acting performance. Dammit, even models get to '*take five.*' Right?

As I exited the poor excuse for a bathroom, Mr. Stunning grabbed me and pushed me gently back into the stinky lavatory. To my complete surprise and utter delight, the charismatic stranger immediately started kissing me intensely and brilliantly. Unable to resist and lost in euphoria, I wrapped my arms around the nape of his neck and pulled him closer. Oh, wow. Goosebumps! Yes, this really happened, and I didn't stop him from continuing with his inappropriate, forward, decadently immoral behavior. I became a coquettish, *old-school,* bad girl as he conquered me. Shame on me, for I loved every sensuous kiss. As his tongue passionately explored my mouth, we felt the fire building between us, and we didn't care to stop. Well, if this wasn't the height of folly? '*What sexellent Hospitaliano!*'

I needed a witness since this kind of wild romance doesn't happen every day, on a plane, or anywhere else. I was so overwhelmed and shy I could barely speak. He revealed he was Italian *(no surprise there),* and was returning home to Rome from an international medical conference in N.Y. He said he was an anesthesiologist, which made perfect sense, as his kiss alone put me under. "Italian, gorgeous, and smart… a deadly combo." He was, categorically, the triathlon of the perfect man. Jeez, I can't believe I said, *"The height of folly!" So disturbing. Who was I, my mother? Ugh!*

Although my inside voice was screaming *"Stranger Danger,"* I could not resist this man who was obviously coloring way outside the lines! By the time we surfaced for air, the other passengers were now quite peeved and banging on the lavatory door to hurry us up. The perfect stranger wouldn't let me go until I agreed to meet with him later that week in Rome, after my assignment in Israel and before returning home. He swiftly entered my cell number and email into his phone. "You promise you will meet me, gorgeous?" I bashfully managed to reply, I promise! He gave me a sexy look, which turned me on even more. I touched his long hair, now slightly tousled and mussed, and stroked the slight stubble on his perfect chin. As this dreamy man gave me one last memorable kiss, I could not help but wonder. How many times has he done this before on a plane? How many thousands of women has he slept with? Whatever!

Walking out of the gross bathroom, with him following close behind, people chuckled, teased, and applauded. Blushing bright neon red, I couldn't blame them. I would have applauded, too. With a phony refined defiance, I returned to my seat and continued to pose like a Vegas party girl or a Kardashian. Unfortunately for me, I didn't sleep a wink the whole flight. The fear of drooling or snoring kept me wide awake, as to preserve the integrity of this crazy romantic happening. I was overly infatuated with this radically charismatic, *all the colors of a rainbow sexy* hunk of a sensual man, who never once took his eyes off me for ten long hours. I grinned, thinking about our tawdry little scene in the bathroom, and assumed this guy had more moves than there were in yoga! I was reckless, just like our moms warned us not to be. Which made me enjoy it even more. Giggling, I foolishly realized I didn't know his name. Did it matter?

With my ego tank filled to the brim, about 45 minutes before we were scheduled to land, this extremely average-looking lady, obviously disheveled from sleeping all night on a plane, approached, and sat down on my future lover's lap. She affectionately pulled back his long, beautiful hair and kissed him tenderly on the forehead. Then, as quickly as she came, she went back to her seat at the rear of the plane. She appeared haggard and so much older than the Italian doctor. I wasn't sure if she was his mother or his wife. Shocked, and bumming hard, I could not believe what I just witnessed after 10 straight hours of him flirting with me. From across the aisle, I looked at him straight in his lovely eyes and mouthed the words in Italian. "Are you married???" The Italian, more handsome than any dazzling Hollywood actor, mouthed back confidently, grinning proudly, *"Yes, but that is not at all a matter for us to worry about!"*

Talk about burying the lead? If this wasn't outlandish enough, he had the audacity to blow me a kiss. Then, the stunning-looking married stranger with the long, silky, blonde hair stopped staring at me (for the 1st time during the whole flight) and started writing something down. When I looked up again, I noticed he was gone. Moments later, he passed by my seat without stopping and handed me a folded-up piece of paper. It read:

"Here is my number and email, Bella. We will meet in Rome, at 6:30 on the 31st, right in front of the Trevi Fountain. I will be waiting for you down below, closest to the water. I cannot wait to be with you and hold you in my arms. Oh, your lovely eyes, your beautiful smile, your sexy hands, and feet. You are like a boom! You're incredibly beautiful, and you will remain in my heart forever. Kisses & hugs, until we meet, Fabrizio!"

My, my, was he ever the typical Italian, right down to his name!

Moreover, *"**What the fuck is a boom?**"* I seriously wanted to know!

As flattering as all of that might have been, I wasn't going to decline his Roman invitation and pull at that thread just then. I feared it could potentially start a scene on a plane, flying 36,000 feet above land, with his wife 2 seconds away from finding us out. It would have been a volatile cocktail and a double one at that.

I'm sorry, but one thing for *damn* sure. This woman should know better than to fall asleep for so many hours on a plane, (or anywhere else in public) with a husband who is so entirely Rolls Royce classy, suave, and *studtacular* looking. And if you ask me, she should sleep with one eye open. I don't care how tired she was. And clearly, "Girlfriend needs to slap on some makeup and seriously do something with her atrocious hair." I realize this sounds a little *'meow.'* But it's not at all the way I meant it. Okay, maybe it was. OK, totally meow, rerrr, and even a loud hiss, in fact!

By the end of the flight, I felt like a disappointed Miss America runner-up, on display with her inferior crown constantly slipping off, and all the while wearing a forced, bogus smile. For 10 long hours, I felt like a Victoria's Secret model tirelessly posing overtime, without the big money payout or the free lingerie. This cad wins the title, "Super Scoundrel."

As anticipated, I arrived in Rome exhausted, sleep-deprived, with a 9-hour time change, which only made matters worse. Just seconds after walking off the plane and running frantically to catch my next flight to Israel, still within eyeshot range, came Fabrizio's encore text. It read:

"I thought last night was a magical night. Can you imagine how few possibilities we had to meet each other? It is incredible. I wait to be in Rome, kissing and caressing you. Baci, Baci, Kisses… Yours, Fab."

"Huh," I thought, "Gosh, is he ever the player!" So, he is *'mine now,'* is he? I wonder if this would bother his fashion-destitute, hair and makeup deficient wife? FYI and still thinking about her, no proud Italian woman would *ever* be caught dead or on a plane looking like that. Then, mid-thought, just as I was going to turn the corner towards my gate, the fab Fabrizio looked back at me one last time. Sly, like a fox, with one final stare, he blew me a kiss, waved goodbye, and walked out of sight with his wife. You know? His wife? The wife, that cheating on "would not be anything for us to worry about?" Yeah, her! *If that isn't the height of folly! I'm diggin' the folly thing now!* Much later that day, when I landed in Israel, I received yet another text from Fabrizio.

"It was fantastic meeting you on the flight. May I please know your calendar? Baci, Baci, Kisses. Yours, Fab."

Wistfully smiling and still shaking my head, I bounced back a reply. *"Fabrizio, you are without a doubt the sexiest man who has ever lived. In as much as being with you is strikingly tempting, sadly for me and perhaps you, I cannot take this romance any further, for you are,* **'MARRIED!'** *Unlike you, Bello, the fact you are married worries me greatly. Please, though, do feel free to call me if, and when, you are single. Fabrizio, I send you so many more delicious, lust-filled kisses that would have been wonderful to share. Baci, Baci. Ciao..."*

Holy shit, PTSD! I flashed back again to our decadent airplane bathroom scene that I would forever remember. What a fab kisser this exotic man was. It was a real anti*climax* letdown. We only began to explore each other, and we'd surely have had a major fuckathon. Damn, it's a bitch being honorable, and having integrity, morals, and principles. Seems it's growing tougher and getting in my way all the time these days.

Walking around Jerusalem eating a falafel, a laffa, and rugelach from the Marzipan Bakery, I thought, "Are there any good, single men left out there? Are there any faithful men still roaming around the planet?" I was quickly losing hope. Fortunately, I was thrilled and content to be in this amazing, vibrant, holy city, enjoying all its sights, foods, and historical spots. It was overrun with wonderful, happy people wandering about. Everyone I met in Israel was joyful, super-nice, and welcoming. I also had a memorable conversation with a group of young people in the Israeli Army, which I included in my report. The satisfying and rewarding ending to this story is, "My serious high-security intelligence report" was received with the utmost praise and gratification.

I reminisce, now and again, about the night of my long flight to Rome. The flight with the gorgeous *Fabriziolicious*, his passionate, hungry, aggressive kisses, his stunning Roman looks, irresistible charms, alluring stares, and my nonstop posing. I like to ignore the parts about his infidelity and his haggard wife. His wife, with her lackluster fashion, and in dire need of a hair and makeup ambulance! Sorry, it's my *nasty-woman* prerogative talking. I must admit, airplane bathrooms will never be the same for me. By the way, I never did find out what the fuck ***"You are like a boom"*** meant! Google and the Italian translator couldn't help me, either.

"Ladies and gentlemen, we have started our descent, and in preparation for landing, please make sure your seatbelts are securely fastened. Kindly put your seat backs and tray tables in their full upright position. Don't forget to take your memories and belongings that you've placed in the lavatory, your fantasies around or under your seat, and your disappointments placed in the overhead compartment. Ba-Bye now. And thank you for traveling on *Air Fabrizio!* Welcome to Roma."

A Fab, romantic, true, moral, ethical, and not-so-plain, plane ride. I won't lie… although I flew away disheartened, I was relieved I was not inducted into the Mile High Club with him!

The best part of the *Fabrizio* story? I will always, now, and forever know, "**I am like a BOOM!**" Whatever the hell that means?

And yes indeed, "I GOT MALED!" Again…
With a "Yes, but that is not at all a matter for us to worry about," Next!

CHAPTER 8

More Crazy Dates!

ENDLESS PRE-GRETS... OTHERWISE KNOWN AS... HELP! I'M DROWNING IN A SEA OF THE "NEXT" MEN. THROW ME A LIFE PRESERVER... *Please!*

"Help! I am drowning and I can't swim. Help!" That said, allow me to paddle through the titanic school of fish in the sea, I affectionately call...

The Next Guys

1. THE WELL, WELL, *WELL* ENDOWED ONLINE GUY...

These well, well, well, endowed guys are marveled by the celebrated myths, legends, and mysteries of the penis, rather than the truth behind the well-endowed privileged few. I'm speaking of those fortunate men who roam the face of the earth with their big, overwhelming, sublime members.

Stone, a handsome man from South America (a country known for this gift) and I began by texting online. After we spoke for a while on the phone, we eventually dated for about a month. To my out-and-out delight, things were moving along exceptionally well. I invited him to dinner with a few friends of mine. He triumphantly passed my girlfriends' and gay friends' approval tests with flying colors. His victory was remarkable, especially with my group. But since he was so disturbingly perfect, I held my breath, anticipating the usual adversity about to blow in. Things were way too good to be true. I wondered what the hell was wrong with him.

Henceforward, I decided to push the envelope, just for fun. I advanced to the next level with my ground rules in place. I invited him to spend the night at my house for a bit of harmless fooling around, but no sex. Not the *"no"* when you mean, *"yes,"* sex situation, either. Purely some innocent, playful fun, to test out the serene waters, or the potentially feared shark in the rough seas. I fancied the notion of putting to rest the mystery of the ship Mr. Stone was sailing. I had my feminine intuition he might be cruising large. After all, he did have exceptionally huge *hands and feet!* I always check that sort of detail out right away. Being insightful and intuitive (in other words, a *nosey reporter*) I was curious and needed to know. On the other huge hand and foot, this could all simply be another one of those old wives' tales. It was irrelevant, for I was determined to find out. Speaking of which, these busybody wives must stop telling their devious, hocus-pocus sagas. Their cunning, deceitful tales are shamefully misleading to the rest of us, who are hoping some of them might be true. In fact, there should be a law against their lies and wicked stories.

Though with Stone, I sensed there was a shred of truth to the old wives' legend. My suspicions were that he hung quite well in the balance.

The following week, Stone took me out for a fancy, romantic dinner. I wore a provocative low-cut dress, red heels, and all. Afterward, we hung out at my house, sharing dessert and coffee. Thirty minutes after devouring the obscene fudge cake he brought, we started messing around. And just like that... O-MA-GOD! Cowabunga! Hello, Mr. Dirk Diggler!

On a cold, rainy evening, there "IT" stood. Like, King Kong in all his glory. I would compare it to the Sky City Building in China, only the penis version. I didn't know whether to shriek, curtsy, salute, or run. A resounding, "Cock-a-doodle-do" and I'm not referring to roosters here, people. Trust me, his woody was as gigantic and hard as a 20,000-year-old Sequoia tree. What-do-ya-know? In Stone's case, the old wives' shadowy tales nailed it. Big hands, big feet, big rooster, and a *Big Stone!* I'm just speculating, but his Rocket Launcher could assist NASA! What else could I say, other than a jaw-dropping, "Blast Off!" His size was intimidating, dangerous, and frightening. There it stood, erect in stunning splendor, and could easily be used as a human shield. It was the biggest penis I had ever seen. Or anyone has seen! It is the Porno "AVN Awards" of penises. The "Oscar Awards" as in, "And the Biggest Dick Award goes to... Stone Wilson!" *(Standing ovation! Applause, applause, applause!)* Holy Peter Pecker, Penis-Man! It took all my strength not to blurt out, "Dude, you've got to be kidding me? Have you entered that thing in a contest? You just gotta!" Talk about the big elephant trunk in the room. Bashfully staring, I spoke. "Stone, I lift my glass for a toast. Here's to your striking, beguiling penis!" I desperately wanted to grab my reporter's microphone. *"This is Mollie Sloan, coming to you live with the man who has the biggest penis in the world. Like ever! Tell us, Mr. Stone, your Real P' Hollywood story?"*

Naturally, at first, I was elated with a flush of excitement. But then, I felt my knees start to buckle from the mere looks of it. "Stone, you could have knocked me over with a feather. Or for sure, with your penis." For survival reasons, I convinced myself to pass. Let me tell you, it tugged at my heartstrings that I couldn't do a thing with it. All I kept thinking was, "Walk away from the eye-popping, Guinness-worthy penis, and you will continue to live!" He was the size of 6 guys put together, maybe even 7! *("Hear! Hear," bellowed outbursts and roaring cheers from the crowd!)*

I was a Stone's throw away from even imagining it inside of me. Simply considering the notion scared the *"F#@%&K"* out of me. It seemed as if every nuance of his Mount Kilimanjaro, Middle Leg, One-eyed monster, his Mount Everest, his Giant totem pole, (And his... *Go on; fill in your own choice of words here!),* shouted out pain with a capital P, which rhymes with flee. I was throbbing and twitching in agony, only seeing a glimpse of it. The way it arched and the size of it resembled the Leaning Tower of Pisa, only bigger. Stone, for sure, needed a huge marina to store his vessel. My harbor would never be able to accommodate him.

Ordinarily, a large Hercules penis would be considered a perk, a bonus, an Aha moment! Disappointingly, after checking out Stone's peak up close and personal, I knew that I wasn't up to the task at hand, or any other place in or around my body. I mean, who the hell would be! Even a well-oiled hooker would surely freak out. But I really believe a hooker most definitely would charge Stone by the yard, rather than by the hour.

Because I'm young and have a strong desire to continue living, I straightaway realized (like duh), I sadly could not be a contender or a candidate. He was monstrously ginormous. As plain as day, I could hear a game show host saying, "Thank you for playing, and a good try contestant number, seven-hundred-and-eighty." I urgently wanted to shout, "Wait, game show host person! Can I at least have what's behind curtain number three instead?" Oh, wrong game show? "Then wait, how about letting me buy a vowel?" I was really frustrated about not playing in the game. I was so hoping to make it to the bonus round, or at the very least, *score* in the lightning round. I asked myself, "What's a *small down under, girl* to do?"

Unfortunately, the answer was obvious. He would break me, or any woman for that matter. Must I remind you? My vagina had already been broken previously by the illustrious Valerio! Don't make me pull out the Bam-Bam card. I feared by the looks of Stone's thingamabob, my hands weren't even big enough to work his thing. What an unexpected curveball. And oh, yes, it was so large that it did curve. How could it not? Many of my reporter colleagues and friends on numerous occasions have said to me, "But, Mollie, you have a big mouth!" But I can honestly say with a *Stone-Cold* expression, "It *ain't* big enough for the colossal man!"

My participation in the Stone caper was humbling. I almost forgot the worst part of all. I'd soon have to march down the '*No Walk of Shame*' to my friends. They'll humiliate, degrade, and dishonor me for running away from the '*Giant Penis Man.*' They'll never let me live this down. I'd have to endure epic laughter and endless ridicule. After weighing my two choices, walking away, and facing my friends seemed the far safer path.

As the wind outside howled and blew, (which is theoretically what I should have been doing tonight), I looked deeply into Stone's emerald-green heartthrob eyes and, for a millisecond, I softened. "I can do this! I'm going to pull it together, be brave, and just go for it. I had to do this for posterity alone. If I didn't, I'd regret it forever. I'm doing it, dammit." (*I heard imaginary porn stars. "Go Mollie, go! You can do it! Get it, girl!"*)

That was all well and good until I once again glared in horror at his overpowering, death-defying beast of a penis. How could a dick get this big, anyway? I thought, there is no fucking way, by any stretch of the imagination, or my vagina. I couldn't. "Your Honor, if it pleases the court, I abstain. I plead all 27 amendments of the constitution, relevant or not!"

Unlike the external wind, there wasn't going to be any blowing, howling, or huffing and puffing inside my house tonight. I speculated, has any girl had and survived sex with this man? And if so, I'd love to meet her, just to shake her hand and say, "Bravo. Job well done, and you go, girl!" Then, I'd ask her to open her mouth and say, Aah. Next, I'd ask if I could watch to see how she does it. It would be like taking a Master Class.

Allow me to say, if Michelangelo met Stone, there would no doubt be a huge marble statue of his penis somewhere in the Louvre in Paris, the Vatican Museum in Italy, or in the heart of Rome, presented in the center of a square. With the Italian's pride, it would be a baroque masterpiece of a fountain, with a waterfall cascading around it. Exactly like the Trevi Fountain, only with his penis in the center. Can you visualize how many coins would be thrown into Stone's fountain? Talk about making a wish!

One thing I knew for certain. They'll be telling stories about Stone and his masculine, inspiring, lucky charms around campfires throughout the land one day. All the while eating s'mores, sipping hot chocolate, and singing (To be sung in the key of D flat), "Kumbaya, my Lord, kumbaya. Stone's big penis, kumbaya!" I clearly understood that "Death, by Mr. Big Dick," was not an option! I could see the Breaking Headline News story… *"Woman Attacked and Murdered by Oversized, Legendary, Monstrous Penis… News at Eleven! Now, back to you in the studio, Wolf."*

My remaining thought was, how the bejesus do I get out of this situation without hurting his feelings? I was upset with myself, for I always had a contingency plan. My mind went frantic with senseless random thoughts and excuses. Necessary to prevent this impossible, *MAN*thrax situation, I gently decided to own up to it. I told Stone the truth. He was not surprised at all, and his relaxed, nonchalant expression told me he had heard it many times before. We agreed to be friends. I'll bet the ranch that Stone has a ton of women friends! I was crushed and saddened by my unfortunate failed trauma. This stone would wisely go unturned.

The following evening, I met up with my beloved gay friends. After hearing my colossal story, they roared endlessly. As expected, they were brutally relentless. They enjoyed every bashing second of destroying and punching fun at me. *"Girl, how could you not have conquered the fortunate man who roams the face of the earth with his big, sublime dick?* Shame on you, woman! You're such a wuss! Where is your pride? And more importantly, **Where Is He Now**?" They all laughed, hysterically.

In my defense, I justified with a giggle, "Cut it out, guys. Back off! If I had had sex with Sir Stone and the weapon he possessed in his pants, it would have turned into a crime scene... yellow tape and all!"

Richie declared pompously, "Speaking of Sir... The Royal House of Windsor should knight him for his kingly jewels. We all roared. He went on, though. "You see, Mollie, this is exactly what happens when you send a woman to do a gay man's job!" Again, laughter filled the air.

Shino chimed in, too. "Yeah, I also have a big bone to pick with you, honey. You have shamefully embarrassed yourself. You're pathetic!"

Our nonstop giggling made my eyes tear. "C'mon guys. Sticks and stones may break my bones, but Stone's dick would've destroyed me!" Endless laughter forced me to run into the other room to catch my breath.

When I returned, Roberto blurted out, "Cocktail, anyone?

Perhaps Scotch on the *cocks*? Heavy on the cock! Sweetie, dahling, I'm guessing no cocks for you. Hon, we so need to cock. I mean talk!" Laughter ensued.

Adonis teased, too. "We bow down to you, divine Stone, and two dicks up for having so much skin in the game! Hey, Mollie, you'd never have to ask him, how's it hanging?" Nonstop merriment at my expense prevailed all night. They never eased up on their steadfast ribbing and mocking me. It was funny and besides, I totally had it coming. Every bit.

And more to the point, where would we be without our amazing friends who are always there, never let us down, love us unconditionally, and forever see the humor in everything? So cute, how they later throw it back in our face and rub it in? Gotta love them, and I do with all my heart!

Richie stopped my loving, tender thoughts, demanding, "Hey there English Rose, you seriously need to surrender your honorary Gay Card for your wimpy, embarrassing, and pitiful behavior! I'm mortified for you."

"No way, Rich! Stone's dick was a marvel from another planet. It was as big and hard as an alien rock. It scared the **dick**ens out of me and blew me away."

"No honeybun," Roberto laughed. "*You* should have blown *him* away, doll! Seriously, now you're just bragging and making us all jealous!" Which naturally brought a belly laugh to all, including me.

"That's one small step of humor for gay mankind, and my running, one giant leap away from this mankind's huge phenomenon of a penis!"

I close this *"ri-'dick'-ulous, gigantic, magic wand tale,"* by quoting the words spoken by Humphrey Bogart in Casablanca.

Stone... "I think this is the beginning of a beautiful friendship." ONLY!

A very big, "Cock-a-doodle, **Don't!**" And **Next!**

2. THE INAPPROPRIATE RISE ON EVERY OCCASION GUY...

One dreary autumn day, Austin surprisingly popped up every which way in my life. We went out a few times, but no matter what we did or where we went, his pouch always popped up like popcorn, a champagne cork, or bubble wrap. Ya know, his sexcalibur, his hockey stick, his Stone!

There it was, always springing up at the most inopportune moments. Like a trampoline, a Slinky toy, or a tulip in springtime, just to say, *"Hello, hi there, look at me!"* During the limited time we went out, I was always in fear of his alarming, ups and downs. And I'm not referring to his mood swings. It was like watching the History Channel on the rise and fall of the Berlin Wall, the Roman Empire, Harvey Weinstein, Ex-Gov. Cuomo, Mel Gibson, Tiger Woods, Paula Deen, O.J., Lance Armstrong, and the winner and still champion, Bill Cosby.

Only Austin's ups and downs were in public, and awkwardly more embarrassing. It seemed to do *'its thing,'* constantly. His Anaconda had a mind all its own, always playing *peek-a-boo*. In her scholarly words, the never-ending wisdom, and insight of Britney Spears... "Oops, he did it again, and again. And again!" Austin was a real-life Pop-Tart, darting up and out of the toaster all hot and ready to go. I was continually self-conscious by Austin and his "Pop Goes the Weasel" antics. He displayed more pop-ups than any children's books or toys. Really, he should protect and hide that thing in his pouch like a mother kangaroo does. Austin took the phrase, "Come out, come out, wherever you are" to a whole new level. This uncomfortable situation was 'hard-on' me. So, I moved on quickly!

A, popping up and out... **Next!**

3. THEN CAME, THE REALLY UGLY ONLINE GUY...

They say, "Beauty is in the eye of the beholder." As I am the beholder, this guy was beyond *Uggg-Ga-ly* with a capital UGLY. I tried. I swear on Versace, I tried with all my might not to be superficial or shallow. I even searched for another tree limb to climb out on. I worked hard to pull out the Zen, philosophical, and moral cards to remind myself that finding the perfect mate is not just about looks. Of course, it isn't! Not at all! But do come on. It is, a little. Oh, stop, you know it is!

Still, I wanted to get past this trivial attitude and give the guy a chance. I promise on Dior, I tried. I benevolently didn't want to slide down that slippery slope or the bottomless pit of meanness and cruelty. Trust me when I say that he is hideous looking, I am being so very thoughtful and generously empathetic. I desperately attempted, because he was such a good guy, and I hadn't met many of this species.

His name was Alonzo, and he was a super-intelligent man. I'll say that about him. He graduated from USC with the highest of honors. But I'm sorry, Alonzo was chillingly ugly looking. He was the "*covering your eyes* or *looking the other way*" kind of awful looking! You just need to go with me on this. Yes, for sure, he's truly a wonderful, kind man. But it took everything I had not to look at him with a straight, non-ick face. I'm talking about the Elephant Man (Joseph Merrick), sort of grotesque. And trust me, Joseph was way cuter! Although an absurd paradox, Alonzo was enormously lovely and genteel. I only wished I could have sprinkled some *pretty-boy fairy dust* on him and, like *poof, Abracadabra,* make the ugly go away. Too mean? Maybe, but I was the one who'd have to kiss him!

I had the most unnerving, terrifying nightmare recently about a horrid, unimaginably nasty-looking man running after me. I believe we were caught up in an old *Bond Movie* because 007, M, and Moneypenny were all there. I don't know how it ended because the man in my dream was so ugly, I woke up petrified, in a cold sweat. All I'm saying is, even the *nightmare guy* was better looking than Alonzo! Can't I just have 007 and call it a day? Still, despite it all, I barreled on ahead since Alonzo was a super-de-duper awesome guy. Unfortunately, and sadly for him, he was the kind of chap you can't bring home to Mother with confidence, for it would rattle and shock the hell out of her. However, if you didn't like your mom much, this could work out very nicely, in fact. Just being honest. The truth will hopefully set you free. Sure, after it scares the devil out of you.

For Pete's Sake, the notorious' Phantom of the Opera' was cuter. But, like the Phantom, how could I possibly ask Alonzo to cover his face and wear a mask? Clearly, that would be downright cruel. It would have been deeply disgraceful for me to crossover that insensitive line. I could never request such a thing from this sweet, endearing man. Totally unacceptable behavior for an educated, well-bred girl, like me.

"He Said No!!!!"

If things weren't unsightly enough for Alonzo, he was also stricken with 'RDNMS!' This condition, known as *Robert De Niro, Mole Syndrome,* appears on his left cheek, only bigger, with dark hairs growing out of it. He really should pluck those. Moreover, Alonzo also had a glass eye. I could tell because there was a crack in it! Nice blue color, though.

I often wondered if this lovely gent realized just how unappealing he was. I wholeheartedly hoped not. I tried enormously to overlook his *"ewe-ness."* In addition, bless his heart, Alonzo had the bonus "ewe-ickness" of thick, black, curly hair over his entire body, plus man boobs. I could see it all right through his shirt. He made the ugly duckling look like a majestic swan, and I'm being generous. Forgive me. I couldn't be with this man! So go on and hate me, loath me, even detest me, but regardless, I still couldn't. Please understand and don't judge me. Take my word for it that you couldn't either! I'm *not* a judgmental woman, but I just couldn't.

I moved on rapidly, into orbit like the Starship Enterprise on a mission to Mars, or anywhere but with poor Alonzo! Seriously, he had a face only a mother could love. Hmmm? Yeah, no. *Not even her*! :0((((!

By the way, just so you appreciate, I'm not totally heartless! I thoughtfully picked out a lovely, colorful, expensive mask for Alonzo. It was from Venice, Italy, and everything! So, don't go shaking your head disapprovingly at me! Oh, come on, be compassionate, and feel my pain.

The ugly truth... And Next!

4. THE ALWAYS COMPLAINING, ONLINE GUY...

Grouchy Griffith appeared grouchily onto my scene. He emulated Oscar the Grouch right off the pages of the Muppets. This guy complained about everything and everybody. I'm guessing he behaved this way since he was shamefully obstinate, insecure, and bitter. I never once, even for a second, contemplated sleeping with Griffith for many reasons. Mostly, I was afraid he would complain about my lovemaking expertise, my vagina, my boobs, my booty, my bed, and my, whatever! He surely would have criticized something. Aside from being cute, he wasn't a lot of laughs or fun to be with. Grouchy

Griffith was about the Blah, Blah, Blah this, and the Blah, Blah, Blah that. He drove me into an exhausting state of ennui.

Mr. Grouchy was all about existing in the "Fester, fester, fester, and the rot, rot, rot, of life." I believe he thrived, basking in a pool of negativity. Griffith would get off living in an ominous black hole if only it were possible. That about describes him in an unenthusiastic nutshell.

One night, way too late to be calling and when I least expected it, the negative man complained and confided in me, "Mollie, just so you know, I only have one ball." Now you see, this in every way goes under the "too much information" category! We never even spoke of sex before, not to mention it was way too soon to be sharing ballgame talk. I gather he never heard of the phrase, *"Don't Ask… Don't Tell."*

Look, I'm not heartless! Even though I never asked him to "take me out to the ballgame," I do feel bad for Grouchy Griffith about his one-ball situation. After all, realistically, they are supposed to come in a set of 2, like gloves, socks, and earrings. Or paired together such as peanut butter and jelly, Bonnie and Clyde, cheese and crackers, milk and cookies, yin and yang, bread and butter, a pillow and blanket, a 65-year-old man and an 18-year-old girl. Wait, no, that isn't right! *Although, it happens all the time!* Thinking about this situation, *2 balls down below,* should go together too. Even though he is a bevy of complaints, this one is justifiably legit. So, I could appreciate and understand his *one-ball* complaint, to be a worthy problem to moan about. But Good Lord, *Not to Me!*

After a few weeks, and a couple of dates with this grouchy confrontational man, I knew I had to end it even before it could get started. I picked the night we went out to dinner for sushi at my favorite Japanese restaurant. Grouchy Griffith never stopped bitching for a second. He complained about the rice, saying it was undercooked. The noodles, he criticized were overcooked. The tempura was greasy, soggy, and cold. The sushi smelled like fish. (You think, Captain Obvious?) The edamame he griped was mushy and overly salted. The green tea he blasted was bitter and too strong. As for me, everything I ate was delicious, perfectly served, and cooked. O-M-GEEZ, he's such an awful, unhappy malcontent.

Then he went off, ragging on me. If you could imagine that! Now, here is where he got himself into dangerous territory. Normally, I would have deflected his new attack target. However, I geared up and got my own bitch-face on. I was so ready for him to, "Bring ~ It ~ On!"

Midstream, biting apart the seaweed from my tasty, nothing to complain about, shrimp and avocado tempura roll with spicy mayo sauce, Griffith targeted and criticized me! "You know, I realize we've only known each other for a few weeks. But it appears we have no magic in our relationship. We need to put some magic into our dating. We need to add some magic, magic, magic!" And just like that, while chomping on a delicious crab roll, eel sauce, and all, *Poof, I Disappeared!!*

Before my grand exit, I wish I had magically responded, "Holy Moly, Griffith. You've got a lot of balls! But then, on the real, you only have one!" Yeah, yeah, people! I understand how that would be too mean. So that's why I didn't go there. Still, he more than had it coming.

A frog and a princess, beauty and a beast, Grouchy Griffith and I were all mismatched in a mystical, not so magical, vanishing story.

A Negative, One Ball, Blah-Blah Complaining, and a Grouchy POOF!

5. "THE CONTROL FREAK, TEMPER TANTRUM, ALWAYS RIGHT GUY," STORMED INTO MY LIFE...

I dated Zachery because it had been way past forever. Plain and simple, I needed sex. Otherwise known as the *"Sexual emergency, in-between, or tweener-guy."* Zac was awfully cute, loving, tender, warm, affectionate, and cozy *'in bed.'* I quantify this by divulging, *"Only in bed!"* Therefore, I saw to it we stayed in bed, a lot. Like, as in always.

For whatever reason, the minute he'd put his clothes back on, Zac became "Super Schmuck Guy." He suddenly morphed into a wickedly evil cartoon villain. He transformed and became cold, thoughtless, aggressive, argumentative, and a straight-out, angry anti-hero. More accurately, stated, a mood-swinging, mean wanker on steroids.

Dating Zac placed me right in the center of a strange catch-22 dilemma. I never grasped what turned him into this nasty bastard character the moment he put one leg into his pants. Gosh, Superman didn't become an ass the minute he took off his cape? He just became a nerd with no game. Zachary's volatile rages and tirades were epic. Perhaps his mom pushed him too hard with the potty training, maybe too many time-outs, or not enough play dates? Yikes, it might also have something to do with weaning him off her breasts too soon. Regardless of why, out of bed, Zac became a paranoid, psychotic, persnickety, pouty, pathetic, prickazoid, and a peculiar, pissed-off guy. Gosh, that was a *lot of P's!*

I wanted to tell this born-again Damien character from the "Omen," that for every hour you are angry, you lose an hour of happiness. Sensibly and cautiously, I decided I was not about to be his shrink. Still, since I enjoyed sex with him so much, I separated in my mind his good and evil, opposing superhero characters. Although not recommended, I placed him into the "It's just sex, with no emotions" file in my brain.

Skillfully and meticulously, I planned all our dates naked in bed. It was the perfect scenario. We sexed and dined in bed. Without exception, my main goal with Zachary was to *stay in bed*. Thus, I spent time, energy, and much ado planning themed events in the crib. It took a lot of finagling. There was the "Good morning, French maid breakfast, (outfit to match, a beret hat, and all) with eggs, bacon, croissants, and pastry, *in bed*." The "Pretty Mexican Señorita themed lunch, serving guacamole, cheese, nachos, tacos, tequila, and cinnamon-dusted Churros, *in bed*. Õle!" The "All American themed stripper girl, beer, ribs, burgers, buffalo chicken wings, with apple pie, à la mode dessert, *in bed*." The "Italian-themed sexy, Bellissimo Senora, serving wine, pasta, pizza, gelato night, *in bed*." The "Greek Goddess, Toga themed Ouzo, chicken kebab, hummus, and baklava night, *in bed*." Lastly, the always reliable, "College Sorority Girl, fruit, Twinkies, cookies, potato chips, chocolate, Jell-O shots, and cappuccino night, *in bed*." (Reminder: True story!)

To be perfectly honest, I started feeling like a cruise director on a sex boat. There were many times I wanted to jump ship, throw him overboard, or start a mutiny on the modern-day bed bounty. It was getting increasingly harder to be bedroom creative. Not to mention, all the food was staining and ruining my expensive Egyptian, 800-thread-count sheets, my Scandinavian Goose Down comforter, and pricey-themed lingerie!

Indeed, it was no surprise the coming of the end was inevitable and inviting. The food and sex love-boat with Zac on board was sinking! It was going down faster than the Titanic! "What? Too soon? Seriously?"

Anyway, Zachery had finally crossed the *"You are just a creep, and I don't care anymore if you are a great lover,"* line. The sad realization hit me hard that Zac, the man, with his perfected sexual skills, was not the slightest bit nice or enjoyable, even in bed anymore. He was now just a mean creep, in and out of the bed. I certainly wasn't going to put up with his super-control, man-freak character for another second. The monumental question I asked myself was, "Exactly when did the dominance and submission games begin, Mr. Zac-Grey?"

It was a long time overdue to throw Captain Hook overboard and off my personal Jolly Roger. Thus, ultimately casting him back to Never-Again-Land! I knew all I had to do was insult him one time and it would all be over. It would be like ripping off a Band-Aid or, in this case, pricey luxurious bedding. Suppressing my stormy anger so as not to blow the sheets off my bed, I pragmatically devised every detail of how and when I'd put my plan into action. Timing is everything in life.

That Saturday night, we did the infrequent activity of leaving the bed, to go out to dinner and a movie. As anticipated, the obsessive otaku man was cranky and irritable all night. This was working out perfectly and was all part of my calculating breakup plans. When we arrived back at my house, even before attempting sex, he was angry, cruel, controlling, and not in a *"fun, anything you wish, who's your daddy"* kind of way!

Lying in bed, having sex, (or whatever that was) I was bored, tired, and I had my eyes closed. This tool of a man protested angrily. *"Hey, open your eyes!"* He looked squarely into my baby blues, all *pissed off,* and asked me point-blank. *"Mollie, were you, Faking It????"* Here was the perfect vitriolic chance to kryptonite Zac. Adding some major attitude, I blasted him with a venomous tone. *"NO! I was really sleeping!!"*

Take that, Zac-Man… Bam, boom, zap, pow, whack, swoosh, and clunk! This femme fatale, lady of the bed, killed it!

And away in a blaze, the "super anti-hero, evil character guy" leaped up into the sky and flew away faster than a loser at the Grammys! Damn, what a missed opportunity. I should have bought him a cape for his exit. It would've been so much more effective and dramatic.

I wonder if Lois Lane ever had this problem with Superman. Oh, please, people, don't act all shocked or surprised. You know darn well Superman and Lois got it on, big time! And for years! Who knows, she might have also done Jimmy Olsen, and Perry White too. Hey, for all we know, she could have done Lex Luthor! In fact, it was even rumored she did General Zod. I mean, he was kind of sexy in a bad-boy way.

Hopefully, Zachary was banished to a far-off galaxy, a distant planet, or into a dark spiraling vortex. My work here is super done. I say, "Yo-ho-ho, and a goodbye to you, mate. The sex-bed-boat has sailed!"

I do declare that online dating is a dangerous up-and-down rollercoaster. I was now so dizzy and about to gag. Honestly, I think I might have hit the online dating wall. That wall really is the breaking point of madness. This frickin' wall was attempting to break my spirit. No way. I quickly pulled myself together and determined this was never going to happen! No guy, neither online nor offline, was ever going to get me that far off my game. I concluded that I had to be the woman who stands up to all this online adversity, full throttle!

> "I proudly flew away faster than a speeding bullet, towards a resounding, *peace out*, villain-less Next!"

CHAPTER 9

Staying the Course

BETTER KNOWN AS HANGING IN THERE AND FORGING ON...

Hanging in there, staying the course, and forging on? A task as easy as being in the ring with an angry bull, wearing all red, and I think we all know how that turns out. "El Toro!" So, after rummaging through my first batch of *"deleted men"* and their offensive disturbing responses, I felt this was all a fait accompli. Hell no, I wasn't about to be defeated, even if I was nose-diving right off the scary dating Kingda Ka Roller Coaster. It was difficult to accept I wasn't experiencing any hopeful feelings, no sparkle, and no exhilarating *Za-Za-Zoo* Pizzazz. There was no magic with any of the men I spoke to or went out with. I wondered, where was *my* quixotic fairytale like the ones I read about in the romance novels growing up? Where were my dreamy emotions of happily ever after excitement?

Like, "I must meet this guy. He sounds amazing!" "I can't wait to go out with *coolguy243*." "I'm curious about, *boylover33!*" "I'm eager to meet *Alec 686*." "I think *bring2youjoy*, could be the one." "*Romance Guy* seems promising." "I hope *Bart36* looks like his photo." "I wonder if *Happyjoe* is as amazing as he sounds." I'm excited with great anticipation.

Clearly, there wasn't a trace of those sentiments above. To be more forthright, I used other, more profound, unladylike words to describe my hopelessness while screaming quietly out loud with each passing bloke. I can tell you though, as disillusioned as I was, I officially wanted to change my name to... *"Mollie, Really, What the Fuck, Sloan."* I concluded, *"Mollie, Really, What the Hell,"* just didn't cut it anymore.

Regardless of all the absurdity I had endured, I realized I had to emerge from the cataclysms of these senseless dating situations victorious. A promise is a promise, even if only made to oneself. I'd keep my vow to triumph, stay focused, and remain determined. I went to *DEFCON 1*, optimistic and hopeful. I went all out with Oprah Winfrey's positive and spirited style. The *"You get a free car & you get a free car, joyful spirit."*

I even pursued Tony Robbins' *optimistic, enthusiastic flair!* *"Why live an ordinary life, when you can live an extraordinary one?"* *"It is in your moments of decision that your destiny is shaped!"* Naturally, I liked Oprah's better! I'll take a free car any day over Tony's, yada-yada. That's just me. Hence, I journeyed on with Oprah's immense free car persistence.

Some people say, to achieve happiness, you should live each day of your life as if it's your last. This way, you'll appreciate every single moment you have. Other people suggest living each day as if it's your first, because this way, every day can be the beginning of a new adventure. I believe that our failures bring us the proper perspective on success. What other option did I have? After all, my Prince Charming, "The perfect-in-every-way guy" (See chapter 18) was waiting patiently, and eagerly expecting me to find him. Being the captain of my man-search ship, I couldn't abandon my vessel in the middle of rough seas! Thus, I remained on the charted course, with all the hope and spirit I could muster!

For you remarkable open-minded men still reading, *"I applaud you with a resounding thank you, and a sidebar of wow!"* Listen up, guys. It's like when you are in a playoff game and you're losing. Suddenly you catch an interception on your opponent's goal line, with 25 seconds on the clock. You are down by 3 points and your team runs the ball back to the goal line for a touchdown and nails the kick for the extra point with 2 seconds left to spare on the clock. That's the type of attitude and optimism I passionately wanted to achieve. It would keep my ship floating safe, confident, and hopeful. While not easy to attain, I was all in.

So, there I was, still Romeo-less, but with the determination of the eye-of-a-tiger, united by the wisdom of the brilliant philosophers, and my storybook dreams. This fusion resulted in a deep, philosophical, positive message. It was so very profound, poetic, and like Shakespeare to my ears.

My friends, I'm afraid that's the kind of fortitude and positive conviction this ambitious dating pursuit takes. Nothing that should, could, or would, was going to stop my quest. With all this resolve, how could I fail?

But despite my tenacity, I had failed miserably thus far. And that's when I heard the "Ding!" Suddenly, I had a revelation, and an Aha epiphany. "Ding," There it was. My guiding bright light. I concede that throughout my pursuit, I've been way too serious. I wasn't having fun at all. None. So, I decided with that tiny "Ding," to look for the humor and the amusement in every part of this dating dilemma. And boy, was there ever a bevy of entertainment to humor me. If you possess an off-the-wall, fantastic sense of humor, with a sadistic twist (very helpful, BTW), you'll surely find online dating to be comically rich. It's a standup comic's Costco-sized comedy of laughs and endless freaky people to make fun of. Humor and levity were the ticket and the missing *Za-Za-Zoo* Pizzazz.

I moved on with confidence and turned over a new comedy leaf. Armed with my fresh, amusing approach in hand and mace in my purse, I boldly set sail with élan. I encourage all hopeful daters to hold on to this comedic and humorous approach for dear life. Go out on a limb if you have to! This is without question your only haven and anchor for sanity. I was done behaving somberly and being decimated by men on and offline. But even with humor, you will still incessantly be tilting your head, raising your arms with angst, and yelling, *"Mollie, really, what the fuck, Sloan!"* (*And please, yell your name, not mine!*) Comedy doesn't promise success or "The One." But it delivers more fun than my dull, humorless technique.

Considering this "Looking for 'The One' journey" to be an essential mission in my life, I was ready and psyched with my innovative "More power to you" positive thinking. I embraced my new search, "Nice and easy," like the iconic Tina Turner sang. I nicely and easily dipped my toes into the water again. After all, at this interval, I had nothing to lose or any desire to settle. I charged in and doubled down with the most sophisticated cherry-picking tool I could ever find. My ego!

Starting my revised quest, I looked all over the country, the world, and globally, in fact, for fresh prospects. I discovered it's not wise to limit your soul-mate search, just in your backyard. For sure, I would have looked on the Moon, Venus, and Mars, if it were possible. It might even be a huge upgrade from Earth. Honestly, if you consider all of Earth's strange, violent, war-hungry, inhuman, prejudiced, little-brained, self-destructive, and ignorant selfish humans, just how far off am I? Perhaps this is the reason why there are millions of alien sightings, but the extra-terrestrials never actually land and say, "Take me to your leader!" Or "Hi! How's it hanging Stone?" Well, in

Stone's case, obviously seeing how it's hanging, they might just say, "Wowza?" Or, if it's a lady alien, she might even say, "Hi there, big fella. Gosh, so that's what the big deal on Earth is all about!" Maybe alien women could handle Stone and his very big deal, easier than Earth women? Anyway, even aliens are laughing and want nothing to do with us, foolish Earthlings. Well, except for Stone!

I had the greatest hopes for the second go-round. I systemically picked the "crème de la crème" of men on four different dating sites. Still, I do appreciate the online, "la crème bar," is disturbingly not set very high. I fastidiously examined (like a Virgo would) each of the men for things I knew I needed for chemistry at first sight. Be it human or alien. Things like breathing, walking, talking, seeing, and hearing, for starters. Next, I got arrogantly bold and finicky as I went for cute, nice eyes, a great smile (with real teeth, not in a glass) under 35, a good personality, and hair. Preferably on the head, and not sliding off. Daring further, I looked for men who were toned, educated, intelligent, successful, fun, and, optimistically with the ability to get it up. Without Viagra! Waxing would be a nice bonus, too. For all of you who don't know, hair below is a telltale sign of a guy over 35. Women too. So, girls, get on with that if you haven't already. Like immediately! And I'd like to add, "Ewe!

As you can imagine, all the above narrowed the field of candidates, plummeting way down rather abruptly. I forlornly deciphered that I was theoretically looking for a needle in a haystack. Which prompted me to wonder. "Why the hell would single, great champion guys put themselves through the drama of being on an online dating site?" Low point and a rude awakening. However, I stopped, humbled by my own tail between my legs and reconsidered. "I personally know there are great single girls on these sites. So why wouldn't great single guys be on them as well?"

Energized and fired up, I stayed eye-of-a-tiger positive, with the added touch of humor and swagger. I was surprisingly eager and giddy on my first day out with a new approach navigating the way. For you men, it's equivalent to losing in a game at the bottom of the ninth. All bases are loaded, and your best hitter is approaching the field. You can plainly hear the organ in the background blaring... ♪ Ba, ba, ba, ba ♫ Ba, ba, ba, ba, ♪ Charge! And Score!!!! Or at least, I was hoping to. You know? Score!

I was all prepared and enthusiastic about my new methodology with a genuine twinkle of confidence in my eye. (Both of them.) I set sail into the rough seas of men who were waiting on the foggy, mysterious horizon. How innocent and naïve I was at this exhausting stage of the game. Aw, so sweet. Warms my heart... even now. "Focus, Focus!"

FAST-FORWARD SIX WEEKS...

Despite all my eye-of-a-tiger positive thinking, with an added sense of humor and perseverance, I nevertheless suffered countless discouraging and exasperating disappointments. It became increasingly challenging holding on to my sense of humor life jacket. I was going through men faster than high school girls go through guys, selfies, mood swings, lying to their parents, texts, and reality shows! With each email, date, or chat, I felt lonelier and more disillusioned than when I first began.

I regrouped and calmed down. Down into the deep depths of hell, down. Yet it appeared I was already in hell. I was clearly seeing a red-horned devil with his pitchfork, fire blazing, and people screaming! *Oh, my bad, never mind.* I was with friends at an Arizona State Homecoming Game. See, this is what always happens around that 3rd shot of tequila. "Mascot Sparky, you're a cute little devil!" Ok, losing it. Whatever *'It'* is?

Back on point, I wasn't about to fail or jump overboard. I wouldn't dream of quitting, for that was not at all an option. I looked my challenge straight in the eye and gave it a wink. "Full steam ahead," I bellowed.

That was scary. I don't remember bellowing before in my entire life. Scream, yell, shout, and holler? Sure, I've done all of those. But bellow? Does anybody really bellow anymore? I'm asking for a friend!

Ok, it's official! I needed a break from the madness. There's nothing better to do the trick of calming one's nerves than chugging my favorite Merlot, with a bucket of popcorn and Milk Duds. This magical ritual of mine erases all the bad in the world and hits the spot every time.

I took a restorative week off from searching online to regain my composure and recharge my stress battery. Searching for inspiration, I reflected on what the magnificent Maya Angelou once said, *"I've learned that no matter what happens, or how bad it seems today, life does go on, and it will be better tomorrow."* How Adorable! Yeah, that worked for about… oh, maybe 10 minutes or so. Maya, Maya, dear brilliant and dazzling Maya, here's the thing. With great respect, you had obviously and fortunately never been involved with online dating. I'll just stick with your other brilliant quote for now… "Life is not measured by the number of breaths we take, but the moments that take our breath away." This one's relatable, true, and relevant. Lovely Dr. Angelou, you're greatly missed!

I appreciated the negative emotions that were now creeping in would get me nowhere. I had to rectify the force of negativity. I'm no Maya, but to quote myself, "I believe the anatomy of love begins with perseverance!" Speaking of which, "Where's My Car, Oprah? Hmm?"

So that you might better understand what you too will endure, I will share a few more of my unforgettable, outlandish experiences on and offline. I trust they will not only comfort and entertain you, but they will also prove to you flamboyantly that, "*You Are Not Alone!*"

Hold on tight to your Za-Za-Zoo Pizzazz. **Swoosh, and off we go!**

CHAPTER 10

More Nice Guys

BUT NO, ANYWAY! REALLY... STILL NO!

"❝T'was the night before more crazy dating, and all through my house, were visions of the next guy, could he be my spouse?"

THE TATTOOED AND PIERCED NICE GUY

I decided to go out with Jeremy, even though we had only spoken a few times on the phone. He was a 33-year-old, innovative, architectural designer for an ultra-trendy, renowned development company. He was coming to town from Ohio to attend a convention. Fortuitously, it was an opportune time for us to meet. I assumed he was going to an architecture convention or *something like that*. I presently live in Las Vegas and since there are thousands of conventions here every year, I never bother to pay attention. Unless that is, I'm assigned to photograph or interview a celeb at one of them. Anyway, I happily agreed to meet Jeremy for dinner.

We met at my favorite hangout restaurant in the city, Mon Ami Gabi, at the Paris Hotel. I love dining outside on the strip at this popular restaurant. No matter what time of year, the weather at night in Vegas is always phenomenal. Moreover, it's by far the ultimate people-watching brasserie in the city. It's remarkable how they successfully copped the Parisian atmosphere, only without the snarky and rude French servers.

When I entered Mon Ami Gabi, Jeremy instantly recognized me from my work and online photos. He walked right over and hugged me with the utmost affection. He had a spectacular smile and was super fine. While on our first carafe of Sangria, I learned that Jeremy was successful, kindhearted, and *sa-weet.* By the second carafe, I got to see the funny, cool, affectionate side of him. He seemed to have it all going on. It was obvious Jeremy met all my foodie standards, too. He drinks wine, coffee, and eats French fries, meat, chocolate, and popcorn. Think about it. What more could I want from a man? And his best features… (Drum roll and try to picture Taylor Swift jumping up and down screaming) he is single, has never been married, is straight, and has no kids. Ding, ding, ding, Jackpot! He was everything I was looking for that night and maybe the next. Who knows, maybe even longer? Then it dawned on me. No frickin' way. This guy had to be bad news. No one is all that and has zero baggage. Meeting someone with no baggage is rare, impossibly so, like living long enough to pay back your student loans. Anyway, I can handle baggage. Well, I can. Especially if it's Prada, Armani, Versace, Birkin, LV, or Gucci. After all, it should be, *"Supercala-Bling-delicious!" I'm kidding. Stop judging me!*

Sitting outside on the patio, from across the street, we enjoyed the Bellagio Hotel's spectacular fountains performing to synchronized music about every 20 minutes. In between the waterfall extravaganza shows, it was amusing watching oodles of hammered tourists stumbling by, with a 10-gallon frozen drink in a plastic boot (guitar, or other ridiculously tacky souvenir container) screaming "Whoo-Hoo. Party Baby. It's Vegas, Man." Evidently, these tourists weren't informed of the town's newly revised legitimate name.

"It's Vegas-Baby-Whoo-Hoo!" Here is the spot one can have fun, eating delicious food, while watching people wearing all kinds of outrageous get-ups and living on the dark side of drunk. I'm talking about plastered and smashed to a whole new level than you've ever seen before. Hence, the film "The Hangover!" I mean, why pay to see a costly "Cirque du Solei Show" when you can get dinner and a show right here? It's the best reality show of all. I find this hilariously entertaining. Especially since the people yelling and the most shit-faced are the CEOs of major corporations. I'd surely make more money taking their photos and selling the pics back to them the next day than I do shooting for the biggest photo agencies in the world. *"Whoo-Hoo, Party! It's blackmail in Vegas!"* It would be a whole other reality show, "Busted CEOs in Vegas!"

Jeremy and I shared a huge pot of tasty, classic French mussels cooked in a white wine and cream sauce base, accompanied by their signature fries and French Baguettes. While devouring dinner, he revealed that he was there for a tattoo and body-piercing convention. I had no idea. Since we were outside on a chilly night, he was all bundled up. Naturally, I was confused, as I didn't spot a single tattoo on him. Soon after, as I was yanking a mussel from its shell, Jeremy, oblivious to the cold, took off his jacket and scarf. He lifted his shirt and lowered his pants. Before I could respond with, "Whoa, what are you doing?" He showed me (and the entire restaurant) he was completely covered, front and back, wall-to-wall (rather skin-to-skin) with multicolored horrifying tattoos and piercings over his entire body. He winked and nodded, adding, "There's a lot more of these I could show you later." I wanted to shriek out in a *marked and pierced voice,* "Check, please?" With all my might, I restrained and kept my mouth shut. I must say, a notably proud and unique moment for me.

Inked all over Jeremy were scary skulls, other symbols of death, and animals I never knew existed. There they were. Horrid faces, reptiles, monsters, sayings, and things no one should ever have to see on a person's skin. Especially viewing them in the middle of eating mussels. "So, what do you think?" He asked coyly, with his poised, refined, self-confidence.

I didn't want to act freaked out, so in an *'all-righty-then voice,'* with a twinkle in my eye (perhaps it was more like *shock and awe),* out came, "Ahhh-Ahhh-Mazing! Aha, wow, incredible, groovy, picturesque, artistic, creative, and way cool!" Those adjectives were the most fundamentally untrue, obligatory, false statements, and the biggest lies to ever (and I do mean ever) come out of my mouth. Even the time when my girlfriend gave birth to an ugly, nasty-looking baby, (So sweet, that's what she likes to call Mia… a baby) and I said, "How cute, precious, beautiful, and adorable, angel baby Mia is," the tattooed-guy lie was equal to that! By the way, my friend's baby is four years old now, bless her heart! She is amazing, incredible, groovy, picturesque, artistic, creative, and way cool? Honestly, she's still wickedly ugly, but getting better every day! Come to think of it, Mia could literally be Alonzo's child. What? Too mean? Whatever. I love her to pieces. Well… *Now!*

Here's my question. I understand the designs and picture tattoos. OK, not really, but I'll let it slide for now. Though, I do question the long sayings. I ask you tattooed people, "Why?" Like, I don't get it! Do you think you're going to forget those sentiments, so you tat them on your body to remember? You can't remember, "Reason and love are sworn enemies," "Some things are better left unsaid," "Never a failure, always a lesson," "Believe the impossible," and "The only way out is through?" You can't remember, "I love mom," inked inside a heart? Really? Or, your ex-lover's name, you wish you could 'white-out' for when the next one comes along. Come on, people. What's wrong with a post-it on the fridge?

Jeremy's piercings, if you can imagine, were far worse than all his eccentric tattoos. I can't adequately describe them. *No one can.* They scared the *ink* out of me. And there you have it. The guy had baggage, after all. Realistically, he had trunks, well hidden. Until that is, he takes off his clothes and, in this case, in public. Luckily, we were in "Whoo Hoo, It's Vegas Baby." Nobody noticed or cared. I love that about Vegas!

The way I saw this situation, I had many choices, besides drinking heavily. I could pull a David Copperfield illusion and escape. I could try a Criss Angel, *"Mindfreak"* disappearance. I could say I was going to the bathroom and split. I could call Ann, "Oh, my God! How much blood did you lose from the drive-by-shooting?" Or "Amy, what? You fell down 6 flights of stairs?" Or frantically tell Jeremy, "OMG, my water just broke, and I didn't know I was pregnant!" It could fly! There was an actual show on TLC all about that. Or I could be a grownup (which I always hate to do, especially on weekends) and just go along with it. This was an opportunity to add new indelible *inkblots* into my finding *"The One,"* memory book.

But dang, he was unbelievably adorable and so cool. To hell with it! Why should over 100 gigantic tattoos and body piercings, covering and hiding his entire body, matter anyway? Although, I was quite grossed out, and wished I could *unsee* most of his tattoos and piercings. Still, my weird curiosity and fascination made me roll the dice and see what happens. Besides, we were really having a lovely time, and he was wonderful to be with. Hell, I liked Jeremy. He's charismatic and such great fun. Seeing him almost naked, I surmised the entire restaurant thought so, too.

Somewhere between the baked goat cheese and tomato sauce dip, the smoked salmon, and the French onion soup with gobs of mozzarella cheese melted over the top, he kissed me. AMEN! I was just skillfully French kissed, eating French onion soup, a French baguette, and French fries, in a French restaurant in Paris. "Whoo-Hoo, Party!" We continued kissing passionately after our first kiss. I enjoyed every ooh-la-la one. It turns out Jeremy, the tattooed-pierced boy, was a mind-blowing kisser. Like the cheese, I melted from his sexy, long, naughty smooches. I was smitten and *in like*. Shamefully, I now wondered if I'd get to see the rest of his tattoos down below. Just to gaze and marvel at the lovely artwork. What! It's like men looking at girly magazines for the articles, only.

Just then, I had an epiphany and became upset with myself. I was acting judgmental and self-righteous. So what? The guy had a lot of tattoos and piercings. I have a lot of shoes and purses. Who the heck am I to criticize Tattoo Boy or anyone else for that matter? Who the hell did I think I was, acting this petty and pompous with someone I barely knew? I was being pejorative and behaving like a shallow, hypocritical snob. Besides, I really liked him. Jeremy was awesome and delectably enchanting, I mused. Come to think of it, I don't muse very often at all? I really should muse more in the future. I must put this muse idea in *ink*.

Sticking with the French theme, the *Coup de grâce,* the *pièce de résistance,* the *Voilà* of the night came during the crème brûlée and the dark chocolate mousse. Jeremy leaned in, caressed my face gently, kissed me fervently, and divulged while grinning. "I think it's important for you to know that I have no interest in sex! Other than kissing. I never have and never will. To be forthcoming, I'm unable to get it up even if I wanted to. Fortunately, I couldn't care less. I am Asexual. Is this a problem for you?"

Mic-drop! Instinctively, with a facepalm gesture of disbelief, I lost my savoir-faire. In a supersonic second, my online dating spaceship crashed down to earth. I had no *inkling* or even a *piercing* suspicion of his Asexual secret. By his sensuous presence, it was unimaginable to me. I never would've guessed Tattoo-Boy among the androgynous chic! It's one thing to date a tattooed and pierced guy, but a sexless one was a no-go. A deal-breaker for this clean-skinned girl, and a no-sex bridge too far.

Mercifully, at that moment, before I could respond to him, my phone rang. Saved by the bell. I had no idea who was on the other end of the phone, nor did I ever come to find out. I only remember my words…

"Hi, Elizabeth. OMG, stop crying! What's wrong? Honey, slow down? Your house burned down? You were robbed? Someone hacked into your iCloud account and deleted your data. Someone stole, all your Ga-Ga and Adele music? Shit, are you kidding me? WHAT? And they took your Vintage Pink Chanel Skirt? No Fucking Way! Oh, no, not the Chanel Skirt. Tell me it isn't true! Please tell me they didn't take the matching jacket too! Where are you, sweetie? Don't move. I'm coming right now!" I didn't dillydally, and this was one of my best escapes ever. Mission aborted.

I never saw Jeremy the Tattooed Boy again, or any other sexless, tattooed-body-suit boys. Bummer, I didn't get to taste the French desserts. You see, there's always baggage, and not always designer ones! *Big sigh.*

"A Tit for Tat, Piercing, And Androgynous Next. I Got Maled!"

THE DULL, DISMAL, DENTIST FROM DENVER, NICE GUY

Rhett, a 32-year-old prominent dentist, was born and raised in New York City. He's been divorced for many years from his New York marriage and has happily moved to his dream destination in Denver, "Rocky Mountain High," Colorado. A nicer, more sincere guy you could never hope to meet. We spoke for several weeks, getting to know one another on the phone. After Rhett passed all my standard interrogation *"get-to-know-you* tests," we made plans to meet. The night before he was to fly to Vegas, he called late in the evening. He nervously divulged, "Look." (Look? That's never a good start!) "I don't know if it matters to you or not? But I have some medical things to tell you. I probably should've told you earlier, but I wasn't sure if it was necessary before we met." In a panicked whisper, he went on to disclose, "You see, I have testicular cancer. But thank goodness it's now in remission." He timidly continued, "There's more." (Isn't there always?) "I was in a car accident recently, which left me seriously injured. I need to wear a colposcopy bag until my cancer has been in remission for a year. After that, I'll be able to have the necessary surgery to fix the damage that was caused by the accident. Later, I won't have to wear the bag anymore."

Interesting how after weeks of conversations and enduring all my interrogations, Rhett never once mentioned anything about his ill health until the night before he was to fly out to see me. This is precisely what I'm warning all of you about. You never know for certain whom you are dealing with, no matter how careful you are. Ergo, never let your guard down. Girl, be cautious when you say, "Wow, I met this really nice guy!"

There was no compassionate way to get out of meeting Rhett. He already bought his airline ticket, booked a hotel, and purchased expensive tickets for the Lady Gaga and Taylor Swift concerts on the strip. I would be a monster to cancel now. I figured since he's had so many devastating things happen to him recently, I couldn't possibly think of canceling and adding more heartache and disappointment to his life. Besides, he seemed to be such a warm, decent man, and I didn't have the heart to hurt him.

When we met the following afternoon, even though I tried, I felt no chemistry with the dentist. My lack of affection for him had nothing whatsoever to do with his health problems. There was simply no magnetic attraction. It's not that Rhett was boring, but I say most candidly with affection, Rhett was painfully boring! The guy would truly benefit from some of his dental laughing gas. You know what I'm talking about, ladies! You're with that guy who is such an agreeable sweetheart, and you think you are having fun. Until you realize it is entirely you who is doing all the talking and joking. Thus, giving you the illusion, you're having fun.

Hold on, there's another kicker to the dentist story. Within the first few minutes of our meeting, I couldn't help but notice that Rhett's face displayed a persistent, dreadful frown. I found this odd and concerning, for no man has ever worn a frown when meeting me for the first time. The second meeting, sure, that could happen. Certainly not the first. So, I got up the courage to ask, "What's wrong Rhett? Why the unhappy frown?"

He announced defensively, "Oh, nothing's wrong. Not a thing. Honestly, I'm very happy. I think I might have forgotten to mention I have Parkinson's. This condition makes it hard for me to smile. Mollie, dear, though it doesn't look like it, I am completely smiling from ear to ear."

Rhett's life was equal to a Greek tragedy! Feeling as badly as I did for all his many health struggles, I surely didn't want to upset him further. Lord knows he's had his unfair share of the dark, negative force going on. Consequently, I made the best of this non-romantic visit. Regardless, we enjoyed a nice time together (allegedly). I hope Rhett had a fun weekend.

He was a good and decent man. I guarantee you'll no doubt have a Rhett or two in your search. But realistically, you simply cannot force love, whether in sickness or in health. It is either there or it isn't, and with Rhett, it wasn't! Big exhale cleansing breath. And the search continues.

Too bad the good dentist didn't work out. I really needed four Veneers. Oh, stop, back off, and remove your fangs! I'm just kidding. I only needed TWO! Tough crowd, tough crowd!

"A Sad, Unromantic, Frowning Next. Once again, I Got Maled!"

JEDEDIAH JONES... THE DEVINE, GAY, NICE GUY

I was under the impression Jedediah Jones, the tall, dark, and yummy 31-year-old man, was my new gay BFF. I swear on Cartier I didn't change it! This was truly his spectacular, spy-novel, given name, and he physically matched it. I begin by reiterating it is an irrefutable fact there are no friends better to a girl than her *gay guy, best friends.*

I met Jones accidentally in an online chat room. After a month of fierce and fabulous conversations on the phone, we finally met in person. He was the perfect, *just friends*, blind date. I quickly discovered he was a total blast to hang out with. We never officially got into the awkward, *"I know you're gay"* conversation. I think, perhaps, he liked the warm, safe, and comforting refuge of the closet for now. No worries because, for me, the magnificent bonus was I could chill and feel protected. With Jedediah, I wasn't going to get hit over the head with sexual *innuendos, prickly* advances (both puns intended), and relationship complications. What an idyllic change of pace. As far as I was concerned, my new pal, Jedediah Jones, was blissfully, lavishly, and fervently a splendid gay man, buddy. Like shoes and jewelry, a girl can never seem to have enough of them. It was entertaining hanging out with Jones. He is a party to be with.

Jedediah was a very successful Power-Gay. He smoked long, skinny, menthol chick cigarettes while holding his pinky finger up. He crossed his legs in a most girly-girlish style. In fact, better than I can. He giggled out of control like Anderson Cooper, whom I simply worship. He always says, *"Girlllll this is everything,"* and constantly flipped his long, gorgeous hair. I think, perhaps, he got that from me. *'Toss, Toss.'* He is outrageously a total fem and I love, love, loved this about him. Jedediah Jones (I just adore saying his whole name) walked like a girl as if he were wearing six-inch Louboutin Heels. He flaunted a perfectly toned, spray-tanned, luminous body. He loved to play trivia, went to karaoke bars, dressed fabulously to the max, cooked, and baked divine gourmet foods and sweets, and always knew about the best and latest hair and skin-care products. Jed (he hated when I called him that) was a foodie, who loved British artsy & foreign films. Though typecast, he idolized Liza, Cher, Liz Taylor, Ariana, Queen, Elton, Taylor Swift, Bette, Barbara & Madonna! To be blunt, he was the classic every day, *gay-best-friend-forever-guy!*

Jedediah and I frequently attended the theatre, movies, concerts, operas, and the latest *"it"* restaurants. We shared endless fun and giggles together. He even invited me to the Met Gala, sending me an outrageous gown, plus the jewels and all. An ecstatic wow there! The guy had major connections. Best of all, Jedediah was the first person to tell me that I had a thigh gap. Geez, I never heard of a thigh gap, let alone knew I had one. "You, my sweetie," he gushed, with his total gay-licious, zealous style, "have the best thigh gap I've ever seen since the Victoria's Secret Angel's Runway Show, at New York's Fashion Week!" What a coup, I imagined. As for his being gay, come on! I ask you, how else could I have read this situation? Besides, I have remarkable *gay-dar*. I'm quite proud of this gift.

All things considered, can you only imagine the utter mind-fuck and confusion I experienced as he reached out to hold my hand at a John Legend concert? I stiffened up like a corpse, didn't move a muscle, and contemplated the idea. I naturally assumed that he was just being cozy like we girls do all the time. OK, so we were holding hands! No worries!? It's just your typical, random, nonsexual, normal friendship behavior at a concert, between a gay guy and his straight friend who happens to be a girl. This occurs all the time. Right? No doubt, this transpires most often. All is good. Nothing to be concerned about. No big deal! Still, I felt confu*sion*, delu*sion*, illu*sion*, and all the other '*Sion*' words combined.

Pointless to say, it was most unsettling that the pieces of the *sexual preference puzzle* we had been making and working on for months did not match the picture on the box. Then, during John Legend's love ballad, "Love All of Me." No, wait. It's "All of Me." Jedediah Jones leaned into me and lovingly kissed me. *"Wha-ha-ha-haaat???"* He Kissed Me!!! He kissed me with a real tongue-in-mouth, very non-gay, very sexual, man-woman kiss! I was freaked out, shaken up, messed up, fucked up, screwed up, and all the other ups! As one would expect, I was rattled. It was as though my vinyl record was just scratched right through my favorite song. I inhaled deeply to catch my breath, for he knocked the *straight girl wind* out of me. Hugely bewildered, I probed in a panicked, awkward tone.

"Hey, dude, what the hell are you doing?"

"What the hell do you think I'm doing? Isn't it obvious? I have wanted to kiss you for like... For like... Ever!"

"But Jedediah," I spoke compassionately. "Honey, you are GAY, and for that reason, you are seriously not on my *fuckit-bucket list!*"

"Mollie, for goodness' sake, what in the world made you think I am gay?" He questioned, flipping his hair. *(Toss, Toss!)*

"Umm, well? Like every, single, thing, and every, solitary, detail about you. You are kidding me, right? Jedediah, you are gay! You are a famous Broadway Director and Dance Choreographer, for crying out loud! Come on, man, you are like *'Fosse, Fosse, Fosse, 5,6,7,8'* Gay! You are 'One Singular Sensation' Gay! 'Torch Song Trilogy, Rent, Prom, and Kinky Boots,' Gay! 'La Cage Aux Folles, Behind the Candelabra, Call Me by My Name, and The Bird Cage' gay! For real you're the first 20 rows of a Beyoncé or Lady Gaga concert, GAY! *Ga-Ga-Gay!* You Didn't Know? OMG, you're classically, divinely Neil Patrick Harris, Anderson Cooper, Jim Parsons, Ru Paul, and Matt Bomer gay! Jeddy, you really don't know you are a fabulous gay man? For real, I had to be the one to tell you? Luv, you're the poster child for *Make America Gay Again!* Please, *Gaysplain.*"

"Girl Stop! Enough, and I mean it! Stop!" He paused and looked desperately forlorn while rolling his eyes like a teenage girl. He went on woefully, "Well, thanks a lot for that piece of info. And Ouch, by the way!" He was visibly scowling, performing his signature hair flip. "I am **'Not Gay'** sweetie. I'm not gay or even Bi, FYI!" He continued while pouting and squirming. "So, thank you! Thank You Very Much!!!!"

"OK, there Elvis!" With that, we couldn't help but laugh so loud that the Legend fans began shushing us. I turned around and sarcastically shushed them right back. "Give us a break. It's an outdoor concert. Get a grip, people. We are not in a church, a temple, a mosque, or even a library. It's a John Legend concert. Seriously, Chill the hell out!"

For the rest of the evening, we spoke about all our blunders and miscommunications with understanding, love, and thoughtfulness. I apologized profusely for hurting him the way I had. Jedediah was eventually cool with it all. Sitting in a 24/7 diner at 4:37 in the morning, we consumed all the fried, greasy, sugary foods we could handle before having a major heart attack. We laughed about everything and mocked each other as usual. The night ended in the morning with a kiss, a big hug, a smile, and a big rainbow question mark still tap dancing in my mind.

Heaven knows we tried, but Jedediah and I were never able to get that romantic moment back. We forged ahead, unlike *"Will and Grace," but rather as "straight-girl* and *straight-boy,"* best friends. The fleeting lover's spark passed us by. The good news is we'll forever love one another and continue to be incredible, "Phoebe & Joey," straight friends.

Thanks to me, Jedediah now listens to trending, up-to-date music (besides Broadway), holds a cigarette with his pinky finger down, and sits like a manly man, legs spread wide open. The hair flip thing? It's his signature trademark and you can't touch that! Thanks to Jedediah, I can go on living with the proud knowledge and joy that I have a great thigh gap.

I was bewildered and unsettled over my slip-up. How did I miss this one? I'm still coming to terms with the realization my gay detector has a glitch! Although Jedediah Jones is a straight man (allegedly), he still looks and acts exquisitely gay! Obviously, I never saw this coming. "La-di-da, la-di-da! All is good." Jedediah Elvis Jones has left the building!

"A Confusing, Straight Ahead, Toss-Toss Next... I Got Maled!"

ROBERT, THE EYE DOCTOR, NICE GUY

Enter Robert, the Ophthalmologist...

"Better like this? Better like this? Better like this?" Funny, in the back of my mind, I was always concerned that he might ask me that in bed. If we had gotten that far, that is.

Though a little too old for me, the 40-year-old Robert was that guy you want to bring home to your mom. You know, a terrific person and a super successful man. I didn't mind that Robert was somewhat pudgy, a little balding, and a terrible dresser. I could have corrected all those things with ease. I know he's an eye doc, but I wasn't fond of his, ridiculous *eye* comments he constantly made, thinking they were humorous. Like: *"Eye* only have, *eyes* for you." "My *Eyes* adore you." "You are the apple of my *Eye.*" *"Eye-e-eye-e-eye* will always love you." *"Eye* will survive." *"Eye* gotta crush on you." Let's not forget, *"Eye* honestly love you." Unsettling me the most was that all those songs were ancient, and he wasn't. What can you do? *Eye* liked him, and *Eye* was going to give him a chance.

Here comes the notorious, *Eye-*opening, *but!* Drats, there always seems to be that other shoe waiting to drop. Annoyingly, I had more than a few major hair-raising issues with his adolescent, lovely (*bratty, spoiled, obnoxious, and just plain mean*) twin boys. They were rude, disrespectful, and impossible to deal with. Truthfully, these boys were so out of control that one might even think they were the precocious kids of a famous star. But Robert was not a famous star. He was just a loving, overindulging dad with his eyes wide shut and his head in the sand. Robert, being entirely in denial, didn't understand it was time to step up, discipline, and control them immediately. He ignored my critical warnings and assumed I was exaggerating. Rob surmised, telling me, "Look, you don't have children of your own, so you are inexperienced and unqualified to provide me with any expert advice." First of all, *that hurt*. And second, I was puzzled by his lack of reason and logic to say such a thing to me. I sensibly decided it best to just buy three vowels, Pat Sajak! 'A, O, and I,' to complete the puzzle, which stated, "*Say nothing*, be quiet, and you'll be safely shrouded behind the 5th Amendment!" Ultimately exasperated, I backed off and looked the other way. Looking the other way concerning things I don't like about the guys I had been dating had become an irritating bad habit, and tremendously aggravating. I was essentially becoming an enabler and I'm not proud of it, either. To keep the peace, I thought I'd just bite my tongue. Edit. I didn't bite my tongue! (Who does that?) I remained silent.

As a man, Robert was worldly, charming, and quite a fascinating, lovely person. But, as a dad, Robert was an entirely different chap. He went brain-dead and illogical when it came to his boys. As far as his kids went, he turned into an overly defensive, overprotective parent. He was a thousand miles past the highways of 'truth and trust,' and believed his children would never do anything wrong. Yet I found it quite telling when Robert got downright frustrated with the boys, he typically foisted them off on the nanny or his ex to rescue him. The ever-present 'X' files!

He never stood his ground or punished the boys. The three of them would constantly debate and argue. He usually ended the many fights or disagreements by saying, "We'll see" or "Maybe." It might just be me, but a harsh, curt, "*No*" worked beautifully for my parents. Ironically, and not too clever, his kids never realized that "*Maybe*" and "*We'll see*" always meant "*No!*" I figured out his trick by the end of our first date. I didn't tell the boys. They'll have enough to deal with in the real world when reality holds them accountable, and Daddy won't be able to buy their way out.

Rob was relentless in his belief that the twins were normal, highly intelligent, talented, and basically perfect and precious in every way. I tolerated his delusions, mostly because I knew he would be in for a huge rude awakening, and sadly, sooner rather than later. Permit me to speak candidly and take in a big breath for this one. Any parent who says their kids are, "Perfect, would never do anything wrong or bad, that they would never lie, cheat, smoke, drink, do drugs, have sex, skip school or steal," is an absolute fool and an irresponsible, ignorant, gullible, ineffective parent. Come on, just think about all the outrageous, dangerous, bad, rebellious, disobedient, punish-worthy things you did as a kid? Things you hid from your parents. Affirmative, I thought so. And I rest my case, your honor.

Then it happened. After only four short weeks of dating (and never sleeping together), Robert's words came smacking back hard, right in his face. And let the shit-fest begin…

One glorious Saturday afternoon, while I was at Rob's house, the darling, perfect children were bored. They asked Daddy to cough up major boo-coo bucks so they could buy some trendy new clothes. Daddy, naively and still living in the past, suggested to them, "Why don't you boys start a lemonade stand, or have a garage sale to earn some extra spending money?" If I started laughing, I don't think I would've been able to stop. His historical idea was so retro 60s, maybe even the 50s. All I could think while keeping silent was, *babe, your age is showing!* How can you tell 12-year-old boys to start a lemonade stand or have a garage sale? A weed or lemon-shots stand, yes, definitely! A lemonade stand? Yeah, not so much!

I knew hell was about to be paid rather quickly. The flawless, treasured children stopped in their tracks, looked up at their beloved, not famous daddy, stared bitterly into his eyes right in front of me, and paused. "*5-4-3-2-1… We Are Live… And Action!*"

"*Fuck You, Dad*," one boy tenderly responded. "*You Cheap Dick Head! Mom Is So Right About You!*"

The other flawless twin lovingly chimed in as well. "*Yeah, Go Fuck Yourself, Dad. You're An Asshole. And a Dickwad!*" And there it was, **Badda-Bing! And cut!** Oh, the humiliating gushes of pain. That was the least surprising surprise in the world and what *I*, the "inexperienced, unqualified, childless one," had been trying to warn him about to no avail.

I couldn't blame the boys for reacting to their dad's uber-lame, preposterous suggestions. Regardless, all things considered, they handled it all wrong and were disgracefully disrespectful. But I knew the dreaded "F" word would eventually peek its predictable, ugly little head in sooner or later. It always does, from ages eleven to twenty-one and beyond. I was dying. I needed to laugh so badly that it hurt, but I didn't dare. With all my heart, I desperately wanted to respond to the little brats with "Wow, gee, golly, gosh, you guys really know how to use your big-boy badass words. Don't cha now?" Again, I decided to stick to the allotted 3 vowels I had previously bought. "*Say nothing!*" I didn't bite my tongue, though! I, the inexperienced, unqualified, childless one, was choking on amusement. I didn't have the heart to say it to Robert, so I hid my "*Eye told you so*" smirk. By the looks of things, it appeared I didn't have to. As Robert stood there, paralyzed under a blanket of shock. It was now clear, he knew, that I knew, that he knew, that I knew, I was right all along. "Quadruple Ouch?"

Poor Robert. His inside voice must have been screaming, "Let me out of here, and I mean right now, dammit!" His eyes narrowed, his brow crinkled, and his anger (AKA, mud on your face), froze him in time. Robert was completely devastated. The painful disbelief displayed on his face was genuinely heart-wrenching. It was evident by his expression he could not believe to save his life, that his perfect-in-every-way, blessed angels could ever speak to him this way. But on the real, I didn't dare tell him it was only the beginning of his torment. To escape Rob's awkward, humiliating situation, *Eye* sympathetically excused myself out the door.

I never saw Robert again. I don't think he had the guts to confront me, nor did I have the heart for him to do so. Regardless, I couldn't help but wonder what became of his darling, perfectly imperfect kids? They probably got rich opening a weed dispensary. Sorry, I am still laughing.

Take note, girls. Never give advice to a guy you are dating about his kids until you are solidly in the family! Probably not even then! "Well, now that's done. Lemonade, anyone? How about a Walkman, VHS tapes, a phonebook, a reel-to-reel? Let's see now, a ghetto blaster, fur coat, a long cord rotary phone, a beeper, or a map? What about a sun hat?" LOL!

"A... 5,4,3,2,1, Perfect in Every Way, 'Eye' Told You So, Next! I Got Maled!"

THE NEW ORLEANS NICE GUY...OR MAYBE, NOT SO NICE?

How could I ever forget Old Avery McDonald, the strange, eccentric, outré cheap, complicated character that didn't have a farm? He was such a stuck-up elitist to the highest power, with no justification whatsoever to back it up. Anyway, he might be nicer in person, I thought.

After speaking on the phone for quite some time, he encouraged me to visit his spectacular city, New Orleans. After all, I had a few days off, and I had never been to the world of Jazz. So, why not? It's interesting, the more I immersed myself in online dating, the more I began to comprehend the many reasons and answers for the *"So Why Not?"*

Avery greeted me at the baggage claim area of the Louis Armstrong, New Orleans International Airport. After our "Hello, nice to meet you, greetings," I couldn't help but notice that he was a flamboyant, showy, colorful dresser who should categorically not be! For one to dress in this manner, you must be a guy who is perfectly built, gorgeous, super young, or gay, and perhaps all the above. Avery was a fashion disaster.

When my bags arrived, he insisted, "Don't get a cart or a porter, you won't need it. My car is very close by." This might have been reasonable had he made any gesture to assist me. On the contrary, Avery allowed me to *schlep* my heavy bags to his car by myself. Lugging all the way I thought, Dude, at no time did I hear myself say, "I got this!"

*Schlep: *Hauls or carries something heavy with tedious difficulty. Example: "This schmuck is not a gentleman and made me schlep my luggage to his car myself! He is clearly a total wanker and a putz!"*

*Schmuck: *An obnoxious or contemptible person. Example: See Avery!*

*Putz: *A fool, an idiot, an incompetent yutz, or a selfish person. Example: Also, see Avery. (Yutz... same as a putz!)*

The kicker? He parked in long-term parking, which was by no means close by. Watching me schlep my bags, he explained, "It was half the price to park in long-term and a far better deal." To my dismay, he was not one bit nicer in person. Unhappy and filled with great disdain, I began wilting from the Louisiana summer heat and humidity. I was exhausted, flying 5 hours and now having to drag two 50-pound bags twice as far as I should've had to. Well, one was 53 pounds, but the baggage guy let it go.

I discovered the hard way that chivalry might well be dead, after all. Profusely offended, I contemplated getting right back on a plane to go home. Then it hit me. All those fancy New Orleans classic cocktails like the Hurricane, Sazerac, Mint Julep, Brandy Milk Punch, Mimosa, and the powdered sugar beignets, the phenomenal jazz, and the original creole cuisine were all calling my name from Bourbon Street in the French Quarter. Hell no, I'm staying. Carry on and keep schlepping, Mollie!

I was "*shvitzing*" like a marathon runner in August, schlepping 103 pounds by myself to Mr. Cheap McDonald's car. Good Lord, how far was his damn car he claimed was close by?

Shvitzing: *When a person is involved in anything that would cause perspiration or sweating.*
Example 1: Trying on bathing suits when just starting a diet, or basically, anytime at all!
Example 2: When looking for a diamond, your fiancée is looking at half-carat diamonds, 'SI-2' and 'L' in color. While you are rummaging through the 3-carat diamonds, 'VVS-1' and 'D' in color, which is what you want. This would make any girl shvitz! Clearly, I was verklempt over the arduous, uncomfortable situation I found myself in!

Verklempt: *Angry, frustrated, irritated, or overcome with emotion.*
Example: I'm verklempt and pissed-off. I had to schlep my luggage 10 miles because this cheap, haza, putz, schmuck, wouldn't help me. FYI, this is an example of a run-on sentence for all the grammar students reading.

Haza: *A greedy type of person. One who acts like a selfish pig.*
Example: Avery is a greedy haza and not a considerate man!

This was the first of many indications to come that this Cheap-Charlie might not be for me. Disillusioned, I was in dire need of some good old-fashioned Tea and Sympathy. Further discouraging since I only met him 10 minutes prior. Still, I was curious about how the rest of this escapade would go down. I feared this was yet another dating debacle. Accordingly, I advanced with great caution, pepper spray, and several escape plans.

Nothing seemed right from our first hello. It's not that Avery lied about his thick head of hair that bothered me. It was that it was somebody else's thick head of hair. His bad toupee must've been on sale for 75% off, buy 1 get 4 free, or something along those "let's make a deal," bargains. His rug floated about, never staying in place on his head. I swear if it was off in the distance and had lights, his fake hair would look like a UFO.

While driving to the hotel, it's not that Avery lied about his age that bothered me. It was that he said he was 35 when he was clearly 70 or older. Remember the rules, readers! Avery was a Dinosaur Smithsonian Guy. I knew if I opened his fridge, there would surely be prunes, Jell-O, Metamucil, cream of wheat, and assorted wrapped hard candies inside.

When he invited me to come out to meet him, I naturally refused to stay at his house. I didn't know him well enough, and I needed to be wise and obey the "Safety-First Rules." Now, having met him, I realize my decision was a smart one. Keep that in mind, fellow daters. Anyhow, he put me up at the Roosevelt Hotel. It was surprisingly lovely and generous of him. I thought at the time. Of course, it was. Well, until I found out, he got it for free. Something about problems the *bargain-basement man faced* the last time he stayed in another one of the hotels in the group. Groan...

Whatever, I was in the exciting city of New Orleans. The

birthplace and hometown of our country's treasured jazz music and the magical iconic Mardi Gras. "I would party regardless of Mr. Scrooge!

Despite his miserly ways, I had a blast at the places we visited, even having to share them with him. I enjoyed the most delectable (early bird) dinner at the famous Gumbo Shop. He demanded that I get the Seafood Gumbo. He specified, with authority, "The Jambalaya is not very good here." To his chagrin, I ordered the "not very good Cajun Jambalaya." Yum-O-La, I wanted to lick my fingers. Which is exactly what I did before devouring my Key Lime Pie. I enjoyed it even more because he demanded I order the pecan pie. Stuffed, I said very clearly with a full belly, "This entire meal was an amazing mouthful of Yum!"

He replied, "What did you say to me? You just ate a mouthful of cum? Well, *BONE* Appétit!" He roared with his nefarious evil laughter and played coy, but he heard exactly what I had said. Gross, and just like that, I escaped to the bathroom, sick to my stomach. It happened. Naturally, he blamed it on the Jambalaya being bad. The guy is repulsive.

When the check came, I was still in the ladies' room gagging from his inappropriate, humorless comment. While doing my thing, Mr. Penny-pincher told the manager I was a food critic, so they waived the bill. When I returned to the table and found out what he had done, I was enraged. Although entirely appalled on the spot, I didn't want to make a scene.

That evening, after having had a chance to recoup some "*normal*" alone at the hotel, I met Avery. I was jazzed to go to the world-renowned, historic Preservation Hall. The brilliant talent of the phenomenal old-time jazz musicians took my breath away. All of us, passionate Avant-Garde music enthusiasts were mesmerized and in the groove. Although unusual for me, I was so into the music I could not stop myself from dancing with a bunch of young girls while jubilantly singing the lyrics to the uplifting, famous songs. I felt like I was being swept back into the past, and the boogie-woogie Dixieland jazzy music was my time machine.

That's when Avery forcibly yanked my shorts down and hollered. *"Shut up! Be quiet. Stop dancing. You're upsetting me. Sit down, Mollie!"*

I looked at him with enraged and flared nostrils, thinking, "Why I oughta!" After 2 notorious New Orleans frozen drinks, (which I purchased myself because he told me to wait till later like I was a child) I declared ferociously, "You talking to me? Are you, for real, telling me to shut up? Because, Avery, I seriously don't think so. Furthermore, while we're on that, I don't appreciate the words, Shut Up! It's worse than F.U. to me."

BTW, this was the 1st time I accomplished the flared nostril thing. Yea, I was jazzed about that, too! I happily ignored him and continued to enjoy the music with the fun party girls. "Whoo Hoo, It's New Orleans, Baby!" Avery was not happy with me! Geez and snap, as if I cared at this point what Donny-Downer thought of me or anything else, for that matter!

At the end of the evening, we moseyed on over to get some famous powdered sugar beignets and cappuccinos at the legendary Café Du Monde. FYI... people really do *"mosey"* in New Orleans. It's kind of cute, too. So, when in Rome! Tasting this world-renowned dessert was a highly anticipated treat for me. Beignets here (like pastries in France) are totally flavorlicious. And girls, they are worth the calories. Just don't wear your skinny jeans the next day. Or maybe even the next. I'll never forget the look on Avery's face when I asked for extra powdered sugar and was told it would be 25 cents more. He snapped at me as if they had said it would be 10 dollars extra! "You don't need it! They are sweet enough."

I snickered, "Oh, no Avery, I Need It! I Need It Badly!" I merrily ordered, "Double, extra powdered sugar for 50 cents more, please." After I left a dollar and walked away, Avery waited for the change. I choked on the powdered sugar, laughing. I realized he wasn't amused by my sweet, powdery antics, which happened to get all over him when I was coughing. "Too bad! That's the way the double powdered sugar beignets crumble!"

The following day, around 11:00, Avery picked me up at the hotel. He gave me an enormous hug and declared, "Hey honey, I missed you!" I couldn't imagine he still wanted to go out with me or ever see me again after all that had gone down the previous day. Let alone miss me?

I positively know that I didn't miss him and responded. "Oh, come on? *Shut Up!*" (Giggle!) Evidently, he didn't think that was funny either. Moving on and going with the flow, we arrived at the fancy, well-known, old-world Court of Two Sisters for brunch. I was downright mortified when he straightaway handed the Maître D' a coupon for a free meal amongst the refined patrons. I lowered my head in embarrassment, for everyone was chic and graceful. Especially the men (and their handheld poodles) with impeccably manicured fingers and paws.

I've always questioned the word, 'Manicure?' A manicure should be a doctor for men. On this subject… Manscape should, in fact, be a woman running away from a man. As in me, running away from Avery. Invariably, Manscape is just another hairy situation to be shaved away. These are among the things that clutter my brain, robbing me of my Zzzs.

To navigate my way through brunch, I imagined Avery was invisible. I enjoyed conversations with some elegant locals sitting at the surrounding tables. One lady gazed directly at me with an expression of, "Been there too, girl. I feel you." We spoke through validating facial codes and exchanged warm smiles. The typical New Orleans southern-style breakfast while being serenaded by jazz musicians was delightful. Drinking away my feelings with a few Mimosas helped to cool off the frustrations and humiliations within. Everything now was coolamundo and hunky-dory. I learned that's what drunk people say in the jazz world.

Following our breakfast, the pre-historic *dinosaur man* and I walked around the *antique shops.* Whoops, that's sort of interchangeable. Forgive me, but I couldn't hold myself back from educating Avery, the *Tyrannosaurus Rex,* that no one under 70 uses the language he had been speaking all day. Like Willy-nilly, squirt, fella, swell, shindig, too-da-loo, and what a doozy! The winner of the most passé, obsolete word he uttered, was, **Dino-mite!** And the guy claims he's 35 years old? I can't even.

In the afternoon, we visited the garden district and went on a taxi bike ride. It was uncomfortable being with this taxing man because of how he treated people. He was rude, demanding, and abrasive. To endure this situation, I thrust myself into a new strategy. My tweaked approach was to think of Avery as a tour guide. It seemed to work out well, at least for the time being. It's not that Avery wasn't a nice guy. It's that Avery *wasn't a nice guy!* Furthermore, he didn't know how to enjoy life or even the meaning of the word fun. He was a bitter old man, whatever age he lied that he was. Despite his behavior, I didn't want to hurt his feelings or offend him. So, I kept my opinions about him to myself. He already had enough hang-ups to last him the rest of his prehistoric, ancient life.

It's not that Avery lied about being an easygoing, fun-loving guy that bothered me. It's that he wasn't easygoing or fun-loving. He was, however, incongruous, controlling, domineering, and bossy! Ironically, as he wolfed down a Muffuletta and a Po-Boy, that we shared at lunch from the famous Central Grocery. It was the first time he smiled since we met. He was happy as an old lady at a Lawrence Welk or Perry Como concert.

It's not that Avery lied about being a wealthy financial broker that disturbed me. As for me, I've always been more moved and impressed by people's kindness, intellect, and talents. Avery bared none of those traits.

It's not that Avery was constantly groping, trying to touch me, and pursuing unwanted, inappropriate sexual advances that upset me. It was the fact that "No" never meant "No," to this nervy man! What bothered me about Avery was basically… Avery! He was unethical, deceitful, and not the brightest star in the constellation! However, I was here and unfortunately committed. Therefore, I was going to make the best of it.

That evening we went to this super cool, legendary place called Rock and Bowl. We sat and listened to a variety of bands playing the most awesome jazz. I got up to dance with a fabulous group of young London tourists on holiday. When Avery touched my jeans as if to pull me down again, I glared at him with a menacing bravado and a look that screamed, "Don't even think about it!" And man, I wasn't kidding around either. Something had to give because Avery, the killjoy, was severely cramping my style. Howbeit, I refused to lose my integrity and character. Instead, I went on dancing and enjoying myself with the fun Brexit tourists.

After enjoying the music for hours, I questioned Avery. "Ok, I'm ready. What about the bowl part? When does that happen? I'd love to bowl. Let's do it." Upon my request, he reluctantly stumbled off to sign us up for a lane and shoes. While bowling, I was confused as to why pushy Avery kept rushing me. That is until the bowling lane shut off. "Hey, why did the lane go dark? What happened? We are only on the 4th frame!"

He admitted awkwardly, "I, uh, I, umm, I only bought fifteen minutes." Oh, wow, did his response ever bowl me over! Yikes, he purchased a fifteen-minute limit to bowl! And, yet there was no limit to how creepy and inconsiderate Old McCheapo remained. And there it was. The final strike! The kind of strike announcing, "You are out!" All I could say to be understanding and courteous to Avery was... Nothing.

I reached my patience level, and this girl was done. I was rockin' & bowlin' out of here. Rock, bowl, and game over! The game was called because of cheapness, *gutter balls, fouls, and curveballs.* Avery stepped over the line and bowled on the wrong alley with a girl far out of his league. So, I scored a perfect split. Not wanting to appear ungrateful, I tried to hang in there with him. Awkward and embarrassed, I found his cruel demeanor and shameful conduct impossible to be around. He was uncouth and offensive to everyone we encountered. I couldn't stand another second in his company. I was super offended that he hurt the feelings of countless people we had met and watched their reactive stares.

"FUJIMO!" After excusing myself, I ran to the bathroom, landed a baby hook, gingerly slipped out the back, Jack, and made a new plan, Stan. I threw a perfect strike outta here and into an Uber. If this wasn't a match made in hell, then I don't know what the hell is? He opened my eyes to see that sometimes, it's better to meet fortuitously, through fate.

I left Jurassic Park and went on to experience two pleasurable days solo in the dazzling city! Luckily, I met up with the London kids from the Rock and Bowl, for fish & chips, and a pint. We had a blast. All in all, I had a wonderful time in New Orleans by myself, being myself, without pawing aggressive hands all over me, and *no one* told me to *shut up!*

Avery, the romantic atheist, the charisma-impaired bore, called me endlessly. However, respecting his request, I decided it was best to just *"Shut Up!"* He sent texts, emails, and left countless messages of apology. Since there was no point, I didn't respond, and I never saw Avery again...

I thought with unreserved indignation that nobody, not even Scrooge or a real-life dinosaur, is going to demand (in a bossy control-freak manner) anything concerning the who, what, when, where, and why of me. Nor will anyone tell me what to eat, drink, dress, speak, or rudely demand anything of me. Lesson learned. I'd never again cave into such intolerable and antiquated conduct. Well, unless I ran into Brad Pitt in New Orleans or anywhere! For him, I would wholeheartedly cave. A lot!

Oh, one last thing... Men, here's a little fashion-disaster tip. If you wear a toupee, make sure it fits properly and doesn't slide around your bald head all day long. This little hair failure will prove to be humbling. You're not invisible. We see you adjusting it all the time, just as we see you adjusting your balls in your pants. We are right in front of you. We see you. You're not Houdini. You can't escape being seen doing this.

I suppose I failed miserably, being delicate in telling my hair- raising, Avery adventure. It's just the way I see it and toupees off to you.

"Old McCheapo was an E-I-E-I-Out!
A Jazzy Next! And Mollie Girl... You Totally Got Maled!"

CHAPTER 11

Taking a Break from the Insanity!

ALSO REFERRED TO AS... ARE ALL MEN FREAKS?

After twelve endless months of enduring online dating, I was thrilled with the opportunity to go on assignment to Brazil, Argentina, and Uruguay. I was relieved to get away from it all for three glorious weeks. In fact, it was a welcomed and needed medicinal gift. I humbly confess I am so grateful for my career. I eagerly look forward to each day with the honor and privilege of being a journalist. Because my work changes daily, I find it exhilarating that I never know where, when, or who I'll be interviewing, shooting, or writing a story about. It's very exciting and keeps me fired up.

So, there I was in the Delta Club at the Hartsfield-Jackson Airport in Atlanta, hours before boarding my flight. I was beginning my beat in Montevideo, Uruguay, for a brief period. Next, I'll be off to Rio de Janeiro. Merely articulating *Rio de Janeiro* out loud sounds profoundly riveting. My last stop is Buenos Aires, Argentina. Despite being a seasoned traveler, I had never been to any of these destinations before, leaving me wild with adventure and stirring emotions.

Relaxing in a comfy beige leather lounge chair with my feet up in the club's, so-called quiet room, I was hoping to get a jump-start on my preparations for a few interviews. I needed to produce relevant and pertinent questions for these intense upcoming assignments. I enjoy pairing such serious topics with some of my traditional signature, fun, and amusing questions. I've learned most readers love to know personal stories and the interviewees typically appreciate the added spice as well.

However, right now, I really needed a place to think and avoid the parents who allow their kids to be rowdy, scream, and cry in public. Why do these parents think the rest of us want to listen to their boisterous little runny-nosed brats? I'm sorry, that was uncalled for. I meant to say, their adorable and delightful children. Still, I beg the question, why do they allow them to behave this way in public? I say, go on and do whatever you like in the privacy of your own home. On the contrary, moms, dads, and guardians, I implore you to pretty-please, discipline your darling little angels in public areas. I totally blame the parents (not the kids) who allow their offspring to get away with this uncivilized behavior. Oh, wait! That reminds me of another gripe. When parents attempt to discipline their kids, why do they all yell at them? Here's how it generally plays out…

"Stop That Johnny! I Said Stop! Do You Hear Me, Johnny? Johnny No! Johnny, No! Johnny, Stop That, Right This Minute!" Then comes the louder and angrier next phase… *"Do You Hear Me, Johnny Samuel Robertson, the Third?"* Uh-Oh! Therein lies the rub. Jeepers-creepers, you know it's serious for real when the very upset and embarrassed parents say the kid's whole name. Especially in public! *"I Said No, No Johnny No!"* It's like the song "Go, Go Johnny Go," only with a disobedient child, instead. Oh, for Pete's sake, and the rest of us having to listen to you shout. "Yes, they, Johnny, whomever you are yelling at, *HEARS YOU!"* They are not deaf, nor are they respectful or afraid of you! They're obviously just ill-mannered, spoiled terrors.

Not to mention quite sick of being yelled at. *"Seriously, stop yelling! Stop. Do you HEAR me?"*

Another trick parents try when that one doesn't work (and it never will), is the notorious next step, counting to ten. This game is typically attempted just before one frustratingly pulls their hair out. *"One... two... three... Do You Hear Me, Johnny? Four, five, six... You're going to get it! Seven, eight... eight and a half, eight and three-quarters, eight and nine-tenths... Nine! Johnny, don't push me, Boy! Nine And a Half... Do You Hear Me, Johnny? Nine and three-quarters... I'm Talking to You, Johnny. I'm Not Kidding This Time!* (What? Like you were kidding all the other times?) *Ten!!!"* After naughty Johnny doesn't listen (and he never will) the parents do nothing! *"OK, Johnny, that's it!* (LOL! Like Johnny, gives a shit?) *One... two... three... four? Do You Hear Me, Johnny? Five... six..."*

And my personal favorite is when parents get so damn frustrated and desperate, they succumb to tossing the child into time-out. Ah, yes, the laughable, ineffective time-out in their room, with their phone, music, television, computer, all their toys, and the rest of their beloved shit. This would also be referred to as "A useless waste of time for the parents. And for the undisciplined kiddies, a get-out-of-chores free card, plus some fun playtime." This is the punishment I wish I had when I was a kid, or even now. Let's be honest moms and dads, time-out is just a play date for one.

Really, parents, we don't want to hear your kids being disruptive. So, plug um up. Here's a novel idea. How about you learn to say 2 tiny words, "You're grounded!" Or perhaps, a simple one-word idea, **"NO!"** Hey, you might like it and your adorable little rascals may learn something. Like respect? Stop the deals and quid pro quo. Just say no!

Back on topic... As I curiously looked around the childless quiet room, oddly enough, I discovered I was the only woman in the "Protection against noise chamber." I detected this could be an indication that women were tired of being paid less for the same job men do! Forget it, let's not unpack that unfair situation right now. But truth be told? I guess it's not all that bad. At least women get to vote now! Hopefully, that will stick.

Still on watch patrol, maybe this was a private room for men only and I took a wrong turn, I alleged. But hell, I didn't care to find out. I was comfortable, and there was no way I was leaving the serene, quiet room.

It was hard not to notice that every man in the childless and womanless room was sleeping. Typical! Classic! Preferentially, in their defense, I should objectively say they were taking power naps. That sounds considerably better. Power Naps, I trust it's the trending word for it these days. Hmm, it used to be called *loafing or sleeping on the job.*

Ergo, out of boredom and personal amusement, I started judging each one of these guys. I found it passed the time nicely. Whatever... I had to. I couldn't help myself. Besides, I suffer from '*Dating PTSD!*'

Then, I silently pondered, "Are all these men 'freaks,' as well?" Was my question fact or fiction? I wondered, yet I didn't know for sure. Still, I saw a substantial number of freak flags flying in this one little room, inside of this one little club, inside this one little airport, inside the Peach State. Sort of like those adorable Matryoshka Russian dolls.

I speculated, is the rather stunning man across the room that looks exactly like a young Liam Neeson, a freak? I reflected, was the man to my left, puffed out from way too much Botox and fillers, sitting in the comfy beige leather lounge chair with his feet up a freak? Or the guy over there who was amusing to watch nodding off, while his head repeatedly bobbed up and down. His actions continued, conceivably for the sole purpose of my personal entertainment. And behind me, there was a cute guy, with long extensions, wearing way too much Guyliner. He was a truly engaging distraction. Wait, a second! "Johnny? Johnny Depp? Psssst, is that you? Johnny? *Do you hear me, Johnny?*" Oh no, it's not you, Depp? It's Rami Malek. Perhaps Rami is playing a character with extensions and Guyliner?

Continuing being judgmental, was that nice man close to me with the ridiculous comb over a freak? I admit it was awfully nice of him to share the only working outlet, so I could plug in my laptop and cell. Besides, it was hilarious listening to Mr. Bad coiffure guy, wearing earphones, and singing painfully loud. In addition, terribly off-key to Steven Tyler's song, "I Don't Want to Miss a Thing." He was not only destroying it but performing a horrendous version of a perfectly great rock classic. As ridiculous as he sounded, was he any less disturbing than the screaming, boisterous kids outside the quiet room? Although I couldn't concentrate on my work, he was far better. "Um, *Sir? 1-2-3-4-5? Sir? 5-1/2. Sir? 6!*" When he finally caught my eye, I pointed thoughtfully to his earphones. He apologetically and embarrassingly, shut the fuck up! Seeing how mortified he appeared, I thought I'd be nice and lie right to his face. "No worries, you sounded great!" Come on, the guy helped me charge my phone. I gave him a break. He's a good boy, but a bad singer.

What about that man way across from me with the atrocious cold, blowing his nose, sneezing, and coughing without covering his mouth? Was he a freak? He hadn't stopped sneering at me for talking on my cell in the quiet room. Whatever. I figured if he could contaminate the quiet room without care, I could quietly talk on my cell without care! Mr. Sicko was for sure a freakazoid, and one without any sense of common courtesy.

Suddenly, hope set in. There he was, sitting on the opposite side of the quiet room. A magnificent man, well dressed, and very kind, judging by the way he spoke to the server taking his cocktail order. He looked to be 40ish and well-to-do, guesstimating by his Versace Suit and his gold and diamond Presidential Rolex Watch. There he sat, the elegant man of my dreams. Or at least for the moment. I was so enjoying witnessing his gorgeous... *everything.* Then, ever so abruptly, my bubble burst when his 17-year-old *'girlfriend/daughter'* walked into the room. To be objective, I am grossly exaggerating. She was eighteen, tops! Speaking of which, it looked to me as though she was sporting 36-double-D implants. Double meow! Meanwhile, I found it positively comical the number of times she posed for the man of my dreams while making duck faces at him. The duck-face pose is an attempt at looking sexy. To do the duck face, you must purse your lips together, combining a pout and a pucker. This gives the illusion that you have larger cheekbones and bigger lips. I couldn't help but wonder, did Mr. Dreamboat notice her duck-face lips were now completely covered by the foam from her hot chocolate & marshmallows? Girl, give it a rest. You can't pose forever. Trust me, I did it for 10 hours on a plane for McDreamy, Fabrizio! *Boom!* It gets old quickly. Be aware. Life isn't a continuous red carpet. Regardless, quack, quack, quack to you!

Mr. Wonderful caught me staring. He gave me a return stare, which clearly implied, *"I know, I know. I'm more than twice her age. But I'm rich, successful, and powerful. Besides, I just don't like women my own age. Moreover, she is no longer jailbait! That counts for something. Right?"* We exchanged friendly grown-up smiles. My smile for him was a posed duck face because I assumed he was used to it. Only mine was without a mouth full of Girl Scout Cookies & a kiddy cup of hot chocolate & marshmallow foam all over my lips. The thing is, someone needs to tell Miss 36 Double D that the duck face is so over and has been replaced by the fish-gape pose! What an infinite bummer, the guy was so handsome and charming. Maybe I could entice Miss Poser off with a 'Toys "R" Us' online gift certificate, or a gift card to 'Victoria's Secret?' Huh, probably not. It's obvious he buys her whatever she wants down to her pleated, plaid schoolgirl skirt, penny loafers, knee-high socks, and the diamond necklace & bracelet she's sporting. That's when it struck me. Are all men freaks or just the online dating ones and the men in this airport club? Contemptable, I had to get away. I acknowledge I'm being super-bitchy. The jig is up. By now you most certainly have spotted my *Dating PTSD!*

After what seemed to be endless hours of sleepless air travel, I arrived in Uruguay, painstakingly exhausted. It was Christmas Eve, day, and no matter how tired I felt, there was no way I would miss frolicking around and seeing the festive sights. I checked into The Grand Hotel Punta Del Este, grabbed some preposterously strong coffee, took a shower, and changed clothes. After a quick glance in the mirror, I confidentially proceeded down to the shops for a stroll in Montevideo. This provocative, fast-paced, electrifying city would make coffee anxious. Driving to the Punta Carretas Shopping Center, the taxi driver gave me a warning. In a very matter-of-fact fashion, he explained to me the town's time-honored holiday tradition. "Miss, I'd like to give you a piece of advice. The men in this country (AKA more freaks) douse people in the streets with water or beer just for some Christmas Eve fun and tricks." He continued in his broken English to disclose, "No worries, little Miss, these tricks are now only a rare happening. Don't be afraid. It would be highly unusual because it hasn't been done for years. It's now basically an old legend!" Carefree and unconcerned, I replied with, "Sir, tricks are for kids!" I added my best fish-gape pose (pursed lips and all), plus a hand gesture to accentuate my point. He looked at me, very confused. Regardless, grown men who would do this would surely be freaks. Nonetheless, I was forewarned, which was troubling enough for me to place my professional Nikon Camera into a plastic bag and then into my carry bag for safekeeping.

Two gorgeous leather jackets and a pair of leather pants later, I stopped at a quaint little restaurant for pizza and a glass of local wine. I found it entertainingly captivating, watching everyone bustling around searching for last-minute, eleventh-hour Christmas gifts. Which logically got me thinking. I ought to buy myself a fab pair of shoes as a Christmas Eve gift for me, from me. How could I not? I'm just sayin' they make some of the best leather shoes in this part of the world. I realized I might potentially be in grave shoe—purchasing peril, particularly in Rio.

Later, as I was leisurely strolling down the street, minding my own blissful shopping business, preoccupied with my future hopes and dreams. Suddenly, out of nowhere, and to my disbelief, I was drenched with what felt like a hundred men, showering me like a category-5 hurricane, with beer. They wouldn't stop. I pleaded with them to stop in bad Portuguese, to no avail. Not only was I soaked from hair to designer shoes, in beer, I was hurting from the weight of the liquid being dumped on me. Just when I thought this traditional dowsing nightmare was over (the legend I was told would not happen), more men ran up and inundated me with buckets of beer, yet again. By now, I was soaking wet, as if I had come out of the ocean. My eyes were painfully burning. Like a good sport, I tried to be cool about this awful ritual, accepting what was bestowed upon me.

Alas, by the fifth group of men drowning me with buckets of liquid, while bystanders were bent over, laughing, and pointing, I grasped by the disgusting odor, amid all the bedlam, that this was not beer at all. This was urine! Also commonly known as piss! *Yes, smelly piss!* This horrific event had brought new meaning to the phrase, "I'm so pissed off!"

Oh, for fuck's sake, I screamed, "Stop it, Carlos, Juan, Jose, and Diego. (Uruguay names.) OK, 1-2-3-4!" It didn't seem to work for me, either. It was so undeniably tragic and beyond psycho. Nevertheless, this insanity was happening. Lord only knows where the hell they collected all this gross pee. Was it solely human or animal urine as well? Disgusting!

Unable to hold back my tears, I lost it and started to cry. I hate giving in to girl tears, especially in front of these barbaric, vile, thugs. Hell, and I thought the boisterous, yelling, crying, *"No, Johnny No,"* naughty kids were bad? Do those little innocent angels grow up to be pee saturating men like these? You see! Their parents should have said, NO!

This was the most horrific thing that's ever happened to me... Not including drunken frat parties, my boring first-year ethics professor, or forced by my college roommate to binge-watch reruns of the *Kardashians* and *Big Brother*.

Thank goodness I saved my camera from this devastating situation. Because that would have pissed me off even more. Every stubborn bone, and tough-girl defiance left inside of me from high school, wanted to egg them on yelling out, "Hey, Mr. Pee-Cock, is that all you got?" Knowing it wasn't, I shut up and ran off like a very stinky, little cowardly chicken.

My hair, clothes, face, and '*my everything else,*' was all sticky and wet with strange men's (or animals') gross urine. I was a hot mess, but grateful my new stunning leather jackets and pants were dry and spared from being ruined. I wiped my tears and ran back to the hotel. After spending what felt like 10 hours in the shower, I still didn't feel clean.

A message from the Sicilian Godfather... "These guys should sleep with the fishes!" My rage over this tradition was seismic, but I moved on without looking back. Ok, that's a lie. I look back all the time. How could I not? *A Merry Frickin', Uruguay, Peece On Earth Christmas To Me! I will never eat pee-za, rice pee-loff, pee soup, pee-nuts, or play the pee-ano ever again. 'Pee-kaboo' is out of the question, too. Peeple, this tragedy happened, and we must never again speak of what occurred here this day!*

After Christmas, I had some leisure time to tour the city (In a raincoat!) before my next assignment. I saved shoe shopping for Rio. Obviously, any shoes bought here in Uruguay would only remind me of the legendary, time-honored, apocalyptic piss shower and piss-storm. Even though I was peeved, pissed-*off, and pissed on,* I decided I had to let it go for now, move on, and have fun on the rest of this business trip.

On December 27th, at 7:00 in the morning, I boarded a flight to São Paulo, Brazil. I was thrilled to be clean, *peeceful,* and out of Uruguay. I don't think I will ever be able to '*un-smell*' that disgusting incident.

Thankfully, every experience in São Paulo was joyful and memorable. Here, all the beer was served in a glass and all pee was dispensed in a toilet! However, I stuck with red wine for obvious reasons.

I spent 3 amazing days finishing my feature stories with plenty of time left over to discover a new city. Which included its traditions, foods, music, history, new acquaintances, amazing shopping, clubs, relaxing on the beach, basking in the sun, and getting a dangerous golden tan. (Indeed, that sentence deserves a runaway adjective ticket!)

Oh, and let's not forget about all the sexy, hunky, flirtatious men everywhere I looked. Ironically, I didn't need my duck face, or even my fish-gape pose to flirt right back. Truth be told, this city should be famous for its handsome men with their spectacular muscles, abs, and butts!

CHAPTER 12

On Assignment in Rio

RAIN FORESTS & BEACHES & FAVELAS... OH MY!!!!
THE CHRIST REDEEMER & FIREWORKS & MARCELO...
OH MY-MY-MY!!!!

I landed in Rio de Janeiro, Brazil, early evening, drained after non-stop fun, partying in São Paulo. I didn't care one bit and harbored absolutely no regrets. Totally bushed upon my arrival, I could barely jump into a cab. I wouldn't necessarily call the zone I was in a hangover. But it is a possibility and reasonable. Ok, you got me. I had a hangover! A big one!

December 30th, the night before New Year's Eve in Rio, always stirs up extravagant excitement. Although I was exhausted, as my driver transported me through the overcrowded streets lined with tourists and locals, it was impossible not to recognize the exhilarating pulse of the city. The mood was abuzz with a highly anticipated, spectacular, monstrous celebration of the year. Oddly enough (especially for me), I couldn't find the strength to recharge my "Let's party spirits." The consummate workaholic within me understood I had to awaken early in the morning, fresh and full of energy. Not only would this be an extremely long day, but I was also obligated to stay awake through the night. Power naps were not allowed here. With no other option, I took the conservative, boring, party-pooper path, and quickly checked into the Hotel, Rio de Janeiro Copacabana. Forgive me, Barry Manilow, because I know this is where the inspiration for your legendary song was born. You'd be so disappointed with my killjoy attitude. Famished, I promptly ordered room service from the Portuguese menu, unwilling to wait for the English one that had somehow escaped from my suite. God only knows what I ordered, but I devoured it. Even while munching away, I couldn't put my finger on what I consumed that night before I rolled over and turned out the lights.

A famous news magazine hired me to write an in-depth feature story on Rio, including photos. It was for a new *"Did you know"* travel section they were test-marketing. My editor, Angela, who I adored and respected, called me early the previous morning, N.Y. time. "OK, Mollie, listen up! I've arranged a private tour guide for you," she rambled on. Angela was not kidding around, as she explained sternly. "This guide has major clout for unlimited access to places in Rio where others are ordinarily forbidden. Be honored. This is a big deal. Now, a cautionary reminder. As you are aware, this iconic magazine has extraordinary power and muscle throughout the world. So please, be very professional as usual. Remember, *it is essential to abide by all the tour guide's rules and directions implicitly.* Please follow his instructions precisely. Do exactly whatever he tells you. One more thing. Be careful, Mollie! Where you are going could be seriously dangerous. Thus, be vigilant and on your toes."

"Angela, I Got this. I can handle it," I stammered! "Oh, and yikes, thanks for terrifying the bejesus out of me!" We chuckled, as both of us knew how totally paranoid and overly protective Angie was about keeping her journalists safe. She was a typical media mom in all respects.

"Wild news flash, Ange. What could be worse than buckets of *human/animal* pee-bombs repeatedly showered over my head?"

"Oh, yeah, Hon, concerning that matter? We are all still laughing wildly about your little epic *'pee party'* here at the magazine. And Moll, I don't think it's going to go away anytime soon, either. BTW, we all just loved the photo you sent of yourself, soaked in pee, from head to toe. Hey, it might even make the cover. You know I'm pushing for that to happen!"

What could I tactfully respond to her? "Piss off, Angie!"

I'd be deaf if I didn't hear the entire office giggling hopelessly. And then I inquired, mortified, "I'm on speaker, aren't I?"

"Yes, you are! No problem, babe, you're loved regardless of how bad you smell. Remember, we are your *'pee*-ple.' Hey, I forgot to ask. Did you brush up on your Pee-tuguese? One last thing, Mollie. Take a couple extra showers before the tour guide picks you up!" From the office in New York, thousands of miles away, came thunderous laughter.

I replied, laughing along with them, **"I hate you all! Goodbye!"**

My guide arrived at exactly 7:00 in the morning as planned. After our initial courteous, "How do you do" formalities, the only thing on my mind was, "Sir, coffee me! Please coffee me, hard! Coffee me, now!"

My private escort picked me up in his purple, broken-down jeep that didn't have a covered top. I gathered this meant no air-conditioning; despite the fact it was 150 degrees outside. He further apologized for the broken doors. "Mollie, is it? OK, Mollie, you'll have to climb in and out of the open window to catch the points of interest outside of the jeep."

"No worries." I smiled, thinking, thanks, Angie! I was grateful Mr. Guide took me straightaway for a cup of café. Perhaps it was more like 3. I swear nothing's better in the morning than getting that vital java jolt with a freshly baked chocolate flaky croissant. Whoa, coffee is crazy strong here in Brazil! I was now content, rebooted, enthusiastic, and ready to go.

His name was Marcelo. He was handsome, but not as much as he was sexy. He had an erotic way about him and appeared abundantly masculine, confident, and fearless. Yet, somehow, he was still gentle and warm. Nice combo, especially in a manly man. Like native-born Rodrigo Santoro (in "Love Actually"), he spoke with a very hot Brazilian accent.

I complimented him. "Marcelo, your English is excellent!"

Pleased, he replied. "I'm flattered. I've been a tour guide for many years, and I, fortunately, learned English from the people I guide. Still, Portuguese to English is a far jump. But thank you for your kind praise."

We started our expedition hiking up to the top of the world-famous Christ Redeemer, better known as "Cristo Redentor." Yes, that happened. If they could see me now, that little gang of mine! I paused, panting and breathless, as I climbed higher and higher. Wouldn't it have been way easier, I thought, to take the train up instead? Marcelo explained, "The Corcovado, better known to the locals, is the monolith, upon which the statue and the tourist attractions are located. The statue itself is about 130 feet high and was 'erected' in the early 1930s." He winked at me, smiling, and instantaneously, goose bumps prevailed. All righty then, I do believe his wink, after saying "erected" was an undeniable flirt. Irrespective, as a professional, I discounted it and pushed away the pheromones. He went on. "The Redeemer now represents the symbol of Rio around the world."

"It's splendid," I responded, snapping numerous photos. Thinking to myself, thank goodness I didn't wear my ultra "erect" high heels, which I ignorantly almost did. I sensibly sported a pair of, white, short shorts, a pink tank top, and pink and white sneakers, with my hair neatly swept up into a rhinestone clip. Since December is summer in Brazil, it was hot as fire. My cell displayed the temperature at 35 to 40 brutal degrees Celsius, which is equivalent to 95-104 degrees Fahrenheit. Making matters worse, it was uncomfortably muggy, with the humidity measuring 100%. I was perspiring out of control, fatigued, and a mess when we reached the top. I won't even discuss the way my silky straight, long hair now looked like freshly spun blonde cotton candy. Honestly, though, the real miracle was not the Christ Redeemer. The actual marvel was my ability to make the steep climb. No doubt, the statue was truly astonishing. Frankly, I was far more impressed by my personal achievement, hiking up to the very top!

Marcelo noticed and giggled, "And that's why they pay you the big bucks, Mollie!" I chuckled. While beaming with self-satisfaction, I was obnoxiously too smug and excessively too proud to show Marcelo just how strenuous this climb truly was. And I'm in good shape, too! But there was no way in Hell, I'd admit (especially to him) that I had *a bit of a go* reaching the top. And why is it, I question, that I am constantly finding myself wet, in one fashion or another, since I left the States? Seriously!

Trying to hide my obvious gasping-out-of-breath situation, I took the last swig of my third bottle of water and condescendingly interrogated him. "So, Mr. Guide, with your wonderful English, where to next? And please, don't insult me by taking us somewhere so easy and unchallenging this time." Marcelo bent to his knees, roaring with laughter, seeing full well that I was depleted, worn out, and entirely full of shit.

I laughed right back when he said, "It's nice that you are so in touch with your primal self!" That's when he gently touched my leg and grinned sweetly. Was that another flirting gesture, I assumed? Was he flirting? Is this spicy Brazilian tour guide interested in me? Even though I looked like a hot mess, I proved to him my athletic talents and skills with ease. So, he might think? Or probably not so much! But why then does he keep ogling my legs and booty? Oh, for the Christ Redeemer's sake, he is clearly hitting on me! I distinctly recall none of this was designated or included anywhere on my media tour itinerary. Not even in a memo. Granted, Marcelo is in no way my type. All the same, he is fascinating and extremely sensually desirable. He's a macho package decorated with a rugged, sexy bow and a trim of softness. Tough, but I stayed professional.

That's when I remembered the strict, implicit orders from Angela. *"Mollie, follow the tour guides lead, rules, directions, and instructions precisely!"* With that being said, I am a dedicated, serious reporter, and a team player, and I respect what I'm told by my superiors. Especially about following a sexy tour guides lead. Was flirting part of this? I wondered!

After a fair amount of tourist time spent up at the statue, Marcelo briskly grabbed my hand and demanded in broken English, "Come now, 69 quickly! We *go down on you,* with the train!"

I was gobsmacked and speechless. What? Come again? What does he mean? He's going to 69 go down on me, in the train? What, now?" Being a girl, the first thought in my brain was, "Shit, I didn't get a Brazilian Wax!" My next thought was, "Shit, I didn't bring a cute teddy!" Thankfully I didn't speak of my confusion in my outside voice, because he then handed an employee two tickets, and we jumped onto car number 69, to go down the mountain on the train. Laughing inwardly, I wasn't sure if I was relieved or disappointed.

What a language barrier! Totally feeling like a first-class fool, I smiled and took the 4th bottle of water he handed me. To his credit, Marcelo is an intensely passionate guide.

We went through the astonishing rainforest, which is the largest rural rainforest in the world. He informed me in his Portuguese accent, "These forests cover almost 60% of the entire area of Brazil. The Brazilian Amazon Rainforests are dubbed as the 'lungs of the world' for the valuable oxygen they release for all humankind during respiration." He continued to explain, "The Tijuca forest, all 46 square miles, situated in the middle of Rio, is home to rivers, birds, mountain peaks, astonishing natural beauty, and some of the best urban hiking anywhere."

Yeah, yeah, and yackety-yak! That was all well and good, but I was blistering hot, and my hair turned into a forest of its own. I felt "Icky, and sticky, and gross. Oh, my!" Though I must confess, this Rio journey was quite an experience. To my complete surprise and paradoxically for a girly girl, I found this rugged, non-luxurious escapade impressively thrilling and super fun. Plus, as a journalist, I believe touring Rio in the raw, without any frills, is the most honest and authentic way to discover its exquisite natural beauty. I'm sure Marcelo's seducing me all day didn't hurt my opinion, either. Throughout the tour, I kept thinking and silently screaming friskily "Oh, homem que você é sexy e quente como o inferno, Marelo," ("Man, you are sexy and hot as hell, Marcelo!")

Next on the schedule, with Marcelo taking me up on my dare of the dangerous, we drove inside a few of the most treacherous and terrifying areas in Rio. He enlightened me… "Twenty percent of the population lives in the city's most underprivileged slum communities, known locally as the Favelas. The residents must be excessively vigilant and brave. They live under the domination of violence, corruption, and drug traffickers. These people deal daily with illegal drugs, arms, militias, and the real possibility of being killed." He described to me what the Favela citizens do merely to survive and provide a future for their children. "If born into a favela, it is quite rare to escape this life. These areas are so perilous and unsafe, even the police enter at great risk and typically, not at all. The favelas are notoriously written off and ignored by the uncaring society outside of them." He said sadly, "As you can see, the electrical wires are dangerously exposed everywhere. It's horrifying that garbage and filth are anywhere you look. It is inhuman to live like this!"

My heart was filled with compassion for these people. I told Marcelo, "I believe the worst slums in America would be considered Beverly Hills and upscale compared to these Favelas in Rio." Being a reporter, I was mindful this was a rare, risky, extremely unsafe privilege to drive through them. Because of Marcelo's connections and tourism status, he is allowed inside safely without our lives being threatened. Regardless, standing up in his broken-down, open purple jeep as I was shooting photos for the story, I justifiably feared for my life with each click of my Nikon. He assured me the countless people walking around carrying large guns knew him and would not shoot either of us dead. Since I didn't completely take his word for it, I stood up in the jeep, quickly took about ten photos, and then hid, slouching down on the seat as my heart pounded in fear. I repeated this approach for the next hour. Judging by the angry looks from men with weapons, I felt much safer hiding like a chicken between photos. Whew! Luckily, only camera shots were fired and not deadly gunshots.

Marcelo recognized I was afraid. "I can understand your fear. But the reality is, most Brazilians are fearful themselves and have never visited the Favelas. Never mind the rest of the world." Marcelo caringly held my hand and looked into my eyes. "I feel your sympathy and I'm touched!"

This was a serious wake-up call for me. Though this experience was highly hazardous, it left me grateful to live in America, humbled, and enormously concerned for the people trapped in the Favelas. It was also a scary reminder that there was so much injustice in the world. All that I encountered today made me reflect. With the many atrocious inhumane situations and tragedies going on in the world today, how benevolent and civilized as a people, have we really become? I feared, not so much.

Continuing the tour, Marcelo took me to the top of the panoramic Sugarloaf Mountain to see the astounding views. These awe-inspiring visions of God's immeasurable natural beauty were heavenly.

I was taken by surprise when Marcelo whispered with his broken accent into my ear at that moment. "You is a sweet, gorgeous, sugarloaf yourself, Miss Reporter!" All righty, then, and there was that! I might be a blonde, but he is absolutely, clearly, without a doubt, flirting. Allegedly! Now extrapolating the tangible outcome that this type of liaison could drastically interfere with my career standards. Cautiously optimistic and in a dither, I wasn't sure how to handle this. For the moment, I demonstrated tactful aplomb in dealing with this awkward predicament and ignored the whole situation. After all, I am a professional journalist on a serious assignment. The disparities in our reasons for being together today might become a severely compromising situation. As horny and flattered as I admittedly was, his behavior was textbook inappropriate. Therefore, I pretended I didn't hear him. Even he acknowledged I was faking it, and grinned with an endearing, impish, little boyish expression. I was kind of anticipating the "wink, wink" eye message coming from him at this point.

Marcelo proceeded to drive towards the renowned beaches of Ipanema. Just like the song, this sexually erotic man started singing loudly from his jeep for all to hear. *"Tall and tan and young and lovely, the girl from Ipanema goes walking and when she passes, each one that passes goes, Ahhh!"* Even though he sang off-key, it was really kind of cute. He followed his performance, turning my way, and in a low voice sang again, "Mollie, you are the loveliest girl in Ipanema, and I certainly know you heard me this time, bela, senhorita!" He radically destroyed the English language as he spoke. I didn't care because it really was adorable to hear. Though he did have a point. As impossible as it seemed, I found no pretty girls walking about Ipanema on this day. To my delight, I did see a lot of tall and tan and young and hunky, toned, attractive Brazilian men walking about. But damn, I hate to admit it, Marcelo was undoubtedly one of them.

Sizing up this Brazilian stud, I noticed for the first time all day that he was not wearing a wedding band, and there were no apparent tan lines around his finger. Profusely flirtatious as he was, it was apparent that Senhor Tour Guide was free, available, single, and wanted me, even looking like an absolute mess. Obviously, there was no mistaking the fact that I looked dreadful, an hour after he picked me up. Evidently, somehow, he still desired me. Hey, far be it from me to fight the opinions of Marcelo. He was so *oomph-sexy* and naturally, I was indeed loving it!

We stopped for lunch at a traditional Brazilian Churrasco. Once seated, I politely excused myself and fled to the ladies' room to freshen up my makeup. Or lack thereof! I quickly slid a tiny battery-operated flat iron through my hair to rid the cotton candy frizz and spritzed on some perfume. I couldn't stop myself from grinning in the mirror, appreciating how much I valued being a journalist. I'm grateful for the privilege of traveling to so many countries and learning about all the diverse cultures and their people. Moreover, it's an honor to share my research with the world. Applying a touch of lipstick and powder on my face, I had a thought, which tickled me even pinker than the Brazilian summer heat to my cheeks. As strenuous, exhausting, hot, and dangerous as this day proved to be, it was easy as pie compared to online dating back at home. This transcendent, perilous day merely involved hiking straight up and down through mountainous terrain, dangerous cliffs, sweating, and huffing and puffing. I was left weak and dehydrated hiking through a rainforest, and Lord only knows how many strange insects attacked me there! I faced a jungle, a maze, life-threatening Favelas, and famed beaches. However, I thought, adding more mascara to my lashes. In comparison, online dating is significantly more chilling and hazardous. Self-confident, I giggled and ignored the odd stares from the 2 young Brazilian ladies in the bathroom.

When I came back to our table all freshened up, Marcelo stood and pulled out my chair. Wine and appetizers awaited my return. Then he spoke softly with conviction. "Mollie, you are a paragon of beauty!"

What could I reply to that? "Oh stop. Please, no more compliments Mr. Tour Guide?" Instead, I beamed shyly. Marcelo continued to flatter me with how lovely I looked all cleaned up. I felt myself blush like a silly teenager and timidly smiled back. As complimentary as all his sweet talk was, I considered, where could this be going? I was uneasy about tarnishing or compromising my reputation, or even being fired. I was apprehensive and worried about my capability of saying, *No!* Obviously, it would be negligent to ruin my esteemed good name, which I have earned in the world of journalism, for a silly, stupid, senseless, serendipitous, secret, sexual, splurging spree. Not to mention far too many "S" words.

After briefly zoning out, I mentally returned to the table. Marcelo questioned with a mouth full of food and lots of it. "Good, to eat?"

I finally adapted to his funny English and realized he wasn't saying I was good to eat, "Yes, it is very good food!" I couldn't identify most of the meat selections I placed into my mouth, nor the endless side dishes. He tried his best to explain each cut of meat, each side, and why they were all Brazilian classics. Yet I did appreciate they were delectable, as I continued to turn my disk green, rather than red, signaling the servers to keep serving away. Surely, I'd remember the tasty flavors long after I returned home.

Changing the subject, I asked my guide, "Why do you spell Bela, and your name, Marcelo, with one L? Isn't Marcello and Bella, *correct*?"

"Well, Marcello is the Italian spelling. I'm Brazilian and proud of my heritage. We speak Portuguese. We don't need that extra *incorrect* L!"

"Good answer!" But recalled that Aubry so needed that extra, "E!"

Feeling stuffed and annoyed with myself for overindulging, I was surprised when Marcelo asked, "Would you like some Brazilian nuts?" Puzzled, as there were none in sight, I wouldn't touch that question for fear it would incriminate me. I didn't know for certain if he was being suggestive or serious. So, I politely answered, "No thanks, I never touch them!" He smiled, knowing exactly what he meant! And so did I…

After lunch, Marcelo with one 'L' took me back to the Copacabana Hotel. I needed to change back into a girl. This required a proper shower, washed hair, and fresh makeup. Then, I'd excitedly slip into a brand new, sexy blue Versace dress for the grand New Year's Eve festivities. The world-famous Rio fireworks show was, likewise, part of my assignment and a vital story to be covered. My guide/

date washed up and changed into a stylish Brazilian tux in the men's gym at the hotel. Afterward, he sat at the bar with a cocktail in hand, impatiently awaiting my return. He called my room several times while lingering in the sophisticated Copacabana Bar, which I ignored. It took every bit of an hour and 1/2 to transform back into my comfy world of fashion. Before leaving my suite, I looked in the mirror to see my reflection for the last time this year. I was pleased with what I saw and quite confident in my appearance, which I planned meticulously to bring in the New Year. A happy, wonderful year, I hoped!

As I entered the bar to join Marcelo, his mouth dropped open, and he only managed to utter, "Wow!" He gushed, expressing, "Vision, my dear. Mollie, my lovely *darling*, you are a magnet, beautiful!"

Giggling, "Do you mean I am a magnetically beautiful vision?"

"Yes, what I say, magnet, beautiful, alluring, and irresistible you."

I blushed furiously. "You too, are a magnet vision, Marcelo!" Now thinking, *darling*? Anyway, I wisely brought a scarf to cover my hair in his jeep. I had to arrive looking like a woman, a journalist, and not a Muppet when reaching the marina. Arriving, as the sun was threatening to set over the Mediterranean skyline, we stepped onto his billionaire client's 328-foot gorgeous yacht. This was a night to party, dance, dine, enjoy the celebrations, the fireworks, and drink away the last night of the year. But was also a night I had to work and shoot newsworthy photos.

This cruiser was spectacular and sparkled brightly under the lovely evening stars. Never wanting to disembark, I contemplated becoming a stowaway on a stranger's yacht. All the guests onboard dressed stylishly chic. They were unimaginably rich and ranked as the most privileged and elite amongst the world's beautiful jet set-ters. But I knew I, too, looked stunning and wasn't intimidated in the least. I couldn't conceive of a more magical way to usher in a new beginning. I sensed that this year would bring with it a clean slate of joy. This was truly a storybook evening and an impressive New Year's Eve to remember. My romantic, innocent heart couldn't stop thinking about how I dreamed of finding my beloved soul mate to share all the rest of my future New Year's Eve experiences with.

Countless champagne cocktails later and at the mythical stroke of midnight, Marcelo leaned in and kissed me on the cheek. I wasn't sure if this was work-appropriate but, I mean, it was New Year's! We watched in amazement as Rio de Janeiro celebrated its illustrious New Year's Eve's massively remarkable fireworks display. Everyone onboard, as well as all the other yachts and ship cruises in the vicinity, observed the extravaganza with childlike enthusiasm. Millions of people around the globe watch Rio's legendary Dec. 31st presentation. The explosions, colors, noises, and visions of extraordinary shapes covering the entire span of the Copacabana beach were so spectacular it was impossible to take it all in. Marcelo explained, "Every year more than two-point-five million international guests gather to witness and celebrate this phenomenon."

Rio's massive fireworks are the most breathtaking, mind-blowing explosions I'd ever experienced. OK, not including my very first authentic orgasm! Then, I thought, what kind of explosions Marcelo and I would make together? I am so incorrigible and a bad, bad girl... a very bad girl! Shame, shame on me, I thought proudly!

Immediately upon the conclusion of the brilliant fireworks production, Marcelo looked directly into my eyes and spoke. "I want to take you back to your hotel and stay overnight with you!" He impatiently shouted and breathlessly explained, "I simply must have you. Nothing would make the start of this New Year more special than spending the night with you, having you in my arms, and everywhere else. I need to kiss your naked breasts and be inside your wetness." Ahem, now that just about puts an end to my thinking all day that he was only flirting with me. And just like that, Marcelo bent down and kissed me passionately, with no invitation or encouragement from me. There was no time for responding with a "Shit, shit, shit" or "Is this part of the Rio tour on my assignment?"

Next, without any guilt or conscience, Marcelo followed his kiss with his groping hand, attacking my breast. A bit off-guard, as I pushed him away, he casually divulged, "Listen, I am sure it won't matter to you at all, but I am happily married for 12 years, and I have 2 young children."

My immediate thoughts were... Mic drop, crash, and are you fucking kidding me? Yet another New Year's Eve colorful explosion, and for sure, the romance bloom had just fallen off the rose! Way off.

Before I could respond, that *indeed, it did greatly matter to me,* and *I don't do married men,* Marcelo completely enveloped me in his arms and kissed me madly. As I forcefully broke away, he crawled his hand up my thigh like the rat that he was. On this serene balmy night, on this showy lavish vessel, as the elegant people all around us watched, he fondled me! I confess it was quite impressive how his pushy aggression didn't seem to faze anyone in the least. That's Brazil for you! When I was finally able to squirm out from his grasp, with my entire wrath I rebutted angrily, *"But you're married! Marcelo! Stop! I mean it, Stop it!"*

He replied, confident, yet confused. "Why so, sweet Mollie? Fidelity in Brazil is only an idea! It is not a big deal. Let's have fun!"

A stunned man oh man, was my silent reply. I really should introduce this guy to Fabrizio! Have men and women, for that matter, become so desensitized to the vows and faithfulness of their marriages, and their monogamous, committed love relationships? To even ponder or consider sleeping with this happily married father would be a total mea culpa on my part. That's where our perspectives started to diverge! I blew him off, probing, "Does that suggestion apply to your wife as well? I feel it would totally matter to her and I do believe she'd think it a big deal."

It was very clear by the scorned expression on his face that this Latin man was not overjoyed by my question. Morally, with the high ground on my side, I confidently understood it was now time for this tour to come to a screeching end. For if it didn't, Marcelo, the Latin lover, and happily married man for 12 years with 2 children, (who was handsome, but not as much as he was sexy) was going to be thrown off this gorgeous yacht, into the sea, by me, Miss Sugarloaf Reporter. Sadly, I was quickly reminded that *men would forever be men!* Even tour guides.

And there you have it, a happy, ethical, New Year's Eve. I can only say it was a lot better than my sticky, wet, insane, Uruguay Christmas Pee-eve. I refused to allow Marcelo's indiscreet evening of unethical behavior to mar my memories of Rio de Janeiro. Truth be told, I found his flirtations flattering. I'll always remember our time in Rio. Marcelo's sexy choppy English, his broken-down purple jeep, the food, the attractions and sights, the fireworks, and the impressive yacht. Exhausted, I went to bed early in the morning, with my reputation intact, a big smile, and a fresh start for the New Year. It felt good doing the right thing. It always does.

Luckily for me, I was able to sleep in, till the afternoon. At 1:00 sharp, I quickly got dressed and gobbled down some fresh fruit and a double espresso when I was interrupted by Angela's call.

"OK, Mollie, tell me! Tell me everything! How did the tour, your research, and the evening in Rio go? Any new crazy stories to report?"

One thing was for sure. I wasn't going to risk any more ridicule or mocking laughter echoing throughout the office gossip pool for the 2nd time on this assignment. I wasn't biting and replied with my mouth full of fruit. "Exciting, dangerous, grueling, risky, lovely, and it will make for a remarkable feature story. You'll love it and the photos are amazing."

Hearing laughter in the background, Angela responded, *"Why are you speaking so funny? Is your mouth full of something? Perhaps some hot Brazilian Nuts? Oh pees, do tell!"* With that, the laughter grew fierce. I couldn't believe she asked me that because I still wondered what Marcelo meant by that same reference. Since there were no nuts of any kind, let alone Brazilian Nuts, sitting on the lunch table when he asked if I wanted some. Making his flirtations on the tour, now even more obvious.

Knowing Angie for so many years as the consummate, dedicated professional, it was nice and quite rare to see her frisky side instead of her ultra-serious, proficient demeanor. Even so, I refused to compromise my integrity and honor by playing along. "Nothing nutty to report Ange, just a late breakfast! Sorry to disappoint the laughing hyenas in the office that I distinctly hear!" Regardless, the boisterous snickering ensued.

Angie touted a smug, "Okey-dokey. Have fun in Argentina. Oh, and Mollie, this time, don't get shit on!" Even I had to chuckle, listening to everyone in the office laughing uncontrollably on my account.

"Touché Angela! Only you would touch on that! I hope you all thoroughly enjoy rhapsodizing on my pain and humiliation!"

"Hey, it's no reflection of our love for you, sweetie!"

"Yeah, yeah, yeah. Love you all too!"

"Goodbye girl, be safe! Now, scram and pees-out!"

Still laughing, I ran out quickly, munching on a raspberry scone in hand. I was tickled that I kept my "Marcelo in Rio story" secret and felt some semblance of my pride unbroken. I've learned some things are best kept secret. "The sun watches me, but the moon keeps all my secrets."

I roamed the city, investigating the best of Rio's shoe, purse, and leather stores. Exploring by myself with no guidance necessary amidst territory, I thoroughly understood well. I profess these people damn well know how to make such remarkable leather goods.

Before leaving for Argentina, I spent the first day of the year purchasing 12 pairs of shoes. That happened. I swear on the Christ Redeemer Statue, it did. Naturally, I was mortified, ashamed, and embarrassed of myself. Shame on me yet again, for I was weak. I let my addiction control me. I totally fell off the shoe wagon! I felt dishonored and degraded, and I shall never do it again. Oh, bull... I will totally do it again and again. I bought the shoes in Rio, and I was taking um back home, with me, when I left! I rationalized effortlessly they would bring me luck, making it a *Shoo-in* (shoe-in) for a perfect year. Give me a break. I had to justify buying 12 pairs of shoes on one shopping spree somehow. And a very thrilling *Shoe-Year,* to me!

With my insane Christmas and New Year's Eve experiences behind me, I would now only worry & fear Valentine's Day!

CHAPTER 13

Don't Cry for Me Argentina
EVITA PERÓN WAS NOBODY'S FOOL AND PROBABLY HAD IT RIGHT ALL ALONG!

Bright and early on the 2nd day of January, feeling fresh as a blossomed daisy, I arrived in Buenos Aires, Argentina. A city I've always dreamed of visiting. It's no wonder why I was happy, overly zealous, and eager as a child, anticipating the first day of a new school year. I was sent to this lively, energetic city on an assignment to write several stories. Featuring the legendary Tango, Evita's gravesite and tomb, the reign of the Perón's, and the mansion they shared together. To be more accurate, it should be branded as a palace, rather than a measly mansion. 'La Casa Rosada' is the elaborate executive estate and the Office of the President of Argentina. The palatial mansion is better known formally as, 'Casa de Gobierno.'

Before noon, after getting my second wind from a hearty late breakfast, I enthusiastically strolled about Buenos Aires. Discovering a new, electrifying city solo is my favorite way to appreciate its pulse and vibrancy. My objective, as usual, is to explore while getting as lost as possible. This always seems to work out perfectly. It's awesome how I typically uncover amazing things I would never have found by following maps, advice, or recommendations. Once I managed to get good and lost, I stopped at a quaint café for a latte with extra foam and a bowl of ice cream smothered with fresh fruit. My opinion and unwavering solid guidance on traveling is to "Eat your way nonstop through a country!" The weight you gain can be lost, but those tasty memories will remain with you forever. The different foods representing each country are distinct and will fervently enhance your travels. I adore sitting outside in the middle of an open square of a city where I have never been before. I find it captivating to watch the busy rush of the locals. It's fascinating to observe that even though people are essentially all the same, we are also quite different. We're each diverse in our styles, behaviors, and customs.

Next on my schedule that afternoon, was to tour the Perón Mansion, Casa Rosada, where Evita and Juan lived. María Eva Duarte de Perón, was the second wife of the Argentine President. There is still much mystery and controversy about Eva's intentions, piety, devotion, and agenda, towards Juan and the people of Argentina. The one thing you can continually count on in life is that people will always judge each other harshly and doubt the sincerity of others. Whether deserved or not.

I stood on the balcony where Eva and Juan raised up their arms and spoke to their troubled citizens. It was surreal having had the unique opportunity to stand in Eva's footsteps on this historic balcony. Sadly, for me, the guards didn't find it funny in the least when I started singing in full voice, "Don't cry for me Argentina!" Tough crowd! Tough crowd!

Eva served as the First Lady of Argentina from 1946 until her untimely death in 1952. Some judged Evita quite severely and strongly disapproved of her because of her scandalous social-climbing beginnings and tainted reputation. Come on, haters, like you're so flawless? "Then, let he who is without sin among you be the first to throw a stone at her."

I say, so what if she slept her way to the top? Allegedly! What famous person or movie star hasn't? Allegedly! Besides, being a commoner herself, Eva understood the needs, hopes, and dreams of the Argentinian people. Allegedly! No matter her reputation, she is admired and loved in Argentina to this day. Her picture hangs everywhere in the city. It was fascinating to learn the younger generation has a more critical, condemning eye toward the first lady. "I guess it takes one to know one?"

Displayed throughout the mansion were selections of her most famous clothes, shoes, and hats. Eva rocked fashion like no one else in her day! Then came Jacqueline Kennedy, Princess Diana, and Princess Kate of England. Scattered about in the rooms of the grand palace are exhibitions of very private, personal, and loving photographs of the dynamic duo.

I know you're wondering. And the answer is yes! I was wearing a pair of my brand-new Brazilian leather shoes that had an adorable bow with a rhinestone centered in the middle. Evita would have loved them.

After my unappreciated, though epic singing performance on the balcony of Casa Rosada, I jumped on the hop-on-hop-off bus. After touring the sights of this cultural city, frozen in time, I stopped to enjoy a glass of wine, a café con leche, and a Rogel, a famous Argentinian dessert.

That evening, following my all-day walkabout, I hailed a taxi to the tourist district of La Boca. This was my favorite spot in Buenos Aires. While exceedingly touristy, it is also flamboyantly colorful, unspoiled, and charming. I dined at this adorable little café called Tango. Apparently, not a particularly unique name for a restaurant in Argentina. I consumed a variety of Asado dishes with chimichurri sauce, and Alfajores for dessert. It was divine sipping the superb local wine called 33, whilst dining outside as a full moon lit up the sky. Obviously, the best part of the evening was enjoying the hundreds of spectacularly gorgeous, amazingly built, yummy Latin men strutting around La Boca. Unashamed, I felt the lust in my eyes as they *lit me up,* walking by with their slicked-back hair, impossibly tight clothes, and their tiny narrow waists. Clearly, this town brings to the world incredibly sexy, luscious-looking men. My self-confidence soared high up in the clouds being hit on, by their flirtatious innuendos and erotic, steamy looks. Throughout the night I enjoyed watching these exquisite creatures strutting about. My cheeks brought blushing, to a whole new level of red.

If that wasn't fantastic enough, (and hell yeah, it was) that evening I had the good fortune of watching several talented and respected tango dancers. Authentic tango artists are passionate and serious as they prance about the stage. Judging by the erotic expressions the couples exchange while dancing, you'd think they were madly in love and having wild sex during breaks. Truth be told, for them it's but another day at the office.

The following morning, after a wonderful night of slumber, Juan Pablo, an esteemed, well-known professional Argentinian Tango Dancer, picked me up in front of the Alvear Palace Hotel, where I was staying. It is important to know that when you pronounce Juan, in Argentina, it is said like... *"HWwwhan!"* It is totally necessary to forcefully blow out air from your mouth with the *HWwwwwhaaa.* There you go! *HWwwwwhan...*

Once again, my reliable editor, Angela, set me up with *HWwwhan,* my guide, and the featured tango dancer for my story. I was thrown way off guard when I first met this dazzling, *stud-tango-ular man*. The moment I laid eyes on him, I vehemently warned myself, *"Mollie, do not gush. Do not gush!* You're a successful, professional American journalist, darn it! Be cool… Do not gush! Pull yourself together! I mean it. *Do Not Gush!"*

Dammit, I gushed! I gushed big time. In fact, my nipples got hard just staring into his penetrating big brown eyes while dripping my *sticky-icky, flush-and-gush* all over him. Worse yet, I was coquettish, demure, and girly like an 11-year-old. For sure, *so not cool.* Ipso facto, I swooned! *I Swooned, people!* Looking back, I might have even cooed? Like a lot. Who the fuck swoons and coos? Pathetic, I thought I was better than this.

Luckily, I don't really think he noticed or picked up on it. Oh, shit. So uncouth. Who am I kidding? He noticed and was smiling that *George 'cocky' Clooney,* "I know you think I'm fabulous," smirk. If that wasn't irresistible enough for me to have to deal with, he wore that, *Robert Pattinson, Ryan Gosling,* Zac Efron tantalizing, enticing grin implying, "I totally get that you think I am beyond hot!" Mercy, this felt like a sexual takeover. Still, I somehow found the professionalism and fortitude to pull it together quickly. At least I thought I did. But probably not. Granted, I'm a professional. But after all, I'm still a girl and human!

Following our warm "Hello, nice to meet you" greetings, Juan took me on a tour of the premier Tango Nightclubs. The highlight for me was Carlos Gardel, a sophisticated dinner and tango club. This is undeniably *the must, go-to, tango,* "It, *spot."* It is also where Juan Pablo dances.

As if casting a movie, *HWwwwhannn,* looked exactly the way you would envision a tango dancer should look. He had jet-black, silky straight hair, combed back with that *"little too much gel look"* goin' on. You could even see the comb lines of perfection. He was around thirty-one but looked twenty-one. His picture-perfect mocha skin gave him a smooth, youthful appearance, making him look years younger than he was. He wore a crisp white, body-hugging shirt, and black skintight pants, which easily confirmed he was very well endowed. *HWwwhannn-na-na-na*, was luminous, built like a god, and wore it proudly, only without the haughty ego! With his unblemished soft skin and chocolate-colored eyes, Juan Pablo is entirely the perfect specimen of a man. He utterly oozes sexuality. Really, someone should be walking behind him with a bucket to collect the drippings. I wanted him in the most "tango-e-ist" way, in every sense of the word! (This is where you should interject a big, long girlish sigh.) He was everything I was looking for and needed in a guy. At least for this assignment. He is luminous "And, cut that's a wrap" movie star gorgeous.

As we worked together throughout the day, Juan explained the history of the dance to me. "When the tango originated, it contained elements from the African community in Buenos Aires, and was primarily influenced both by ancient African rhythms and the music from Europe." He continued, "Although the tango evolved to exemplify the glamour and elegance of high society, with women in lustrous, glitzy evening gowns and men in tux and tails, it began in society's underbelly. It all started in the brothels and low cafes of Buenos Aires at the turn of the century. Originally, the tango dance developed as they acted out the relationship between the prostitute and her pimp. The dance is still relevant today."

Certainly, I visibly recognized *HWwwhhan* was saying more than, "Blah-Blah-Blah." Fortunately, he assumed I was listening to every single word with a deep fascination and interest. Honestly, I should have been for the sake of my article, as well as the security of my job. In my defense, I did hear sounds that signaled English words, as well as complete coherent sentences of vital information. I appreciated everything he was saying was evidently important to my assignment. But *"Ay, Caramba!"* The guy was lightning in a bottle. I couldn't concentrate or comprehend a single sentence. Not even one word. Luckily, he provided all the literature I'd need for the article to take back home with me. To be clear, I was far more interested in his plump cushiony lips, which I presumed were pronouncing pertinent words, but not 100% certain. He was royally getting in and under my skin. Even my breasts stood at attention watching him. Now, feeling hot and horny as I could see his hard, circumcised penis saluting me through his mischievous tight pants. Let the record show. *These reactions were not my fault!* My career & professionalism had no other choice but to escape me. I hope I kept all this under control. But not 100% certain I did.

With him leaking sexuality right before my eyes, I couldn't care less about the tango, unless he was doing it to me, in me, and on me! His face, his hypnotic, penetrating eyes, and his sensuous, kissable mouth mesmerized me. I was spellbound and entranced by his charisma. By this point of the interview, I was mainly content knowing I was performing the illusion of a high-level ethical correspondent. Or, at least, I thought I was. But not 100% certain. As a professional (well, I WAS before I had laid eyes on the alluring, *HWwwhan*) I was reassured knowing I had been recording his dialogue. This guaranteed I had a shot of quoting him correctly in my article. Drifting deeper under his spell, giggling inside, amid my naughty behavior, I thought, "Toto, we're not online *anymore!*"

Escaping my private thoughts and returning to reality, *"HWwwwhan"* continued to speak in a serious, apodictic, confident tone. "The tango's very beginning was a ballet-like dance between two men. Shortly thereafter, the dance became distasteful and offensive, since both men and women had the opportunity to rub their bodies together."

I spoke sarcastically, "I shudder to think! And yes, dance me, Juan!" This was the first time I heard this debonair man laugh out loud. Every move he made, every gesture, his every expression caused me to yearn with an insatiable desire for him. "Mr. Tango Don Juan" controlled me and pulled my strings like a French marionette! I humbly say, in the most refined, ladylike way, that I had no ability to obstruct his powerful force that urged me to want to fuck his brains out! It's not my fault! I am just an innocent puppet. A puppet that wished he'd pull my every string!

Ironically, I wasn't sure if I wanted to kill Angie or thank her for this assignment. Honestly, spending the day with this striking man was personally the real *climax* of this entire assignment. Especially after the "Princess & the Pee, and the Married Marcelo in Rio," fiascos! All in the past week, alone! Regardless, I knew for the first time this whole trip (and unlike before) I desperately wanted to be wet! Very wet, on top of Juan!

Still, I wasn't telling Angie about any of this. With *HWwwhan* still speaking in the background, I wondered what the '*over and under*' was of my winding up in bed with *him! Over or under, either was great with me.*

HWwwhan went on explaining. "As Perón rose to power in 1946, the tango reached the high point of popularity in Argentina. Juan and Evita embraced it unequivocally. The tango became widely fashionable and a matter of national pride under the government of Perón."

I was confident every word he spoke was completely enthralling, and I'd describe it just that way in my story. Pathetically and to be candid, all I heard was, "Johbg, AJpojnegakn, Dflngaklny, Tzxy%$#!*ep, @*)+=, Goaubfoqboebge, Zethroxios, Obgobfbdwt, and Blab-la-la-la Blah, Blab!"

"Mollie, do you understand what I'm saying to you? Do you have any questions? Miss Sloan? Do you hear me? Miss Mollie! Hello?"

"Yes, absolutely, Juan! I understand every historic word." I lied!

I knew right at *"Hello,"* the illustrious Juan (or now, as I lovingly refer to him, HWwwhann) was single and free, unlike Marcelo and Dr. Fabrizio. What's more, I was informed, he planned on remaining that way for life. His gorgeousness was the only reason I wasn't exhausted from listening to all his "Yadda-Yadda riffs, Blah Blah speeches, and rhetoric.

I gathered from our "Nice to meet you" introduction that Juan was a huge womanizer and a relentless player. I liked that about him! The guy was up-front, straightforward, and did it so well. He was silver-tongued and silky smooth, like a baby's tush. He possessed an abundance of erotic, exquisite panache, arousing every feminine sensation in my craving body.

Having the opportunity of spending the entire day with Mr. Tango, I gathered he was a "no-complications, no strings attached, (except for the ones he had controlling me) and a no-drama guy." He most definitely had me wanting to be all in. Very in! For HWwwhan was a delectable hunk of sweet sexiness. His *formula of sweet* had no calories. A total "win-win."

I knew the instant he introduced himself to me, I was his for the taking. And he knew it too. If nothing else, I wanted to experience him as my own personal Argentinean erotic souvenir and tango memento.

"Jello, Mollie, I'm *HWwwwwhan!*" (Blowing on me with all his

W's.) Come on. Understand. People, I haven't had sex in like... Forever! Even longer than that for great sex! The last time was with the mean and only nice in-bed guy, and before that Bam-Bam. So, have a heart. I was looking through horny-colored glasses for a tale as old as time. And this tango dancer was unquestionably a prelude to a humongous orgasm!

That night, I had the honor of seeing Juan's tango show at Carlos Gardel. I observed, with awe, the suave, impeccable, "Studtacular, *HWwwhan.*" Awe was hardly the correct word for what I was thinking, but adequate for now. How astonishing and beautiful he was to watch. His seductive moves were precise, artistic, graceful, and fastidiously perfect, like a sensual swan. I couldn't take my eyes off him and his hunky, entrancing, drool-worthy handsomeness. It appeared there was an entire audience of adoring women who yearned and lusted for him as well. It seemed I was among a long line of worshipping ladies (And Men!) who longed and hungered to be with him. I had a big girl crush going on here. I barely even noticed he was dancing the tango until I shamefully reminded myself this was half the reason for my being here. Stop gushing, Mollie!

After the show and all our business had been completed, we went out for a typical Argentine late dinner and a nightcap. While we dined, the only thing going through my mind was, "Tango man is going down!" And preferably on me! I had to be with him! If only for the fact I wanted to call out his Latin-as-hell name with all the extra H's and W's during sex.

"Harder, Juan Pablo. Give it to me, Juan Pablo! Faster, Juan Pablo! Don't stop, Juan Pablo! Deeper, Juan Pablo! Slower, Juan Pablo! Yes, yes, and yes, *HwwwHannn* Paaaablooo-*OOOH!*" It was all so very Hollywood Boulevard, XXX. I was desperate for *HWwwwwwwhannnn* Pablo and rapido! I wasn't exactly sure how I would feel about all my inappropriate actions tomorrow. But for tonight, "Wheeeeee! And XXX, ME!"

Yes. Oh, yes! Late that night, what I needed, Mr. Tango gave me great! I got a tango lesson from a pro, and I wasn't even standing on my feet. While flat on my back, he tangoed my ass off and gave me the best *Tang~Gasms"* I have ever had. Talk about hot salsa. I had an itch, and *he* scratched it over, and over, and over again. My dance with Tango-Juan was never-ending, and he never stepped on my toes. He led. I followed.

They say the Argentine Tango dance is fruitful when you are in the heat of desire. When all kinds of emotions are flying, such as passion, lust, anger, and even humor. Indeed, all that and everything else was flying this night, including some sexy, expensive lingerie I bought in Rio. I believe in the "Just in case" and "A Girl Scout is always prepared, book of rules."

Breathless and sweating, as we continued *knocking boots*, I gazed into Juan's eyes, and out of my mouth, unexpectedly, came Darth Vader.

"Obi-Wan has taught you well!"

Apparently confused, he uttered, "HWwwwwwhat?"

"Sorry, never mind, it's a Star Wars thing. Remorseful to have stopped you. Please, please, do tango-on!"

After hours and hours of tango-sex, at last early in the morning, my tango dance card was full. I was so *overcum,* that I desperately wanted to run back to Evita's palace balcony, throw up my arms in front of the guards, and belt out my new hit song, "I Got Tangoed in Argentina!"

Maybe a breaking news story. "This is Mollie Sloan, CUMMING to you live from Argentina. I'm here to report the Tango is an orgasmic dance. I would seriously love to learn to dance the tango, standing up one day. It looks like great fun, whether standing up or lying down."

George Bernard Shaw once said, "Dancing is a vertical expression of a horizontal desire." How very innovative and accurate he was.

I learned from my sexy *HWwwwhann*, in those 24 hours we spent together, that it's true, "We enter this world alone, and we leave it in much the same way. But, in between, there is a whole lot of life. And we should create a whole lot of fabulous, dancing our way through it all.

"And if you're lucky... *You Tango!*"

I learned in Argentina that it fundamentally, and most certainly takes two to tango and to dance it, as well. Therefore, I convey my well-researched, educated hypothesis about men. All of them, no matter what the culture, country, education, background, wonderful, dreadful, good, bad, online, or off, "Men are basically all the same! You just need to find the one who can tango your world with the greatest passion and ease."

The following morning, after the best night's sleep (I haven't slept that well since biology class), I was on my way back home to the good ole USA. I couldn't hide that cheerful, glowing, and peaceful look on my face. You know the, *"I just got tangoed, and had endless tang~gasms by the most stunning dancer in Argentina, look!"* Aha, and everyone saw it, too!

By the way, remember the little brats (I mean the darling children), I was complaining about in the Delta Club in Atlanta? The ones yelling, crying, and screaming with their parents, who think we all want to listen to them? Surprise, surprise! Returning home, I was surrounded on the plane, sitting next to all of them. They were shouting, kicking, and crying for twelve dreadful nonstop hours!

Oh yeah, sure enough, it was obviously karma, and the dreaded Murphy's Law. I just hate that Murphy bastard!

I didn't let them bother me very long, for I had my own special memories of Argentina to bask in. I visualized my spicy affair, listening to the tango playlist Juan made for me, beaming all 6,088 miles to America.

When I arrived home and got into bed, I vividly remembered the erotic moments we spent together and sang out loud one letter at a time, laughing underneath my blanket, "*T-a-n-g-o, T-a-n-g-o, T-a-n-g-o, Juan Pablo was his Name-O!*" **Bingo!**

FYI, my feature articles on Argentina, the Peróns, and the Tango came out better than I even hoped. However, to write my story about the Tango accurately, I undoubtedly required the assistance of my mini recorder, as well as all the literature Juan provided me with. No doubt, he must have to provide a lot of literature to journalists. Alas, realistically, I excluded the very best parts from the story. Like all the "Tang~Gasms!" For those were my secret, personal bonus, tango-twist, and my very own happily ever after memories and erect perks. I adore these "workcations!"

In the end, no matter how hard Angela tried (and boy did she ever), I never discussed anything about HWwwhan or Marcelo with her. I kept it all very hush-hush and on the down low! Although, I did tell her the song, "Don't Cry for Me Argentina" has a whole new meaning to be treasured.

♫ 𝄞

"Don't Cry for Me Juan-gentina, the truth is I never left you.
All through our wild day, my tango existence, I kept my promise,
happy Juan didn't keep his distance!"

And, for the rest of my life, I smile whenever I hear the words... Argentina, Jello, HWwwhat, Juan, Tango, *Tang~gasms*, or *HWwwwwhan!*

HWwwwwhannnn is still exquisite, single, living in Argentina, and happily tangoing his way through the dance floor of life. To this very day, we keep in touch. After all, we have history to answer to...

OMG, in the most delicious Tango-ish way possible...

"I GOT MALED!"

CHAPTER 14

Back Home in the Online Saddle and Starting Over, Yet Again…

THE PLAYAS… AKA, THE PLAYAS

DEGENERATES, LOSERS, PERVERTS, AND POLITICIANS (SORRY, I HAD TO THROW THAT LAST ONE IN!) ALSO MEDICALLY KNOWN AS…

EMAILS FROM: "THE FUCK YOU AND LEAVE YOU, GUYS!"

Home, after multiple *sexual tang-gasms* in Argentina with *HWwwwhan*, (my tango souvenir) I opened my laptop to discover I had been bombarded with oodles of disturbing emails from online guys. How refreshing and wonderful it was escaping them for a few weeks. Finding it difficult to sleep because of the huge time change, I read as many emails as I could stomach. Surprisingly, I had a laugh-fest reading them. I pinky-swear, I couldn't fathom how ignorant these "playa men" are, who send these vulgar and outlandishly disgusting emails. I mean, are they that ignorant to believe this will entice a woman to go out with them (or more) by sending these vile kinds of emails? Does this really work out for them? I was so grateful most of the guys didn't know who I was.

They likely never watch the news. After being shocked and repulsed to my maximum level of disgust, I gladly went to bed. Closing my weary eyes, I decided to deal with this offensive online situation tomorrow. For now, I had my erotic recollections of "*HWwwhan and his sexy, big, hard tango,*" on my mind.

I awoke early to a beautiful Sunday morning. I adore traveling, but I love returning home as well. There's no place like it! I sat outside in my backyard and enjoyed the calm of life while sipping my heavenly coffee, a tablespoon of peanut butter, and a grapefruit for breakfast. Later in the day, after paying my bills, food shopping, and laundry, I jumped on my treadmill and began to tackle those distasteful emails. It was necessary to deal with these repulsive 'Playa' messages and confront them before going back to a very busy workweek ahead. I became so frustrated reading, I switched the speed on my treadmill to the max, and accidentally fell off. Big ouch, there! Meanwhile, after 20 or so of these depraved and ignorant communications, I repeatedly pressed delete, delete, and delete. And that's how I chose to deal with the situation. Let's be real, it's all they deserved! Presto! Problem solved! Relieved, I caught up on the new season of my favorite shows on Netflix, Prime, Hulu, Max, and Apple TV.

Sister daters, luckily, these "playa guys" are easy to spot from the very first email. Just be aware some of them are cunning and deviously skillful. Pay attention, as the sly ones can get past the emails and phone calls, still having you believe they are one of the nice guys! They shrewdly hide who they are till mid-stream on the first date, which is usually around the salad. I say, don't leave. Finish the rest of your dinner. In fact, order another cocktail. If nothing else, you'll be able to laugh while telling your friends about yet another fanciful story. When out on a date, you discover he's an overt "playa guy," activate and heed all your warning alarms. I promise, if you continue to go out with a playa, you will be heading right into the storm of online devastation. Nevertheless, if you like this kind of mental tornado, well then, go have fun with that!

In other related news, and still on "playa topic," let's chat about the new clinical disease some playa guys hide behind called, "*Sexual Addiction Syndrome.*" This medical diagnosis is the *biggest* **cock** *of shit*! Sorry, I meant, "the biggest crock of shit," diagnosed by the medical field in any decade. This newly, "con**cock**ted" ailment is complete gibberish, gobbledygook, nonsense, rubbish, garbage, hogwash, baloney, poppycock, bull, phooey, and hooey even! I do hope you're getting my point.

Speaking scientifically, based on my own "theory of relativity research," this so-called addiction is nothing more than your "typical, horny, married, or committed guy, who simply got caught cheating and needed a flawless, ironclad excuse to save his sexless, boring relationship!" Yeah, Sexual Addiction, I bet? What a farce. What a hoax. This is merely an easy, *get-out-of-monogamy-fee-card* for guys who are just tired of the same monotonous flavor! I.E., the same lady, every day. The same ole, same ole woman, just equals *the Sexual Addiction Syndrome, lies.* Period!

You know who you are! You guys fooling around beneath the bedsheets, with the façade of loyalty and responsibility, while hiding your flimsy obsession. You're so busted. Surely, even you are chuckling out loud right now. Let's be honest for a Tick-Tock, shall we? There is nothing ambiguous about this, *"A-Dick-tion!"* Obviously, this is only transparent bullshit, based on defensive justification and pretext! No guy in the world's history (which includes other planets, in any galaxy) has ever once complained or considered the notion that he suffers from too much sex. I.E., *"Sexual Addiction."*

Never, not ever, nada! Unless he was caught cheating and needed a great lie and a perfect escape clause!

Ladies, listen up! Men typically spend time behind your back frequenting porn sites. Sorry to be the messenger of smutty bad news, but they most likely won't ever stop. Uh-huh and yes, topless strip clubs are part of this horny male behavior as well. (And not just for a bachelor party, either.) It's nothing more than your traditional good ole boy attitude! Assuming he isn't cheating on you with another woman (or man) then just "Let It Go," like the Disney song! I equal this behavior to women using vibrators. Which, essentially, most of the time, is necessary. Going to Chippendales is part of this equation, too. Oh, come on. Seriously! We all have a vibrator and have gone to a male strip club at some point, even if it was just for a girl's night out party! You girls know who you are out there! You know I'm right. To be sure, I can see and hear you snickering.

Anyhow, it's absurd to give any credence to this "*Sexual Addiction Syndrome*," fabrication, as being legitimate. You just know some clinical psychiatrist came up with this ruse for himself and used it to make money off others. I can see it now. Joe Blow, AKA Joe Winston, confiding in his buddy Winthrop at a local pub, over beer, chips, and a football game. (To be read with a British accent, for greater effect.)

"Winthrop, ole chap, I don't know what I am going to do with myself! There is undeniably something dreadfully wrong with me?!?! Dreadfully wrong, I say. I need sex all the time. I desire sex with fat girls, skinny girls, and beautiful girls. But not ugly girls. That's a lie. Them too! Winthrop, my good fellow, I crave sex with brunette girls, blonde girls, and even, by-golly, gee willikers, red-headed girls. I scandalously confess, Winthrop, I want sex with them all! Girls who are black, white, or any color at all! I want sex every day, in every way, and in every position. I want respectful sex, tender sex, and especially very naughty sex. I admit, dear friend, I want the dirty, erotic sex that you only read about in books, with 'Whips and Chains and Masks, *Oh My!*' My loyal mate, I am an appalling, vile, human being. I am an animal, Winthrop. My dear pal, I'm an animal, I say! Woe to me! I'm sick. I am sick and gruesome. What shall I do, Winthrop? Don't just sit there laughing at me! What can I Do?"

"Well, Joe Winston, my dear fucking bloke, Fuck 'Em! Fuck 'Em All. Fuck Um Well, And Fuck Um Hard. You're a guy, my good pal, Joe Blow Winston, and it's totally normal! Just make sure you're a warm, kind gentleman. Thank them afterward, wear a condom, and don't get caught! What you're feeling, dear mate, is natural and common! Joe, my opinion, and humble advice? Enjoy 'em, fuck 'em, be fruitful, and don't multiply!"

"Truly Winthrop? You really don't think I have the dreaded, (Melodramatic pause) *Sexual Addiction Syndrome?*" (*Insert now, a mysterious "dant-dant-dan-dah," and a loud, crashing noise.*)

"What the fuck are you talking about, Willis? I mean Joe Blow Winston. Ah-haaaa, yes, I see it clearly now! I understand entirely. Alas, you were caught cheating on your wife! Ha-Ha-Ha- Ha-Ha! OK then, it's a perfect idea! Go ahead and claim the *Sexual Addiction Syndrome.*"

Yep, caught with your dick in the cookie jar! I say to you busted cheaters, mumbo-jumbo, it's nothing more than a whole farm load of bullshit. All righty, I feel much better now that is out in the open!

Returning to the original point of this chapter

Ladies, sexual red flags are vitally important to observe. If an inappropriate sexual flag is raised, don't continue any further with the playa-creep who raised that flag! Well, unless you are into these kinky boots, kinds of games. In that case, "playa on." Girl, be careful, have a great time, and prosper. Who am I to judge?

I have received hundreds of sexually disgusting emails. As well as the flattering bullshit emails, hoping to get into my pants. "You're very beautiful. I'd love to go out with you." I have heard more than my fair share of "la-di-frickin-da," pushy, horny, white noise from countless online men. I have read and listened to more rhetoric than a politician spews out when running for office. *In an election year!* Very scary!

I want to reiterate. *"You're not alone!"* You are not the only one getting these shocking, filthy emails! To unpack this for you, I've included a handful of these unsettling, **dick**sgraceful messages. Truthfully, I have personally received and endured an infinite number of repulsive, shamefully troubling, and wickedly indecent, X-Files-Alien-creature, lewd emails! Trust me, Winthrop, and Joe Winston. It's horrible.

Sorry for my adjective, hurricane. They are impossible to describe in a word. These vulgar, nasty men prove, "There's no such thing as half crazy!" Verifying once again, when one door closes, we should bolt down the windows! Here's a smattering of sexually inappropriate, insane emails that you, too, will probably receive, prompting you to shake your head. I refer to these moments as *cray-craygasms. Try to Laugh it off and run.*

Note: **These are all authentic, genuine emails I received!**

Double note: Because I didn't feel it necessary to extend an olive branch, I never did respond to any of these savage, uncivilized animals! However, I included what I **would** have said, had I done so, purely for my own fun, entertainment, and mental well-being.

Triple note: As indicated by the endless **highlighting,** none of these men are Rhodes Scholars! *(Or what I assume they might say Roads Collars.)* I left their emails, as sent to me, for your pleasure.

Here is a small but tasty assortment of the hideous emblematic messages that blew my mind the most. I promise, on Louis Vuitton, they're all true!

Warning: These poetic (?) writings may not be suitable for any normal person to read. But go ahead anyway. Enjoy, and have fun.

1. *hi you know how I fell abut you .....I right you's for 3 weks. I did give you my phone numer but you didn't call! as I say I think you look fantastic ....and I will like to no moor a butt you. But if you continue to ignore me like the cunt bitch hore you probly are then just go fuck youself now. Yu CUNT FACE! Michael!*

   Reply: "Aw, Michael, I'm over the moon! What a darling man. But stop. Behold my virgin ears. I wonder, did you finish elementary school? Well, at least you spelled cunt, fuck, bitch, and your name correctly. Mr. Crazy Cakes, you just might need to increase your meds! You know, I can now totally understand the principle behind tarring & feathering, or the stoning of people in the dark ages! Just a suggestion, but it might be a good idea to bring it back. Dude, I'm just thinking out loud, but someone must commit you. I can help with that! OMG, I need some deep-fried Oreos and stat!"

2. *You are beautiful, striking, sexy, sassy and I cents completely grounded in strength, soul, and intelleckt! I would love for us to explore our chemistry together and see where it leads us. I am talking about chemistry, in the bed. I am not looking for love just want to fuck you and I can tell you that in any language. I want to tear apart your pussy! I want to fill you to the brim of your pussy with my come. Does that offend you? If it does, you are not the one for me. Let me know your thoughts? Jr.*

   Reply: *"Yikes, I felt raped just reading this shit! I might even be pregnant! I think that was a bit of emotional terrorism there, Jr. This darling prince among men was so sensitive that he worried about offending me. Ah, now fancy that. Simply precious! Junior, aren't you just a Yankee Doodle Dandy. Mr. you are so far off the beaten track that your 'Little Train That Could' is leaving the station, and I suggest you be on it! Let me say this, all wrapped up in a nice bouquet of thoughts… Go F$&#@K yourself! In every language, do piss off! (Been there, done that.) You are a repulsive lunatic. What can I say, Jr.? It could be a 'me thing,' but I highly doubt it."*

3. *By the way: You look amazing…are yu really as beautiful and youthful as your pix suggest? wow, u have that peter pan gene I guess. I do to In a different way. I have always wanted to have sex with my mother. She is hot. I grew up peaking through her door to see her naked. I loved looking at her huge boobs and hairy pussy. I didn't like at all when she shaved it. She looked like a little girl and that ruined it for me. If we go out please keep your pussy hairy the way I need it. I hope you right me back. Stu*

   Reply: *"Geez, if that isn't a telltale sign of Satin at his best, then I don't know what the devil is! Your email gave me pause to wonder.*

Are there any sane men out there? My response to you is gross and in your dreams. You are a revolting demon. I'd rather have elective dental surgery without Novocaine. By the way, your photo should be hanging on the Post Office's most-wanted list. Your email far exceeds the boundaries of any aspect of normal. You, evil incarnate. Oh Lord, your poor, poor mother!"

4. *Hi gorgeous I hope you like the center of my attention? I will show you unconditional love and care. I'm a big-hearted kind of guy!! so hook me up? What do you look like under your pretty clothes? You look like your breasts are purky. I would love to suck your nipples all the time. Babies are so lucky they get to do that. You look like you have a small vagina. I love that. I want to shove my big hard dick in you. I hope you don't mind it hard. That's the way I like it. No tender fucking for me. I want to ram my cock into you so it hurts.. I want to pinch your nipples till you cry. I want to come all over your pretty face. If you didn't come by the time I did, sorry. Can we go out this weekend? Looking forward to hearing from you sune! Chris*

   Reply: *"Tempting, and as much as I might regret this decision till the end of time.* **NO!** *Your text was as dirty as a petri dish on a bus station's floor of the men's room. Good for you! You've made me never want to meet a man again. You might get some decent play out of this crap of yours with other women, but seriously, it is a big No, with me! Your email is perplexing and disturbingly chilling. Chris, you're a pig. And news flash, the only women with perky breasts are 12 years old. So, don't even think about it! Your letter freaked me out. If this was your goal, you reign victorious. Dude, you're flirting with some real danger here. Chris-Off!"*

   I did my best not to dwell on or pay much attention to his ominous comments. Ladies, these men are real and out there. Lord knows it could be your gardener, mailman, or perhaps even your senator or governor!

5. *hi gorgeous, what u doing? I'mJurking off loocing at your pitchers online. Cum is everywhere! I do it everyday. An other think, i suck on alott of lollypops. I gues i was not weened off moms brest write? Smith*

    Reply: *"**And Scene!** Dear Lord, not even in an X-Rated porno film! And, apparently, that's when the wheels fell off my wagon. I'm so totally grossed out and horrified!!!! You are a clown show, all by yourself. I feel like I need to take a shower! Smith, going out with you would be like a chicken, going out with Colonel Sanders! You're a conduit to hell and the socially amoral. Help, 911! Wait. Wait, a second. Is this my EX-boyfriend?"*

6. *Hi, I can cure you. relly cure you. havving sex with one spoon full of coKEaine makes the cumm go down. Better in the rane. You don no hu i thik i am. Leds du a 3sum! Pip*

    Reply: *I am now convinced I need to kiss many, many more frogs. "Hey, Pip, 3sum? You can't even spell it. How can you do it?" Pip surely has restless asshole syndrome! Oh, and BTW, why don't sexual perverts know how to spell? Why? Just wondering. Oh, the humanity! Pip, "i no hu u r!"*

    People, I'm not making up this stupidly.
    These grammatically incorrect, insane, scary, emails are all
    authentic. I have reported and blocked so many guys.
    Each one was more offensive than the next!

7. *hi I am Gus, I am a Pilot for a major airline. You are very pretty and have beautiful legs. I noticed you're shoes too. I would love two see your pussy willow! I like really high pumps. I like studs, on them.*

Red very high heels are my favorite. If we hook up, I wood want you to leave them on when we have sex. I would like you to scratch my ass or whatever you want to with the heels. Getting aroused now, I will stop. Talk soon I hope.

Reply: *"What? I mean whaaaaat? Gus, scratch this. Not on your life. The only heel you need is the one that can heal you." With my ears clogged with rage, "I pray you are never, ever the pilot on any of my flights. Not even flying my kite. Take off Ace and fly away into the void. Word out!"*

8. *Hey sweetie heart ya wanna go out w me? I am 89 yers old. Gotta say you are a beautiful woman but I think I am beyond your age range - darn! But I assure you I can have sex with you all night long. I take Viagra. It works great. I know you young girls want multiple cums and I can do that for you even though I am much older. I will have to stop in betwen going down on you and fuking you? I like you youngr ones cause I don't like the old lady skin, its not nice the way it just hangs bad when they fuk on me. Thir pussys look old and ugly to. Gimmie a chance. You wont be sorry. thinking of you with a big fat comey hard on. Sidney*

Reply: *"I've lost my will to live. Your Honor, may it please the court? I seek the death penalty here! Sidney, the crotchety old man, has seriously lived long enough. Hell, can I at least make a citizen's arrest, your Honor?*

I really need to believe the Constitution is on my side here, Judge!"
What can I say? Vomit! No… Really! Vomit! "So, Sid, thank you for your enchanting offer, and, as enticing as it might be to some, I'd rather be a prostitute in a nursing home!"
The funny thing about Viagra is it's mostly for old guys. Here's

the dilemma. What the hell can they do with a 4-hour erection when these old farts finish in 3 minutes or less, then fall asleep? I guess perhaps you could hold up a tent with it! Great, if you're camping. I'm so grossed out!

9. *I'd like to scare you and bite you! What are you doing in this site full.of.sharks?;) Sew you know, I will fix all the shit u need me to fix for you for a sex trade. but I mean dirty, XXX-rated, vulare sex.No what I mean. Whadaya think? Fuck me and I will fix for you. Doug*

   Reply: *"Mr. Fix-it, aren't you the sweet talker, and don't you just make my little girlish romantic head swoon? I spy with my little eyes a sicko! Doug, do you truly believe saber-rattling a girl is a great way to catch her? Ah, yes, you also added the tempting Quid pro quo! I'd rather have my entire car keyed than be with you. Your email was more than a little out of line, even for online dating, don't cha think? Oh, and please Doug, don't stay in touch. Do you see me rapidly swimming away from you?"*

10. *I have been searching. I lived for a year in London looking for you, but I couldn't find you. I travelled to America about 30 times over 20 years looking for you, where were you? I ran with the bulls in Pamplona like a super action adventurer looking for you. I hate bullfighting but I did it to find you! I thought I found you there, but you ran off with some arrogant yappie South Africa bloke. I was in involved in the rescue of 36 False KillerWhales at Cape Leeuwin, and whilst I loved the experience, I was looking for you. My heart has been empty, searching, hollow, searching, fragile, searching... It's you? I want to show you sex in every sick Jacked Up Hideous way. I want to do things that you don't want to do. I want to have scary, painful sex with you. I want you to cry and be afraid! I know you*

want it. You know you want it. I know you want me to. You know
you want me. Fuck me baby. Mr. Jones

Reply: *"Wow, Mr. Jones, you can't back up from that! You are as*
charming as a monster in a scary movie. Parish the repulsive thought.
You are a mindless, half-witted lamebrain animal! You're a wrenched
creep and a corpulent fuck. Not for all the money in a movie star's
bank account. Hell, No! In line with F&%@K Off! Wait, are you the
crazy guy who flew over the cuckoo's nest? Is this all because your
parents wanted a girl?"

Holy cow. Reading these emails made me want to hide behind a terrifying mask of denial. Because I twigged the reality of this horror all too well, I can't go on with this chapter. I'm disgusted! Please, just gag me with whatever you have handy. By The Way, my poor trustworthy laptop spellchecker quit and threw in the towel from these illiterate emails.

Furthermore, I want to apologize to all the holy cows, reading…

I say to these awful goons, "Shame on all of you evil-minded little perves! You need to contemplate the error of your repulsive ways. I must ask, where were your parents when you were growing up?" I'd pair that with one of my scornful sweeping hand gestures. In closing this sickening chapter, if only these devils wrote their emails from the slammer, I'd feel so much better right now. There should be an online dating prison.

I tried to wipe away the sick feeling I felt after reading those emails. However, I learned all too quickly that I couldn't put the genie back in the bottle. To help erase those appalling thoughts (you, too, will experience), I binge-watched every one of my favorite romantic movies and basked in the beautiful artistic quotes, to cleanse my palate from the vulgarity of the Looney-Tunes men emailing me! Sort of like an intermezzo frozen sorbet, in a fancy restaurant, does. I needed the film writer's tender words to help me believe in love again. As clichéd and corny as they are, romantic movie quotes help bring optimism and hope that passion and love still exist in the world. Men, pay close attention and don't roll your eyes. The wonderful, dreamy quotes in films are the types of messages women long for and crave to hear. So, bring it!

Although sentiments of passion and romance share a touch of the *overkill* factor, they are real! They are found capsulated in the hearts of genuine love. Both men and women could learn a few things from silly movie lines. Forget about the 'Playa's,' people, and their bogus *Sexual-Addiction Syndrome!* True love is out there and waiting with open arms. So, look for the love within, then open your heart and believe.

CHAPTER 15

Hold Everything, Dammit!

MEN, AFTER MUCH CONSIDERATION... CLASS IS NOW IN SESSION! DAMMIT!

After peeking through the latest herd of unsettling, perverse emails, I was completely dumbfounded. How could men think it's fine to write women in this obscene, disrespectful, crude way? Aren't they aware it is offensive and wrong? Even if they were raised in a forest by wolves, it's still **not** ok!

I sat in my office for the longest time, thinking about these men while staring into space. The more I thought, the more confused and aggravated I became. After being caught in a "blonde vortex," I decided there was only one possible conclusion. Alas, I felt the absolute need to teach an online dating course for men. *Hence, Chapter 15!!!!!!*

To be clear, I was downright troubled and disturbingly burdened by having this need. Not to mention riled up, incensed, and outraged having come to this titanic conclusion. Seriously, you men out there have *no idea what the hell you are doing!* How is this possible in the modern-day world? I promise every single one of you guys (If you're still reading, *and, **aw-shucks, thanks!***) that you will never connect with your *Wife-Fi* like this. The tactless way you're logging on is forcing her to log right off! Consequently, leaving you continuously *Wife-Fi-less,* with no connection, input, hot spot, and no giga*byte,* yet again.

This unimaginable situation gets my Irish up. Which is blarney, as I have no Irish heritage. There is not a drop of Irish blood in my entire family bloodline. Hell, I don't even drink Irish coffee! Sorry, but you men out there don't understand women or have the foggiest clue what we need or want. You're doing everything wrong. (Excuse me, Guys, are you still there? Oh, awesome, good, you stayed!) Moving on, it appears most of you don't comprehend the most banal, ordinary things about courting.

Forgive me, but this is outrageous, even for the most naïve, inexperienced men. What's wrong with you? Are you high when you write these sorts of emails? Do you hate your mother? Are you afraid of women? I don't mean to be unkind. I am only trying to make some sense of your awful, contemptible communications. Somebody needs to help those clueless men who are dangling somewhere in the abyss of love. Someone needs to guide you, and I don't mean your ignorant, doofus buddies while sharing a drunken *"bropocalypse"* night out, either. They know less than you do about women and romance. If that's at all likely. So, guess what? I became obsessed with trying to break this ignorant cycle of ill-informed men. Even with an already full plate, I'm going to step up to your plate and help you. Willy-nilly, I had to get involved, because honestly, I can't deal with it anymore. And neither can the rest of the girls on these sites. I fear my reasons for this decision might be slightly selfish.

I must ask, why are you guys so ignorant about love, wooing, and romancing a lady, or women in general? It's impossible for me to comprehend. Moreover, why are you so blind and incapable concerning everything necessary to execute on a dating site? I'm referring to, (among everything else) your ghastly pictures, ridiculous, poorly written high-schoolish profiles, your 1st offensive letters of contact, dreadful questions, and your inappropriate, disgusting sexual responses and interrogations.

I hate sounding like a nasty woman, (I really do! Ish!) but you leave me no other choice. I have too much gumption, and this topic drives me to the point of being possessed. I mean possessed, like the girl from the films, "The Ring!" or "The Conjuring!" It was obvious someone had to get involved. Little did I know as I began this reckless online charade, it would be me. It became clear I'd be safer in The Ring or The Conjuring.

"**OK, men**, *I'm here to cheer you on. Besides all that you are doing incorrectly,* you're doing just great!? *I'm not trying to insult, hurt, or put you down. I'm trying to bring you some knowledge and along the way possibly make you laugh. Still, stay away from the light & be afraid!*"

CLASS IS NOW IN SESSION!

To make it feasible to guide you men, I first needed to overcome my, "Once upon a mentally, emotionally, physically, and I can't accept all this lame, ignorant attitude" anymore. But I overcame it. Guys, pay close attention, reboot your minds, and let's do this, shall we? Listen up.

Posting Your Pictures:

I will start with the worst (And I do mean the worst.) of your problems. But make no mistake, not the only one! Seriously, good God, men. Really? Really! *No, really!* It never ceases to amaze me just how truly awful the pictures you choose to put up on your profile are.

What's up with that? Can't you see for yourself just how bad and absurd they are? For Pete's sake (and yours), I beg you with all my heart that you only post **"Recent Up to Date"** photos of yourself! Let me be more specific. *"Current, Present-Day, Up-To-The-Minute, New, Now, Today, photographs of you, that actually look like you!"* Allow Me to Repeat, "Photos Taken... **Now, Now, Now!!!!!!!!!!!!!!!!!!"** BTW, don't try using all those exclamation points on your own. I'm a trained professional. It could be dangerous, especially for grammar students. *We don't* want to see any photos you took back in high school, college, or those ten-year-old vacation photos with your kids, or without them, for that matter.

Please, no photos with hands on your face or chin. Don't cross your arms hoping to look more buff. Go on and work out for that look. If you have fantastic muscles, great, we'll see them when it's time. Just so you understand, *it's what we see first that forms our impression of you.* Therefore, don't look like a psychopath or a serial killer by making crazy faces. It's just weird. And for the love of God, don't act like you're drunk in your photos while crouching over a beer. We won't get to your profile if we see creepy pictures. That's an absolute guarantee. Wouldn't you feel the same way seeing bizarre photos of women? You have a two-second window to impress a girl with your photos before she clicks next and goes on to another guy. Two seconds, and that is if she is slow on her laptop.

For your information!

1. No one is interested in seeing your stuffy first business or corporate photos, childhood photos, or any photos where you are like, twelve months old. No, I promise. We aren't! Your mother will show us those darling photos of you one rainy day when it's appropriate. Don't cheat your mom like that. She lives to show

off your childhood and baby photos. We don't want to see any pictures of you, shot more than a year ago, max!

2. Don't post a photo that shows you thirty pounds lighter or heavier than you presently are. This is a big No, and it will immediately turn, us girls off when we meet you for deceiving us. Just be honest with your photos. What we see is what we expect to get! It's irrelevant to us that you just got back from a 3-week cruise and gained 50 pounds. On the contrary, you should also know we really don't care that you were sick, or in a coma and lost 40 pounds. In either case, lose the weight, gain the weight, or change the deceptive photos. I'm striving to be upfront here because it is true.

3. Don't put up photos wearing a hat, a cap, or any other head covering in every photo you post. It just screams that you are bald or balding. It's so obvious you're hiding something under there. Just show us candidly who you are "Now!" After all, lots of women like bald men. Ergo, you could be cheating yourself by hiding under the covers. My hats off to you!

4. When shooting your photos, do attempt to look your best wearing nice attire. By that, I don't mean an old, oversized worn-out sweatshirt, baggy jeans with holes, and a backward baseball cap covering perhaps, your baldhead? Show your best look. If you feel that is your best look, then I must interject, "Are you OK, man?" Remember, you have *2 SECONDS!*

5. Don't put up a selfie photo. I repeat, don't put up a selfie! It makes you come off looking lonely as if no one would take a photo for you.

6. On that note, don't take any photos pointing your camera at a mirror, capturing your reflection to get the shot. You must know one person in the entire world you can get to snap a friggin' photo for you. This type of image sadly tells us you don't have a single friend to help you out. Which, in turn, could explain why you are still single. I think it's fair to say, this is not aerospace engineering, people. Get over it! Ask a restaurant server, a bartender, the person at Starbucks making your Double Chocolaty-Chip Crème Frappuccino, or a stranger walking by if you need to. These photos look extremely asinine. Particularly the ones you aim at in the bathroom mirror! "Just, don't!" I mean it. Jeez, why do I even have to explain this?

7. Don't even think about posting any type of photo displaying beautiful scenery instead of your own picture. Why do all you men do this? Hello, you're not even in the photo! We are looking for a man, not a mountain. If we wanted a scenic photo, we would Google it. No matter how much you honestly believe that you look like a sunset over the ocean, snow-capped mountains in Switzerland, rainbows in the desert, a sunrise over the Himalayan Mountains, or any scenery whatsoever, and so forth… Well, take my word for it, **Ya Don't**! It basically makes it clear to prospective women searching online that you don't think you're attractive and want to post something that is. Sweet Baby Jesus… just don't!

8. **Do not** post a picture posing with your mom, father, your beloved children, anyone else's children, grandparents, siblings, or any other family member, including grandkids. Moreover, don't post photos of your dogs, cats, or any other pets. Also, fair to say, don't post photos of you on a sheep, a donkey, a horse, a water buffalo, or on any other animal, whether it is yours or not. We

don't care about any of this at the picking stage. The beginning of the online process is very much like America's Got Talent. Women are weeding out the bad ones! Since we are not going to date any of the above animals or people, we only want to see a clear and recent photo of you at this phase of the process. Photograph yourself, your face, your body, your eyes, and your smile. Try to limit hats and glasses.

Post a photo of little ole you! Seeing you on a dolphin, an elephant, a camel, a giraffe, or with another person, I can assure you, will not make us want you more. It won't win you any bonus points, to be certain. We might possibly even choose the elephant over you, and assuredly the giraffe. Here is another one of my photo pet peeves. Don't post a photo of your ex-wife, lover, or girlfriend. Especially one where your arm has been chopped off at the shoulder. Your arm that once had lovingly been draped around her. Trust me, you're not fooling anyone. This in toto is laughable, tacky, and all-around stupid.

9. Don't post photos with other guys in them. Good Lord, how the hell are women looking online supposed to know which one you are? Why the F%&@#K, do you men do this? And when we find out which one is you, we will probably like the younger, cuter-looking, fun guy in the photo much better than you. We might even opt for the camel. What makes you guys think putting friends in your photos, who are far better looking than you, will somehow make us want you more? Or that you'll appear far better looking than them by comparison. These buddy pictures are not too slick of an executive decision. Unless, perhaps, you're trying to hook those guys up. That's my opinion, whether you agree with me or not.

10. Don't put up photos of just your eyeball, your nose, a hand, a leg, or any other body part. We are looking for the total package here. Don't try to act all mysterious in your photos because it only makes you look wacky. Don't post a photo of you sucking on an olive, a chicken wing, a peach pit, an ice cream cone, or any other food item, especially a cherry. This is just gross, tasteless, and disgusting. Do you really think this is your best look? Hence, any woman who responds to this sort of photo deserves you! If your goal is to be clever, then, dammit, *just put up a great shot of yourself, sporting a brilliant smile on your profile.* Done!

11. Do not post photos doing any activity or sport where one can't easily see your face because it was taken a mile away. Dude, just jot down the sport you love and enjoy so much in your profile, under *sports and hobbies.* Reviewing photos without being able to see your face because you are playing tennis, scuba diving, kayaking, horseback riding, skiing, or whatever, isn't going to wow us unless you are Roger Federer, Bode Miller, or Bill Shoemaker. Don't put up shots holding a mug, a rake, a vacuum cleaner, awards, a bird, a turtle, a dead fish, your bowling trophies, a football, a taxidermy moose head, or any other random item. Don't post a picture of your car, boat, motorcycle, bike, house, and so forth that you aren't in! We are looking for a man, not a moose head. UGH! Remember to leave your sunglasses off in at least one photo. We want to see your eyes! They are the windows to the soul. I get that you guys think you look rock-star cool in your shades. Regardless, we need to see your eyes. Good grief, you are not Tom Cruise or Johnny Depp incognito, hiding from the paparazzi or the stalkarazzi! *Leave um off.*

12. Don't post a photo where you used to have facial hair and now you don't. Or vice versa. Again, show us who you are **now!** Understand we are not interested in what you looked like 10 years ago. Did you notice *"Now"* is the running theme here with photos? I really need to talk to your moms!

13. Don't, and I mean don't, post photos where you are basically naked. Or your muscleman photos in which you are mostly nude. It's a bad start, and a fundamental rule, especially if you don't have an amazing body. And even if you do, avoid it. Show a little mystery and control. Keep your clothes on. We'll find out about your body you feel is, oh so perfect, when we're ready. This goes under too much information and is usually unwanted. That's the naked truth! Well, unless you are Chris Hemsworth, Channing Tatum, or a young Hugh Jackman. Then, of course, rip um off!

14. Now, for another one of my photo gripes, if not, **one of my biggest grievances of them all**…

    Do not, and I cannot stress this enough, put up photos where in the first one you look great, and then it goes downhill with each picture that follows. I can't tell you how many of you men out there do this. If you only have one good photo, then, shit, dammit, *put up one good photo!* We don't want to see the bad ones. Why do you think we would? This photo scenario drives me bonkers. The smart girls look at the last photo first as it saves time. Men, listen up. Allow me to illustrate what goes on in our female heads looking at your photos, starting with the good photos.

    "Wow, not bad" or… "Awesome, he's actually cute!"

    Followed by your further horrible pictures where we gasp, blurting out, "Ewe, gross, oh fuck no, who's this guy, hell no, and spare me, No!"

Then laughing as the photos continue, "Ugly, barf, fugly, fucking ugly," and then the inevitable "OMG, I'd rather die. No can do! Next!"

Honestly, I'm trying to explain to you guys that we girls turn into a fusion of Simon Cowell, Gordon Ramsey, Bruno Tonioli, Tyra Banks, Michael Kors, and Heidi Klum shouting, "You're out" and "Auf Wiedersehen," in unison! What I'm saying here, guys, is you foolishly let the genie out of the bottle after one bad photo. Before you even start, you've lost. *Warning.* "Make certain, however, that the one good picture really looks like you. ***Now!***" So, if you're wondering, why you don't get dates, or they turn out badly? This right here is why! Man, I can't even!

15. Caution! If you don't put your pictures up, you're not fooling anyone! It sends up a red flag, which only means one of three things...
    a. You are married, which makes you an asshole for even being on a dating site. Stop it and go home to your wife, Mr. Sexual Ad**dick**tion!
    b. You think you're so ugly you didn't want to put your photo up.
    c. You are currently in a relationship, and you don't want her to know you're still online, dating others. Which also makes you a dishonest dick. Just break up, or work it out with your girlfriend, or whoever!

You must be mindful. Most of the time, no one responds to the 'no-photo people.' Let's be honest, would you? There isn't a get-out-of-photo-jail-free-card for not posting photos. "I see you, but you can't see me" is an unfair scenario that will leave you empty-handed and dateless.

YOUR PROFILE

Please, Lord, *help me!* Watching you single guys with every online task, including writing your profiles, is like watching an old man parallel park his inner thoughts for two hours. It's clear that you want to meet the challenge and *'run with the bulls.' But guys*, you're running in the *Wrong Direction!* Your inner light should coruscate like a bright, shiny diamond.

It is essential to stand out with your own personality, wit, kindness, and intelligence. Though you may find it difficult to boast about yourself, it's essential to put great effort into writing your profile with confidence to meet with success. Glass ceilings are like a barrier, just as finding love online is a huge barrier. But glass ceilings are meant to be broken, and your doubts about finding love need to be shattered. Believe that you are a bright star, and don't forget to shine. A candid, unique, fun profile, filled with a dazzling personality, is key to victory. Therefore, don't take this task lightly. Here are a few suggestions that hopefully will lead you running in the right direction, like Saint San Fermin running with his bulls.

And do Be Careful with any of Your Bullshit, Alternative Facts!

1. To begin, sorry to burst your bubble, but grammar and spelling count here, guys. Aha, I can clearly hear you moaning from here. It's not a test, but since we don't know you from Adam, this will be the first sign of your education, intelligence, or lack thereof. And BTW, who is this Adam guy?

2. Don't lie about your age, but if you do (and you most likely will), no more than 5 years. Honestly, any more than that won't be forgiven.

3. Don't be afraid to write precisely what you are looking for in a mate. Straightforward honesty will work best here. Even though your many requirements may seem arrogant to the reader, you are better off putting it all out there from the start. You will gain respect from the right person, or an eye-rolling, moving on, from the wrong person. Explain all the things you seek, want, and need in a partner. Present your desires with finesse, and don't be rude or vulgar. It's best for a potential candidate to be aware upfront of what you require and hope for, rather than beating around the bush, so to speak. This scenario only wastes time and energy for you both.

4. Don't lie about your height, weight, your job, or your salary. You can't hide the truth forever and to lie about these things will only make a girl resent you for it later. (FYI, she shouldn't ask about your salary. It's rude!)

5. When writing your profile, be amusing, creative, and don't compose the ordinary gibberish every guy online writes. Be imaginative, original, and clever. Just be yourself! Don't babble on in your profile or emails about your woes, problems with your mom, siblings, your kids, your exes, how you hate your job, and all your other baggage. Especially when you meet.

    Quite frankly, we really don't care about all that nonsense at this point. Go to a therapist for that shit. Ask yourself, do I want to read or hear all that drama about a girl I've only seen online and haven't even known for ten minutes? Exactly. Zip it. Keep your baggage in the vault.

6. This next one is a biggie. Don't drone on, and on, and on about your ex being a bipolar bitch. Don't put her down or discuss how

much money she stole from you. Too much info and besides, we really don't want to know, anyway. (At least not yet and perhaps never.) This topic includes how the horrible woman (Never use the notorious "C-U-Next Tuesday" word. *Though tempting*) turned your kids and friends against you. It only makes you look bad and turns women off. Be positive and optimistic. Online girls are your future, not your past! Turn the page and move on to a fresh start.

7. Don't write anything risqué, sexual, how big your penis is, or boast about what a fabulous lover you are. Unless, however, this is the sort of site you are on. Not a big turn-on. Besides, if you had to brag about it, then it's undoubtedly false, untruthful, all talk, and no action. Fake News!

8. Don't come off sounding insecure, bitter, or unhappy. It is a huge downer. Don't be negative! I repeat, don't be negative. There is enough negativity in the world already. We don't want or need you to add more stress, drama, or extra problems to our lives. That's a hard, no thanks.

9. Try your best not to be braggadocious by stating things in your profile such as, "Hey ladies, I'm the bomb!" By the way, no one says, "the bomb" anymore, other than a real one. And for sure, never say that out loud at an airport, or anywhere else! Plus, you most assuredly aren't the bomb, or you wouldn't be single. Mr. La Bomba, let a woman be the one to tell you how wonderful you are. Humble is a good thing and the new black!

10. I suggest after finishing your profile and feeling confident in what you wrote, read it out loud a few times. Then ask yourself, "Would I want to go out with this person?" If not, fix it till you'd say yes. But be honest.

11. Listen to me well. When you start contacting women, if they don't answer you right away, don't immediately write a second, or worse yet, a nasty letter. Give her a chance to return your email. Girls are busy out there, juggling the world on their shoulders. And mind you, for a lot less money (for doing the same job) than what men earn. Just saying!

If she doesn't answer by your fourth email (Which should take about a month. And to be truthful, you should never send that many anyway, without a response) then buddy, travel on. She's so not interested. You're not her type! Accept it! Not everyone is a match. Don't keep writing to her. Quite honestly, if she liked you, one text would've done the trick, no matter how busy she was! You must trust me about this.

One experience I had on this subject was with a guy who wrote to me 100 times without exaggeration. I was out of the country and didn't answer. Here are 3 *actual* letters he wrote. I cut and pasted them below.

1) "Hi, I am crazy about you. I can't stop thinking about you. I'm in love with you. I need to be with you. Please call me. Please write me. Oh, Mother Mary, I need to be with you. I love you. I need you, and I want you. You make me grow. I am growing hard right now!"

If that wasn't enough 'ewe' to make a girl run some track and field, he went on to scare me further. He wrote the following letter, ensuring he would never receive a reply from me.

2) "I see now. You are just a fake bitch!"
And the lovely as well, follow-up letter:

3) "Go fuck yourself, you big fat whore!"
Ah, how romantic and tender. Oh, goodie, I just can't wait

to meet him now! Mother Mary, someone is wearing his bitter-colored glasses.

These types of guys will drag you to the dark side! My response. Delete and Blocked!

12. Don't be pushy, aggressive, or needy. None of this is attractive. Seriously, don't write things like what a loser you are, how depressed you are, how you hate your sad little life, how insecure you feel, and life just sucks. We don't respond well to the pity of a total stranger. Memo, this kind of profile is in no way alluring or sexy. Just so you understand, we girls never meet our gal pals for lunch and say things like:

"Listen, Joyce, I met this totally pathetic, nervous, loser, with no self-esteem, online. Golly, gosh, I am just dying to go out with him!"

"Hey Barb, I met this guy George online. He seems like a real zero. He's all about living in a world of despair, tragedy, unhappiness, and deep depression! Do you want me to ask him if he has a friend for you, too?"

We also never pick up the phone to call our BFF and say things like:

"Wow, Richie, I've been texting this guy online. He's very pushy, excruciatingly hopeless, loathes himself, and hates life. But he might be good in bed, and I totally cannot wait to go out with him!"

Just to be clear, our friends never respond back with:

"Bloody hell, who is he, what's his name, and where can I get one? Wait, do you think he might have a desperate loser friend for me, too?"

To you single men out there, I assure you, we don't think like this!

13. Let's finish up with this last lesson, which I should not have to teach you! I appeal to your senses that you refrain from getting sexual during your first, or shortly thereafter, conversations. Girls will dash away, I warn you. OK, perhaps desperate, lonely girls will play along. And yes, possibly an out-of-work prostitute will like it because she's looking for some work. But that's about it. *We don't* want to read sexual, lewd, and nasty things from a total stranger, as I demonstrated in a previous chapter. Such as:

> *"Hi, I want to fuck you."*
> *"You look good enough to go down on, can I?"*
> *"I want to eat you. Then you can suck my dick. If you're lucky!"*
> *"Hey, want to have phone sex? What are you wearing?"*

Hey, don't shoot the messenger. Those were among some of the emails sent to me. These disgusting creeps are clearly a waste of oxygen! Yes, people, all the above and more were sent to me. I cut and paste more of them for your entertainment pleasure later, in another chapter. They are so repulsive. If you are among the sexually squeamish, you'll want to skip that chapter altogether. Again, I'm just the messenger. Warning: you may also receive them. With all that ick, I must go in search of chocolate cake!

Do not compose anything whatsoever along those naughty lines. I guarantee it will cost you any chance you might have had. Don't begin or end with anything at all sexual. Hear me when I say you don't sound badass. You just sound hardcore, ignorant, and desperate. If these written responses are because you are excruciatingly horny, then give yourself a hand. If you know what I mean, before responding to any emails or dates.

If she likes your photos and profile, your first interaction is a make-or-break deal. Don't blow it. FYI, below is an example of an email most girls would like to receive. It's respectful, and complimentary, and shows you took the time to read her profile. It also reveals you are looking for a girlfriend and not just looking for sex. Don't misunderstand, women like sex too. However, we are also in search of a meaningful relationship.

AN ACCEPTABLE, FIRST MESSAGE...

"Hi there. My name is John, (Fill in your *own* name. I'm a bit worried that I needed to tell you that. Ugh!) After reading your profile and seeing your beautiful photos, you seem to be lovely, highly intelligent, and a fun person to be with. I'd really enjoy the opportunity to know more about you. I think we have much in common, and the makings of a good match. Who knows what could happen next? It would be great if you would take a moment to check out my profile. If you are interested, please, by all means, do email me back. If not, I wish you all the best in life and hope you find the one you are searching for.

With great respect and I'm hoping to hear from you,
John."

With any luck, this example should give you a clue. I hope, I hope-A!

Men, Don't Send a Message Starting with Any of These Below! And I mean it!

1. Good Morning, good night, or any other good time of the day! We most likely won't get to your email for those greetings to be

accurate. Here is an authentic email sent to me illustrating this issue. Btw, I fixed his grammar.

"How are you doing this afternoon? Having a good week? How's the New Year treating you? Any fun plans for this upcoming weekend? I just wanted to tell you I really liked your profile. What time do you get up in the morning? I am just going to wish you a good morning now. Can I? Could you please take a glance at my profile this afternoon? If you'd like to chat, shoot me a message back this evening. Will you? Have a great day. Hope you have a good time tonight. Just in case I forget to tell you (on the actual day that we go out) I had a wonderful time today! Grayson."

"Lots of questions, Grayson. Nice name though. Good day and bye now!"

2. Don't start your communications by only saying, hello, hey, ciao, or hi. You sort of fall off a cliff after expressing only one word. It tells nothing informative about you other than the assumption you're shy, and not a man of many words. It won't stir up any interest for most girls to want to reply. Well, except if you are drop-dead gorgeous. In that case, we won't care one bit about whatever you write. Also, don't just send a smiley face with no other message. Well, unless you're ten, and even then, don't. And, OMG, if you are ten, why the hell are you reading this book?! Where the fuck is your mother? Great, now I'm going to get flak from your mom for saying fuck to you. Whatever kid, back the fuck away from this book.

Don't send a text like, "I *hope* you're having a fun weekend!" You genuinely don't know her well enough to really hope for anything. Save your good solid hopes for when you need them for something real. Hope is a terrible thing to waste. But *I really do hope that kid put the book down.*

Lastly, don't start with, "Hi, sexy lady, I like your sexy lips." "Hey, sexy, I really like your hot body." "Hey, sex kitten," or other, sex girl statement you might think is clever. It's not. Moreover, you come off sounding like a player! Instead, write that you like her photos and profile. She's a whole person with a mind, a heart, and a soul. A little clue for ya!

3. Don't ask, "What's new? What up? How's it going? What's happening" or any other nosey questions? You don't even know the woman for any possible answer to make sense. Don't ask, "How are you," because, until you get acquainted, you don't really care how she is, and she knows it!

4. Don't say, "Lovely day, lots of snow today, beautiful sunshine today, it's been raining for days, glorious weather we're having" or anything at all concerning the weather. Unless you're writing to a woman over 50 who is a meteorologist and uses the word "glorious!" Correction! Maybe 60.

5. Don't ask, "How was your Thanksgiving, Christmas, New Year's Eve, Hanukkah, Easter, Purim, Passover, Valentine's Day, Fourth of July, Halloween, Rosh Hashanah, Yom Kippur, Veterans Day, Memorial Day, Labor Day, Presidents Day, Martin Luther King Day" or any other holiday. It's just a first communication email. Settle down, cowboy. You needn't know any of that yet. Still, Happy Chillax Day!

6. Don't beg, plead, or say how much you adore a girl online. Don't declare feelings such as, "I think I love you," or "Will you marry me because I am certain we are soul mates?" How can you

adore, love, or want to marry someone you've never even met? I must advise you, any of these sentiments make you sound like a fool, full of shit, or clinically psycho. It is clear you are judging her purely by her looks alone. Women want to be adored for a multitude of reasons, besides their physical appearance. On a related note, don't tell her you are obsessed or infatuated with her and especially don't claim you are crazy about her, either. That is scary, disturbing, and rather creepy! None of it is cute and won't win her heart. You haven't even met her yet, and with all your BS, if you get the chance, she will never believe you. If she does, she is insane too, like you! And that won't work out well. Just don't. Get a grip? All in good time!

7. Try to live in the modern world. Know at least twenty male and female movie stars of today. Be able to talk about ten movies that were released in the last few years. Know a minimum of ten female and male singers, as well as ten bands from this decade! Recognize a few names of popular television shows, whether you have seen them or not. I don't care what your age is, just make the effort to stay up-to-date and informed. I abhor people who use their age as an excuse for anything. Including laziness, ignorance, or being uninformed, whether it is someone young or old!

8. Men, I beseech upon you not to communicate with any facts you may think shows off how smart or funny you are. And, for the record, I hate beseeching people about anything. So, thanks a lot for making me go there! Beseeching? Do people do that anymore? Anyway, I've received endless stupid comments that were sent to me by online men who believed they were standup comedians. I didn't reply, but I really wanted to.

9. When you are scripting your profile, don't use words like zafty, gorgonize, daddy-O, snollygoster, made in the shade, what's buzzin', radar-range, dungarees, spiffy, ruckus, get bent, knuckle sandwich, spaz, Frigidaire, Hobo-pants, pedal-pushers, hoodwink, ado, gobbledygook, finagle, beatnik, brassiere, threads, beauty parlor, and valise. If you do pops, and you write that you are 31 years old or younger, we'll know immediately that you are 70 or older. Old words equal older generations. These sorts of words are basically Viagra needing words. Sorry, Daddy O!

SUCCESS, AND GOING OUT ON A FIRST DATE

WOW and a big Congrats there! On your date, *don't say any outrageous, strange things, Even If They Are True!* Especially then! Oh, how I just adore a Crazy Fest, always lots of laughs. Pathetically, here are some of the little ditties that have been said or written to me in online messages.

Here Are a Few Classic Examples of Things You Should *Never Say on a First Date*

1. Don't admit that you see zombies. *(Besides, they prefer undead.)*

2. Don't state that you have super paranormal experiences all the time. *(Even if it's true, save it later for shits-and-giggles.)*

3. Don't tell anyone you hear, see, or talk to dead people. *(Actually, we all might do some of this. Still… Don't!)*

4. Don't admit you are certain your house is haunted. Particularly, don't reveal you have Ghost Busters on your payroll. (Seriously, *WTF did you do to piss these ghosts off so much, anyway?)*

5. Don't confess you've had an exorcism to remove your demons.

Specifically, if you did. This kind of talk won't end well for any-one! *(Meanwhile, just asking for a friend. Did it work?)*

6. Don't state you've experienced an alien encounter or abduc-tion, even if you think it happened. Worse yet if you did. *(Cool though!)*

7. Don't divulge you slept with your last girlfriend's mother, sis-ter, or brother. Moreover, don't admit to sleeping with your own mother, sister, or brother. Especially if you did! *(Like, gross, and shame on you! "Tsk-tsk!" That's just downright Jerry Springer, crazy! What's up with that? More to the point, what's wrong with you?)*

8. Don't tell anyone you went to see the wizard. *(He can't help you!)*

9. Don't declare reincarnations that you believe you were King Tut, Jesus, Moses, or anyone else you think you were in another life. *(BTW, Charlton Heston and Ewan McGregor were. So there, liar!)*

10. Don't state when you were a kid, you did weird, strange, and cruel things to animals. *(But if you did, %#@* and FU@? I just lost my vocab. Seriously, you monster. Why, I outta, %$#@*&!?FU@!)*

11. Don't disclose you are a peeping Tom and watch the lady and man across the street. *(If true, you have a dark underbelly. Stop it now!)*

12. Don't state you can move things with your mind. *(Hey, wanna-be, Copperfield, you've created the illusion of deception and bullshit!)*

13. Don't reveal you bite your fingers and toes. *(No one wants or needs to know this about you. No one!)*

14. Don't divulge that you like to steal things. *(You're so lucky, Mr.*

Kleptomaniac, you haven't been caught. BTW, if you tell her, you'll never be invited to her house! Cut it out, you thief.)

15. Don't state that you have random thoughts of murder. (*On that topic, you might want to seek some immediate help. You should probably do that very soon. Like now. Run!*)

16. Don't announce you're a Republican, or state you're a Democrat. Don't admit you are a Libertarian or an Independent. As a matter of fact, don't talk politics on a date, even if you both are of the same party. Wait till later. Because no matter what, it will not lead to fun, romance, kissing, or sex. Except if you are a married politician. But then, what the hell are you doing on a dating site? Oh right. Sexual addiction syndrome! (*I hope you get caught.*)

17. Don't admit you relate to, understand, or like Hannibal Lecter. I don't care if he is your hero. You will see your date running away faster than a cheerleader runs to the quarterback after a game. Or a loser, leaving the Oscars. Faster than a Twinkie or an Oreo disappear in a room full of Overeaters Anonymous! Faster than a hundred-dollar bill disappears at a blackjack table in Vegas! Faster than saying shit after stepping in a wad of gum in the middle of the street! (***"Isn't that right, Clarice?"***)

18. Don't ogle, gawk, or stare at other women when you are on a date. Women hate this if you didn't already know. (*How could you not?*)

19. Don't say things like, you save water by taking a shower once a week. (*Even, and heaven help us all if it's true!*)

20. Don't share your past, strange, and nasty dating stories with prospective online women. Particularly the tales about the ones you claim are Satan's sisters. (*We don't give a shit! We don't. Case*

in point, it only makes you look idiotic, and it won't get you any further dates, because you'll probably talk trash about them too.)

21. Don't think you are clever or comical by saying asinine things like: "I love chicken. My favorite parts are the breasts, thighs, and legs. That's why I eat at Hooters." (*Riveting! Mr. Chickenshit. You go to Hooters and strip clubs because you like boobs and booty, and you can't get them any other way!*)

22. Don't tell a potential woman all about your "X-BOX!" Women don't want to hear about your last partner, what a great lover she was, or her astonishing beauty. When you first meet, she won't be interested in your "X-BOX," how much you miss her, or how it ended. On the contrary, your date will want to talk about you and her, and not about the one that died, ran off, or got away. I mean it! If you continually talk about this, and if your date likes you, she will live in fear of the Ex worming her way back into your life. (*Put a lid on the "X-Box." Play with your Minecraft Box instead.*)

23. When you meet, you can disclose your religion. Since you might not want to continue if this is a huge deal for either of you. But if not, don't talk about religion until you are more serious. Even if you both are of the same religious persuasion. Discussing religion in the very beginning is an unmitigated romance killer, especially if you are both very religious. See if you like each other first. If not, it's a moot point. (*Unless, however, you are a priest or a nun. But then, what the hell are you doing on a date? I swear to God!*)

24. When you start dating, ask her what she likes and doesn't like. Ask her questions. Make a real effort to get to know her. She'll like that you care enough to know. (*Unless you are clairvoyant.*)

25. For The Love of God, if she doesn't like you, she doesn't like you! Move on and don't harass her. Don't leave her voicemails saying, "Ok bitch." Or "Shame on you, whore." Or "You are a phony liar." Or "I get it and fuck you." Or the always nice to hear, "I hope you die." If you do, then you are a 'POTUS' guy. You are considered a **P**ompous, **O**bnoxious, **T**hickheaded, **U**nethical, **S**tupid guy. I say with all sincerity, move on, dude. She doesn't like you, OK! OK? Shit happens. (*Ladies, there are hordes of these angry, bitter men. So, pay attention, heed the flags, and then sprint!*)

GUYS... HERE ARE SOME OBVIOUS HINTS:

When you find someone, you think you like, give her what she needs and show her genuine care and affection. Why do I have to teach you this basic shit? I refuse to empower such unawareness about love. Where was your dad when you were growing up? He should've taught you this stuff.

All the things mentioned below are not a mystery. In fact, pretty much every woman wants the exact same thing to some degree. It's sometimes the small things that count, as well as the grandiose ones. Here are some things women want, need, and desire from you! Please, listen up! (Maybe your dad should listen too.)

LET'S CUT TO THE CHASE...

Men, you can't just dish out the following things during the honeymoon stage and then stop. You must continue throughout the entire relationship. Sorry, guys, it's just the way we are. But also, know that we understand and care about all your many needs as well.

Here are just a few things that all women want.
And a lot, all the time, and forever!

1. To be loved. To feel loved. To be respected.

2. Romance, and not just once in a blue moon.

3. To be cherished, appreciated, and adored.

4. To be admired and know that you are proud of her.

5. For you to be her best friend. This is important to most women.

6. To be treated like a lady, a princess, and in the right places, your whore. We really do sometimes enjoy getting kinky and XXX dirty with you.

7. To feel your warm affection, kindness, and your loving passion.

8. To feel secure, cared for, and taken care of. Try a little tenderness.

9. Sharing special times and knowing you are present and in the moment.

10. Your faithfulness and loyalty. (Meaning, not fucking another girl!)

11. To know you always have her back.

12. For you to be fun, playful, and even spontaneous at times.

13. Shoes and jewelry.

14. To see your sense of humor more often and to laugh together.

15. To feel your warmth, gentleness, sensitivity, and compassion.

16. *TO NEVER BE ABUSED, Sexually, Mentally, or Physically!!!!*

17. Receiving surprises and gifts on important holidays, birthdays, anniversaries, and just because. (The just-because ones are the best!)

18. To never hear you say, "Yo, bitch, do you have your period cause you're severely PMS-ing?" FYI, *never start anything with, "Yo bitch!"*

19. To be wined and dined, go out to movies, concerts, the theater, and for you to surprise her by making all the plans yourself, every now and again.

20. Massages and foot rubs. You rub ours, and we'll rub your... *Hmm.*

21. Shoes and jewelry. (I know I said it before, just making it quite clear!)

22. For you to share your thoughts, feelings, and what's on your mind. Women want to feel connected and not left in the dark. We care.

23. For you to really listen, to hear, and to be understanding, or at least try. You don't have to fix everything all the time. Just listen.

24. For you wanting to help now and again, without her having to ask.

25. Honesty and truthfulness.

26. To make her your priority. To be treasured and valued.

27. For you to learn to say you're sorry and truly mean it, from time to time. Or at the very least, try to fake it, well!

28. Being mature, dependable, steady, and responsible. To rely on you.

29. For you to be a man with honor, morals, integrity, and dignity.

30. Now and then give her kind, sweet compliments, and words of praise.

31. For you to communicate, to be open, to share your heart, words

of love, and emotions. Men, we know you have a hard time with this, but try.

32. To understand that even the small things count and why they do.

33. To not be yelled at, criticized, or taken for granted. This is huge.

34. For you to make a real effort to develop inventive, creative, exciting, passionate, tender, and even naughty sex. Not just going through the same-ole-same-ole, monotonous, boring, ho-hum sexual motions.

35. Your time and to be able to talk to you freely and share feelings without fear of an argument or ridicule. To be understood without judgment and with love.

36. *Finally… Never* (not ever) tell her she looks or acts like her mother! That will be the end of you forever!

Oh, and this just in! In case you haven't picked up on it yet?

"Women Want and Need to be Wooed and Courted!" For us girls, sex is the total package, the whole ball of wax, the whole enchilada, and the whole shebang. Foreplay doesn't just start in bed for women. Surprise, surprise. It is the dinner, the movie, the concert, and the romance! It's holding hands, cuddling, tenderness, and so forth. Sexual intimacy is all the attention, way before the bedroom and the sex. Dammit, men, why do I have to explain these basic logical skills to you? I guess this should be taught in school. Because, dads, let me tell ya, you are not cutting it. That means you too, Bam-Bam's dad! Guys, instead of thinking that dating, and love are chores, try to think of your dating venture as the gateway to a new frontier. Courting isn't just about opening doors, pulling out her chair, helping her out of the car, or providing and putting on the condom. We can do all that ourselves. All the chivalrous stuff gets old rather quickly. Well, except for the condom parts. Go ahead and carry on with that.

For the record, a girl feels loved when she feels safe and taken care of, and that includes her children if she has them. Frankly, what disturbs me the most is that I sadly had to include this chapter. This is just your straightforward, elementary, 'Dating 101-class.' Having to teach this class to anyone over 18 years old is preposterously troubling. Mamma Mia, I can only say, where was your dating guru guide after teaching you those few initial things? Why did they stop at, "Here's the vagina, here's the condom, put it on, then just go in and out, and in and out until you've cum!" Dag Nab It and *Geez Louise*! My work here is never done. Sigh!

Good luck men, go forth, happy trails, and don't fuck it up! One more thing. I really feel bad for that Louise girl who gets blamed and pulled into every preposterous situation. Really sorry, Louise!

P.S. To you men still reading, WOW-WEE! This effort alone will ensure your success. I'm so proud of you guys. You've shown great promise. Good for you! You now possess a fountain of knowledge and have become a student of romance. Amazingly, you stuck with the whole chapter. Now, rules in hand, go out there and find your princess!

CHAPTER 16

About My True Love. "The One!"

HE'S FLAWLESS AND PERFECT! WHEREVER THE HELL HE IS? WORDS BY AN UNREALISTIC, ROMANTIC DREAMER...

To understand my dismay over the men I've met on, or offline, (I imagine, just like you have!) I feel it's important to take a moment to explain about my true love. It will justify why my results have been so disheartening.

To define my one true love would take countless adjectives. Therefore, just deal with it! And you as well, you judgmental grammar teachers! You can roll your eyes, shake your head, and 'yea right, me' all you want. I confess I don't blame you one bit. Before you continue reading, I suggest you put on some melodramatic, romantic music.

Go on. I'll wait.

You're back? OK, cool. Here we go…

I envision my eternal love and I will stay awake all night, far too many nights to count. For the rest of our lives, we find ourselves talking about everything, discussing diverse topics, from politics to aliens. I don't mean aliens like Lady Gaga, Joaquin Phoenix, James Franco, or Steven Tyler. I'm speaking of the Area 51 kind.

We speak about random spiritual thoughts, only to be shared

with each other. Mostly for fear of being committed by reason of weirdness. Sometimes when we're together, we don't speak at all. Our love has a language all its own. I call this language 'Lovelish!' Our childlike souls embrace spontaneously, and our carefree, bohemian spirits have no limits or boundaries. Oftentimes we get up at 4:00 am to enjoy fresh doughnuts at Krispy Kreme. Or we run to get hot bagels before they cool down at the bakery around the corner. My love always gives me the better doughnut. You know, the bigger one that's perfectly shaped, with more glaze over it.

We have mind-blowing crazy sex 14 times a week. Okay, 12 times Fine, being honest (if I must), 7 to 10. We not only share sex in our bed, but in the most unimaginable, foolish places with no concern about getting caught. On the contrary, we hope we do. This is the childlike spunk and moxie, which created our relationship, transforming 2 people into "us."

His gentle touch manifests the power to place me under his spell, bringing me to a state of mesmerizing helplessness. What an awesome, fantabulous lover he is. My "sexpert" makes me quiver and finds new, creative moves and styles to pleasure me. He captivates me now and forever. Our lovemaking never gets old! Sex with him is like a gigantic plate of double chocolate chip cookies, caramel fudge, and every flavor of Ben & Jerry's combined. After hours of intimacy and rapture, we snuggle and cuddle until we both fall asleep, fulfilled, and happy in each other's arms. We become 'one' all night, every night, and for the rest of our lives.

OK, readers, stop shaking your heads and laughing at me!

Seriously, it's offensive and juvenile. I don't want to go on sounding all Pollyanna, but you never know! It could happen! Obviously, I won't *climb out the window and foolishly hang onto a tree. But I am willing to go out on a limb with hope. Indeed, we may fall-down and get our hearts broken. But it's worth a shot, isn't it? The odds might be greater in our favor than against us. So, what if the odds are even a trillion-to-one? Not to rhapsodize endlessly, but my man is comparable to a thrilling adventure at Disneyland or a shopping spree at Chanel. Whether it be a tiny chance, there's still a chance of finding him. **Oh, stop your arrogant snickering!***

My man doesn't always rely on me to plan our social activities. He finds the time and imagination to arrange all sorts of exotically inventive fun and *dreamazing* activities. Not your typical humdrum movie and dinner dates, like most couples. Our love is different. We travel to places overnight on a whim. We fly to Bali or India to experience a spiritual pick-me-up. We attend Milan's, La Scala for a night at the Opera, or even Spain for an imperial gala. We travel to Paris just for a romantic dinner at Les Ombres with the view of the Eiffel Tower as the backdrop. I tremble with exciting anticipation of the fun adventures he'll come up with next. Unlike most men, he never protests or complains about the number of suitcases I pack, or how heavy they are. Truthfully, he thinks it's adorable.

Come on now. Stop! *Don't be so negative and cynical. These are my extrapolations, dreams, delusions, and I'm basking in them. Bask off!*

Meanwhile, my love generously offers me three-quarters of the closet and drawer space with his *cutesy* affectionate smile. He admires my shoe collection. Actually, he encourages it. And not because he has a shoe fetish, but because he loves me immensely! He showers and dresses after I do and, of course, he never leaves a mess. When I purchase a new outfit, he not only notices, but he tells me how stunning and *thin* I look wearing it. Very smart how he elongates the *"TH,"* in thin! He worships my silly idiosyncrasies and explains they're all part of what makes me irresistible.

FYI. Now would be a good time to change to more gushy, passionate music. Hurry! Go on. I'll wait!

About fighting or arguing, you ask? It never happens. We are too close and past such a ridiculously childish waste of time. Our mutual respect and communication skills prevent such immature behavior. We never think of interrupting or completing each other's sentences. On the contrary, we crave hearing one another's thoughts and opinions in our own individual manner of speaking. We listen intently to each other for hours on end. We marvel and grow from our individual philosophies and beliefs.

He is energetic and forever on the go. He does this to ensure that we have all the time we want to enjoy being alone together. My love is so full of vitality. I couldn't imagine him ever taking a power nap, catnap, micro nap, mini nap, caffeine nap, Nano nap, or any other nap category. Now meditation, that's a world of difference. That he does. Namaste!

Women walking by, catch a glimpse of him and notice at once that he's elegant, sophisticated, charming, chic, down-to-earth, and magnetic. The guy is clearly catnip to women! He can't help it, so I'm never jealous.

Really, people? Cool it. Stop laughing! I can hear you from here, and it's a book! Perhaps I'm a dreamer, but it could happen! It will. It has to! Stop laughing! Don't make me get all high school principal on you!

To continue, I really need to buy a ton of adjectives. Here goes…

He is loving, kind, sensitive, caring, nurturing, well-endowed, understanding, patient, funny, classy, successful, easygoing, emotionally sound, (*Reader, pause here to take in a nice deep cleansing breath. And stop laughing!*) proactive, creative, even-tempered, affectionate, well endowed (*I Know I said that already, but it is worthy of repeating!*), and loves spoiling me with expensive jewelry, cars, clothes, and fancy gifts.

Furthermore, my guy is unable to look at or even think about another woman, because he finds me beguiling. He thinks I'm sexy, hot, and wondrously stunning, as I do him. Don't get me started on his loyalty, devotion, and faithfulness. It is unwavering, like a stone. Cheating is unthinkable. So very refreshing a virtue not found in most couples today.

I suspect if there are any men still reading this novel, it's now being thrown into the trash. *Hey,* wait a second. Please, at least recycle the book! We need to pass this planet on to the next generation. Of course, I know there're some steadfast male exceptions still reading. And they would likely be my loyal, beloved, fabulous gay men. They will faithfully continue reading, as they are looking for the same fabulous man that I am!

Moving along, my mate has a large, loving, and devoted family, all of whom accept and embrace me completely with open arms. They flower me with affection, love, and adoration. *Ok, whatever? Surely even I can vividly see how this might be a smidge unlikely and perhaps not feasible or accurate!* I don't care, it's my vision and I'm sticking with it!

Above all, there is laughter. There is an overabundance of it! We both credit that laughter is the fundamental and pivotal secret to life, health, happiness, and everlasting love. This philosophy stands, whether the Dali Llama agrees with us or not!

For those of you who are still with me and didn't already throw the book away, I thank you respectfully. "Come on, though, let's be real. Ladies, (and gents) don't lie! You know you want him too. Go on, admit it! Yeah, I thought so. What woman (or man) in the entire universe isn't looking for this guy? Too bad. He's mine! *Maybe there's more than one?"*

There are lots of other traits to tell you about my guy, "The One!"

1. Unlike most men, my Prince Charming politely asks for directions when he is uncertain of where to go.
2. He always puts the toilet seat down.
3. He never puts dishes in the sink. (He knows there isn't a magical Sink Fairy that cleans them and puts them away.)
4. He gallantly leaves the room to fart.
5. He only watches sports that we both enjoy together.
6. He never asks, *"You wanna do it?"* This question only implies that the asker doesn't want to. He's far too elegant to be so unromantic and crass.
7. He religiously puts his dirty clothes into the laundry bin instead of leaving them all over the floor for the Laundry Fairy to put them away.
8. He always takes the garbage out without waiting for the Garbage Fairy.
9. He always remembers where his keys, phone, wallet, sunglasses, reading glasses, and where everything else is.
10. We are the couple everyone wishes they could be.
11. We're the duo they write love songs about. I don't mean Katy Perry or Taylor Swift. I'm talking about Sinatra or Air Supply love songs. Perhaps not that extreme. Music more along the lines of Adele, Michael Bublé, John Legend, Savage Garden, Bruno Mars, Usher, or maybe Keith Urban.
12. We bask and luxuriate in the cradled sanctuary and warmth

of our love. We only need to look at each other and know all is right in the world. Or at least in our world. Our love is timeless and surpasses the restricted boundaries of this simple, mortal, Planet Earth.

13. We live on for all eternity, for we are star-crossed lovers. Eternity as in, Fa Eva, and Eva, and Eva! (Yes, Dahling, this is to be spoken in the style of Garbo, Dietrich, or Davis.)

14. *My prince keeps my heart beating like a symphony of joy and happiness. He is my Avatar of Love.*

Hey, quit giggling, and stop judging me! *Wow, you are so jealous, aren't you? Fine, I get it! Overkill. Frankly, even I'm getting nauseated.*

In my defense, romantically, I believe we should reach for corny. Why not? Though sadly, at this point, I had not even come close to meeting my true love. Regardless, I vow to never stop searching for my flawless, perfect man, who will forever hold the keys to my heart. *And moreover, knows where he placed them!*

I wait for the man of my dreams, for I am 100% certain he is out there looking for me! Knowing he is there waiting patiently is what pulls me through this devastatingly preposterous online search for *"The One!"*

Everyone out there, hoping and dreaming of finding "The One," please trust me when I say your love is waiting for you, too! You must never give up! For that would be your supreme loss.

Now, let me continue teaching you the pertinent, relevant, and essential lessons to be learned through my real-life, true stories! Read on... Enjoy.

CHAPTER 17

Alas, the Guy with Extreme Idiosyncrasies
The Brainiac Pseudo-Intellectual
BETTER KNOWN AS A GRAND BORE...

His name is "Brice, Academic, Brainiac" and very likely his given first, middle, and last names at birth. We spoke on the phone numerous times. Rather, he spoke, and I listened, with my laptop religiously accessible to the Webster's and Urban Dictionary sites. It's not that Brice, the Brainiac, meant to be obnoxiously bumptious, smug, and subsequently arrogant. Nevertheless, he oh-so-self-importantly was. Yet, I found it appalling that a small part of me immeasurably liked this about him. And just so you know, I was justifiably sickened with myself for these feelings. Brice was a paradigm of ego and possessed his own version of personal gravitas. I couldn't exactly put my finger on *why I was so entirely intrigued and enticed by his odd academic and intellectual behavior.* He pulled me right in, like a cowboy roping a calf at a rodeo. "Yee-haw!" Egad, that was ultra-humiliating. Yee-haw? You see, this is precisely the sort of thing that occurs when you deliberately hang out with an alternative universe. It triggers a short within your cerebral cortex, causing your brain to overload and burn out just enough to say, Yee-Haw!

My foolish behavior repulsed me. Regardless, I was unequivocally certain Brice would never attend a rodeo to witness a cowboy roping in a calf or for any other rodeo reason. I wouldn't either unless I could wear my extremely cool Howard Knight Cowboy Boots, I couldn't afford but bought, anyway. I couldn't help myself. I suffer from the medical condition, *F.D.P.S. "Fashion Designer Purchase Syndrome."* Don't criticize me, and trust me, you don't want this ailment. It's ugly, people. I've inquired, but there is no known treatment or cure for this disorder. Instead, have a little pity on me, ok?

Brice seemed to be quite enveloped in his braggart, scholastic, narcissistic, personal glory. After all, he graduated from Princeton. (As he had pointed out repetitively.) "Wowwww," and might I interject further a simultaneous, "Oooooh," to make it a set! He's a diehard (without Bruce Willis) egotist. Snobby, Brice, embodies the perfect semblance of the urban word, Ludwigvanquixote, (It's an actual word. Google it.) with his massive delusions of grandeur. I learned from our conversations that he must be always in total control of everything. He behaved like King Canute, sitting on the shore, commanding the oceanic tides to reverse and rescind back, to no avail. In fact, his self-appreciation was blinding!

I quickly learned Brice was more than a handful. Nonetheless, his supreme intelligence intrigued me. I was attracted to his amazing intellect and beautiful long hair. Intelligence and long hair are my Achilles *high-heel* and the 2 things that forever turn me on about a man. Ergo, I had countless infatuations and embarrassing crushes towards my high school teachers and college professors. Anyway, that's a whole other hardcover!

After many phone chats, we agreed to meet in Las Vegas. I shared with him the updated and official name of the city, now commonly known as "It's Vegas-Baby-Whoo-Hoo!" Vegas is the

"Literati Haven" where all the other pseudo-intellectuals live. Hmm, perhaps I'm confusing that with hookers, gamblers, magicians, and the mob? Either way, that's where we met. Ironically, the "NFR" (National Finals Rodeo) happened to be in town that week. What the hell, Yee-haw!

Brice is a 36-year-old man, which is older than I was looking for. That said, he was adorable, had an angelic face, long curly brown hair (the good-shiny curly hair, not the frizzy, out-of-control curly hair), and was stylishly well-groomed. He was keenly on-trend. He arrived for our date wearing extremely pretentious, bang-on hipster fashion. There he emerged in a flowing long black jacket, a Hamburg Hipster Hat, and a pair of thick, black-rimmed glasses. Although he didn't need spectacles, it was totally irrelevant to him. Style is style, fashion is fashion, and this poser was proud of it all. Brice was extraordinarily cliché, which absurdly defeats his purpose of professing to be a true intellectual! Paradoxically, I found his scholarly bravado both disturbing and super sexy. He was light-years past, conceited. More, Defcon-4 superior, which was puzzling to me. I typically avoid this superior, affected species of men. Well, Lah-dee-dah.

We met at one of my favorite cozy outdoor restaurants. It's a place that only the locals frequent and is well-known as a real foodie's hangout. The cuisine is deliciously obscene. Yet, not so gourmet as to be considered nouveau riche, missing The Avant-Garde mark. We talked as we wolfed down a lovely array of scrumptious small plates. Thank goodness, just in time since I was borderline hangry.

Although we were off to a good start, our date was becoming increasingly frustrating by the second. Brice was loud and a ginormous intellectual bore. People sitting by us heard him rambling on and on and were incisively rolling their eyes. I couldn't blame them, as I too felt a bit animus towards Mista-Dude who needed to chill down. Downtown down!

It was evident that someone had fed him too many ego-cookies. Yet, oddly enough, his prosaic cockiness was arousing to me in a sensual, enticing way. Still, I was angry with myself for having these feelings. The burning conflict within me couldn't fathom how Brice, the arrogant, flinty, impervious egotist, was turning me on. I'm not impressed with snobs, but he was just so good at it. I kept thinking this peculiar situation I found myself in was unlike me. On the other hand, I loved these surprising dates which were refreshingly novel. I am sure my silly fascination had something to do with his long hair. But dang, he was really, really, cute! Even so, I was disgusted and disappointed in myself.

It was impossible not to notice people kept staring at us. I assumed their stares were because Brice was noisy, and we looked as if we came from 2 different worlds. He sported Acne jeans, an American Apparel plaid shirt, a very cool vintage coat, a trendy-preppy-hipster Pendleton Bag (as described in his own words), and his kicks shoes from A.P.C. Naturally, I'm only assuming about all the labels above, but quite certain I am accurate. So confident, in fact, I thought of betting on it. I mean, it was doable, as we were already in, "It's Vegas-Baby-Whoo-Hoo!" In complete contrast, I wore a Versace Dress (I couldn't afford, but bought anyway), Jimmy Choo Shoes (I could not afford, but bought anyway), and my Birkin Bag (I really could not afford, but seriously should not have bought anyway). Understand, people, I had no choice. As I already mentioned, I suffer from chronic, "Fashion Designer Purchase Syndrome." Perhaps it's not one of your well-known syndromes and charities to sponsor or fight for. Still, it's a real disorder and I'm riddled with stylish guilt! Note this excuse isn't equivalent to the fake *"Sexual Addiction Syndrome!"* 'F.D.P.S.' is serious. It's not pretty, and I have a severe case of it. I'm a prisoner of this sickness. Alas, I have courageously admitted and accepted my ailment, which is the first step, and it feels so good to come out!

Brice did all the talking, which, *if you knew me,* was unusual at best. The brain-man spoke, as I silently ate and drank wine. It appeared this scenario was mutually beneficial. He droned on about politics, foreign films, scientific discoveries, taxonomy of cognitive dissonance, intelligent engineering, informatics, chemical and biological engineering, intelligence control systems, COVID-19, financial management, risk analysis, and more, Blah-Blah-Blah! I thought it was very polite of me to listen to it all. I kindheartedly considered it *free, blah-blah-blah, psychotherapy.* I was so frustrated I thought of asking him to stop! But I realized it wouldn't have ended his blabbing away vigorously with his know-it-all, yakety-yak-yak. I really do think he missed out on a wonderful opportunity. He seriously should've been a contestant on Jeopardy, instead of wasting it all on me!

Brice appeared to possess an encyclopedic wealth of knowledge. Everything he spoke about seemed mysterious. Because of his ego and vast expertise, I believe he thought I should be honored to be privy to his secret knowledge of the CIA, FBI, FCC, FDA, DEA, and KGB files. (And all the other 3-letter organizations he was probably bullshitting about.) The way he spoke with precision and low vocal undertones, one would think he was disclosing classified government intelligence. Or lying!

He raged on with assurance about quantum physics, cosmology, physic-physics and the nature of consciousness, astrology, reincarnation, Shakespeare, Dali, Picasso, Michelangelo, and Chagall's works of art. As well as everything discussed on the history, science,

PBS, entertainment, news, and sports channels. He certainly had superiority running through his veins. Brice continued talking non-stop with his overconfident facts about politics, religion, and education. Despite his gorgeousness and stunning long hair, I became dizzy from boredom and the cheap wine.

Since there was no way to stop him, I childishly amused myself by trying to distract him. I kept touching his leg, making annoying gestures, random noises, and messing with him as he spoke. I was like a mosquito on his face, a bee by his ear, or a red ant on his toe. Poor dear, Brice didn't know how to handle my antics. It was so much fun responding to his monotonous monologues of knowledge and spewing out comments to screw with his brain, which freaked him out. Comebacks like, "OMG totally awesome," "Really, Kemosabe," and the always reliable, "No shit, Sherlock?" I think somewhere inside his head were millions of atomic, molecular particles exploding, one by one. It was comically epic to watch. Like a 4-year-old, I couldn't hold it in and had to say something to lighten him up. Futilely trying to muzzle him, out came, "You know, Brice, hugging leads to spooning, and spooning always leads to forking!"

He had a panicked, clueless gaze across his face. Likely the same look as the 12 publishing houses exhibited when they passed on and rejected JK Rowling's series, "Harry Potter." Only later to learn it became a multi-billion-dollar famed piece of literature, mega-hit movies, and an iconic franchise. Those fools must've read the book upside down. Oopsie!

With a flustered, confused voice, Brice protested, scratching his head. "Excuse me, what does that mean? Forking what? I don't get it?"

He sat there unnerved. Becoming unglued and terrified not to know something. I Almost felt bad for the guy. Regardless, I merely chuckled and clicked his wine glass with mine. "Cheers, Hon!"

"No," he said in a perturbed voice. "What does that mean? Are you being condescending? Are you patronizing me?" He experienced a total meltdown, whilst his intellectual pride seeped out of control, all down his neck and out of every pore in his body. He feared these unfamiliar dummy moments. I almost got a rag to soak up his oozing overflow of insecurity.

"No, Brice, I was simply stating when you use table utensils, it leads to sex and other unexpected consequences!" The poor guy erupted like a volcano in a blaze of mass confusion. As he freaked out, I admit, it only made me laugh harder. Hey, one can't always take the high road!

Brice disregarded me like a bagel in a doughnut factory, like chewing gum in a dentist's office, or vanilla in a chocolate factory. I blew it, for my laughter only infuriated him more. He began saying a copious amount of ostentatious, big words. Preposterous unknown words, just like the vocabulary section of your college acceptance, SAT tests. Fancy words, you had absolutely no idea what in the world they meant and just went ahead and guessed on the exam. Such words as: abligurition, dactylion, cheiloproclitic, groak, euneirophrenia, hebephrenic, horripilate, misodoctakleidist, neanimorphic, timmynoggy, and zenzizenzizenzic, to name a few. Vocab words, to this day, you still don't have the foggiest idea what they mean or should ever need to know. Yet the Brice-Man used them, knew them, and flaunted them like intelligence daggers!

"Whaaaaat?" Silently screaming, I had no idea what this crazy man was talking about. However, I now wore the same panicked, clueless, painful expression on my face that he had displayed. But, like a lady, I didn't ooze. I waited patiently, hoping to jump in at any point. But I didn't have my laptop to look up any of his hoity-toity, narcissistic showing off so I could educate my interruptions. And I am a reporter! I knew, in my heart, I could've added something to those topics, even if it were only knowledge about fashion, journalism, travel, photography, music, politics, life, and sex. By the way, I did not misspell any of Brice's words above. They're just not recognized by my Apple Computer tool capabilities or the spellcheck. I'll let you look them up for yourself, and please do enjoy that.

As the evening slowly progressed, I kept wondering when this braggadocios man would lose his voice and quiet down already! Judging by the apparent glares of the other patrons in the restaurant, I surmised it was their thoughts as well. Good lord, how pompous and full of oneself can a person be? Granted, I'm a tolerant modern woman, but this was way outside-the-reality-box, and too much grandiose, bullshittery even for me. Though the wine was not at all up to par, I was grateful it never stopped flowing. I didn't care anymore to fake my disinterest in him or his conversation for one. By this juncture, there wasn't a single drop of *"Phys-Brice-ical"* attraction left on my part. Surprisingly, neither his hair nor his brain could keep me captivated any longer.

He interrupted my thoughts, declaring, "I have done, experienced, accomplished, and have learned everything important there is to know in this world! I'm a role model for what others strive or hope to become!"

Snickering while quietly sipping my lousy wine, I replied. "I mean, Gee-whiz, Brice, that's a whole barrel full of arrogance. Don't ya think?"

"Not at all," he reacted. "For it's all true and accurate. *So, I win!*"

"Oh, gosh. Dear me, I didn't realize we were playing a game. I wasn't aware I needed to keep score. Wow, my bad! OK, I'll play."

He declared, "It's the game of life, babe, and I am the winner!"

I thought, subtle much? But darn, he was so cute! I rarely enjoy meddling in other people's lives, but he had it coming! Even though I felt sad for him, as he was so insecure, I had to strike back.

"Life is not a game, Brice! Life is about giving, sharing, loving, helping, experiencing, and most importantly, appreciating family and friends! Even though it's your nature to use bombastically complicated, over-the-top, verbose words, my words are unpretentious and true. I sense you understand nothing 'real' about life or the genuine meaning of it. I'm referring to the most simple and beautiful things. You, dear sir, have unmistakably run out of game!"

He bounced back defensively, spilling his entire glass of wine. "You are wrong, Mollie! I understand everything there is to know in life. And more to the point, with the highest of intelligence."

Without realizing it, I laughed aloud. Come on, I had to!

Miffed, he said, "Why are you laughing? You laughing at me?"

I swear I tried to remain silent and reserved. Nevertheless, unable to continue this approach, out came, "Oh, I was just wondering how much extra they charge you at the airport for your overweight baggage of ego?"

Lashing back self-righteously, whilst trying to wipe the entire spilled glass of red wine off his now-stained pants, "What do you mean?"

I paused and impishly looked up to the gods, thinking of various responses. Though I kindly kept them to myself, smiling at him sweetly.

I learned a few things from his nonstop babble, which I found very depressing. Brice, the pseudo-intellectual brainiac, had never experienced true love and evidently knew nothing about good wine. Including how to remove it from his pants. He had few real friends, if any, and had never been close to his family. He never went to the circus or the state fair, where one gets to enjoy taffy, cotton candy, fudge, caramel apples, funnel cake, and greasy corn dogs. He never frolicked around Disneyland as a kid, eating a smoked turkey leg from Frontierland, while laughing with Mickey and Donald! Worse yet, I discovered Brice has never consumed a Milky Way Bar, Mallomars, Girl Scout Cookies, a peanut butter & jelly sandwich, Pop-Tarts, S'Mores, or a Reece's Peanut Butter Cup. Goodness, I consider that to be several forms of child abuse. What was wrong with his parents? Even more tragic, Brice never had a fake ID or got drunk in college. That's downright heartbreaking. I was also surprised to find out Brice has never traveled outside the country and barely traveled around America. With all his bragging, he had missed out on important childhood memories and failed to experience so many magnificent pleasures of life.

I explained to Brice in my slightly tipsy state of mind (from the atrocious nasty wine,) all the wonderful and important things he had missed out on, regardless of his extraordinary IQ. Upon finishing my speech, with an immature giggle, and a girly toss-toss of my hair, I tenderly whispered, *"Perhaps, I win Brice! So STFU."*

Rather amused with myself and just shy of rolling on the floor, I heard thunderous appreciation from the surrounding tables, now applauding, supporting, and laughing with me. It was most validating.

Likely, for the first time in his brilliant scholastic life, Brice was humiliated and mortified. Of course, I knew it was wrong. Still, I couldn't stop laughing. I strained to stop. I really did! All right, I suppose I didn't try *all that hard.* I loved the moment far too much to not revel in it.

And, just like that, the brain-man, in a crazed rage, threw his cell phone at me! All I could say to that, giggling hysterically, was,

*"Oh, no you **di'int?**"* Huh, that hasn't happened to him since, well, ***Never!*** "Dude, people who live in academic glass houses shouldn't throw cell phones!" Everyone in the restaurant was bursting with laughter. I was all the while laughing so hard, I snorted! Gee, I've never been a snort-laugher. This would have been awkward if it weren't so hilarious to me.

With bloodshot eyes, enraged with fury, he blurted, "You're lucky to have gone to dinner with me and blessed to have been in my presence!"

OK, the gloves were off. I was all set and ready to rumble. Such a bummer, he really was eye candy. I responded, snort-laughing. "You go right ahead and tell yourself whatever you need to, Sir Isaac Newton!"

And, with that, the red-faced, irate Brice picked up the many pieces of his now broken phone and ego. He frantically grabbed his trendy-preppy-hipster bag (Stated in his own words. But to be clear, there is no such thing as they are two different fashion styles) his hat, glasses, and jacket, all the while scowling. Before he could run away with his brain between his legs, I called out, "Hey, Brice-Einstein, this is the cessation and denouement of our future together. Ta-Ta and game over!"

With a petulant huff, Brice made a run for it, leaving me alone with the check. Reaching into my oversized Birkin bag, I pulled out my Visa, thinking, "There really is no such thing as a free lunch. Or *dinner,* in this case." He did, however, get a giggling ovation from all the customers who were dining, and I got a ton of high-fives. "Potato, potahto, tomato, tomahto," I was ecstatic to call the whole damn thing off! The brainiac's skedaddle was worth paying every penny of the bill.

Although in the end, I Won! So, STFU!

Escaping Brice-land, situated in the heart of Elitist-Ville, was a tremendous relief. Still, though, the evening thoroughly tickled my funny bone. More importantly, I was thankful no one recognized me. It's always a concern for me in moments like this to be spotted in an embarrassing situation as a notable journalist.

I couldn't stop laughing all the way home. I really need to start doing stand-up! Dating positively delivers endless comedy material. I mean, it writes itself. And the laughs just keep coming.

Damn, too bad though. He was, so darn cute!

AND A YEE-HAW, NEXT!

CHAPTER 18

Dating is No Bed of Daisies

THE FIVE KINDS OF MEN

Then, just like that, I heard the ominous sound. "Dant-Dant-Dan-Dah," and my hopes were shattered. My faith was crushed by reality and my positive attitude was overshadowed by epic failures and disappointments.

It's *"Loserageddon"* out there, people! The bloody gates of Hell have opened! It's an honest-to-goodness real-life, *"Bloody Rocky Horror Show!"* Delivering the fundamental truth, I've determined dating off or online nowadays is dreadful. I'll tell you, these dating sites (all of them, there are no exclusions) are riddled with phonies, imposters, scammers, and liars. And that's just for starters. "Online dating is the equivalent of the Antichrist of matchmaking." Hmm! That statement could be a bumper sticker. Even so, I believe love is hiding out there amidst all of it, patiently waiting for us to come find it, no matter what the obstacles and hurdles.

I warn you, though, save yourself and stay cautious! There should be flashing warning signs on all these dating websites. *"Buyer Beware,* to infinity and beyond," in every sense of the word! Yes, indeed, Buzz Lightyear had it right all along. He apparently went on one of these dating sites, too. However, I am super confident he didn't meet Jessie online.

There is good and evil in the world, and online dating is no exception and a perfect example. After numerous online encounters, I learned I'd rather go out with an alien and have a close encounter of any kind! So, then I tried to ponder. Yep, aha, I did. I took a time out and uncharacteristically pondered. Which is most unsettling because I never do, or say, *pondered.* Honestly, I've never pondered before! I'm not at all a ponder person. I don't really know how to ponder, even if I wanted to!

Nevertheless, there I was, all alone, freaking out and pondering. Like someone being held in solitary confinement. I questioned, once more, "Am '*I*' the only one going through all this crazy?" Again, "Is this just a me, moi, myself, and I quandary?" This surely just had to be a *me thing!*

I declare and thank the Lord, or whoever is your spiritual guide or holy leader (fill in the blank here), as far as all of us seekers of love go, *"We Are All"* floating in the same crazed, unsteady, wobbly boat. I'm telling you now, you will lose your direction numerous times. There will be moments you'll desperately and willingly want to jump overboard. Allow me to enlighten you. This information is not merely a hypothesis, but an absolute fact. Like any voyager searching for true love, your other half is your constant north and your center. Let this thought navigate your "cupid vessel" toward love. A little, gag me? Sure, but go with it anyway! I'm trying to keep your heart and mind afloat. What? You'd rather drown in a bottomless ocean of sorrow? Take the life raft! Trust me, you're going to need every bit of the help I'm offering you. And then some!

"Johnny, Do You Hear Me?????"

I came up with my analysis by interviewing oh, I don't know, thousands of other women and men too, who were all looking for true love. I was pleased to learn that most of them were still rational and sane at this juncture of their pursuit. I discovered we, you, and I, collectively are all suffering and steering our way without directions or the aid of a "Love-GPS" through this dating labyrinth!

OMG! Note to self, what a great idea, a "Love-GPS!" Who wouldn't buy that? I gotta talk to Apple! Maybe even Google Maps! Wait a sec, how about a freak alert too? For sure, I must schedule a meeting.

"In matters of the heart, all single people are in this dilemma together." This simple conclusion is not only eye-opening but the good news and the comforting silver lining! Next, I begged the question. And just so you all know, I hate begging even more than I hate pondering!

"Are there any unmarried (which, for you men who dared to keep reading, means **single**! *And thank you for continuing. Read on!*), well-balanced, stable, heterosexual, healthy, loving, kind, intelligent, caring, great guys left on this planet?" I ask in a panicked, shrill voice, "Where is my betrothed?" I can't express just how much I despise it when that shrill voice happens to me. As do all the surrounding people, I have noticed!

For those of you who are truly adventurous, fearless, and not already frightened off by previous chapters, (And you really should be, because it gets worse!) please focus and hear my words to the wise and unwise alike. "When entering online dating, be prepared for madness and lunacy. Brace yourself and acclimate. Above all, understand "You're not the only one meeting weird, bizarre, disturbingly strange, creepy losers, and crazies. If you haven't already heard, they live among us!" Funny, it turns out the "Men in Black" movies were not entirely wrong or fiction.

The "drama brushstrokes" of dating are so broad and peculiar. No one tells you this, so I will. Always keep your eyes and ears open. Be prepared to listen to an abundance of rhetoric, lies, and very tall tales of deceit. Not unlike the rhetoric and tales spoken by your governor, senator, House of Representatives, and the POTUS. In other words, don't believe everything you hear, or perhaps anything you hear! Take it all with a grain of salt. (Use sea salt, it's much healthier!) You'll find yourself, as did I, living in the middle of an uninteresting, dismally boring, sometimes dangerous dating storm, which I enjoy referring to as, "Smorgas**bored.**"

I'd like to recommend that you think of your search for love as the ultimate cherry picking, the Oscar, Tony, or Grammy Awards of cherry picking. Picking, as if you're looking for the perfect cherry, like when you picked your friendships, career, hairstyle, and birth control. Only, multiply the difficulty in cherry picking times a billion, to pick "*The One.*"

Remember, he or she is your reward and infinite focus. Hold on to this thought and remind yourself daily. Appreciate that finding your one true love, "The One," is worth every bit of the drama, heartache, and eye-rolling moments you'll endure traveling the uncertain footsteps throughout your pursuit. To be victorious and unscathed with all you'll experience, cradle in your mind this non-wavering point continuously.

Should you be afraid? You *betcha*! But get in the game, anyway. "Nothing ventured, nothing insane." (Or was that gained?) I, in no way, want to obfuscate your hopes and dreams of finding "The One," in an easy, delightful, hassle-free fashion. I only want to alert you, going online is not going to be a "bed of roses." Which is not to be confused with, "A rose by any other name would smell as sweet." Quite the contrary!

About that famous phrase, "Bed of roses," why roses? They have thorns that'll prick you in the bed. And not the good kind of prick in the bed, either. Why not a bed of daisies, so much friendlier and safer? What I'm saying is, this will not be a walk in the park or a trip to Wonderland.

Yet, the simple fact you're going online indicates you are at a crossroads in your life. Reaching the decision to search for "The One" is the cornerstone of finding true love. Just make sure you begin your glass of hope, not only half-full but rather with your hope-glass completely overflowing. Give it everything you got. It's this kind of intense degree of commitment you'll need. Are you in the game? Are you all in? If you answered yes and yes, then let the cherry-picking games begin.

Before we continue, allow me to inform you about a few things, so there will be no shocking surprises ahead. Yeah, you know what? I take that comment back. There will be a plethora of never-ending bombshells and shocking surprises coming your way. This is simply inevitable, and it won't necessarily help one bit to duck and cover. In fact, there will be many alarming, outrageous, disturbing, mind-altering blows. One moment you might feel safe, secure, and filled with optimistic expectations, positive hopes, and excitement. Then, the next moment, when you turn around, you might be worried about your safety, feeling forlorn, defeated, or hopeless. These are some of the reasons why I caution you, so your surprises will be somewhat detectable, expected, and skillfully anticipated.

It's equivalent to being prepared for a scary film. When you start your search, think of me as your guardian angel, sitting on your shoulder screaming at you to avoid the terror. Sort of like you do when you shout out at the screen during a frightening movie scene. I will become the screaming voice in your head. "Hurry, run!" "Don't go there!" "Turn around!" "Don't go out with him, he's crazy!" "Watch out, he's got a knife!" "Get out of the shower, he's psycho!" "Look out, he's behind you!" "OMG, you fool, don't go in the closet!" "Are you stupid, don't go down into the basement?" Loving simple, helpful warnings, just like that.

So, you won't be woefully unprepared. Allow me to coach and enlighten you with some necessary training and crucial guidance.

BASICALLY, THERE ARE FIVE KINDS OF MEN:

(**Note**: *Sometimes, there are rare exceptions which provide a sixth kind of guy. This is essentially the combo guy, otherwise known as a tweener.*)

ONE...
The Perfect In Every Way Guy... "TPIEWG"

The Perfect In Every Way Guy is the man who will always make your heart smile. He is often stunningly gorgeous and magnificent from head to toe, inside and out. He is physically, spiritually, and emotionally luminous. Moreover, he is typically kind, loving, humorous, generous, creative, fun, and worldly. He is globally conscious, charitable, and has many talents. This guy is respected and adored by all, whether they know him personally or not. He runs in many different social circles. TPIEWG can charm and get along with anyone, from a homeless person to the wealthiest individual in the world. Including presidents and leaders around the globe. And he has.

More good news! This prince among men can predictably have sex without pausing for hours on end. He is quite experienced in this arena. However, he is altogether classy, so he won't likely brag or let you know in advance about these most fortunate talents of his. But when he does, he will push all your erotic buttons and have you begging for, "More please!"

He has no baggage or any dangling psychological or emotional issues of any kind. He's essentially the "golden ticket" among men! Aha, "ding, ding, and ding again! Winner! Your willpower will desert you?"

TPIEWG, was raised in a loving, well-to-do, close-knit family. He is a devoted family man and will be the best father ever. He's highly educated, successful, charismatic, wealthy, and, overall, fabulous. You are his everything, his world, and shows that he appreciates you daily. He will melt your heart and leave you feeling moonstruck! (Just like Cher was!)

His home is expensive and spectacular. It is rich looking, clean, and decorated with unparalleled taste and refinement. He drives a Ferrari-esque dream car, along with a few others. His idea of a fancy dinner for two is dining at his favorite restaurants such as Noma in Copenhagen, Solo Per Due in Vacone Umbria Italy, Le Louis XV Alain Ducasse in Monte Carlo, the Le Gavroche in London, Restaurant Le Meurice in Paris, and El Celler de Can Roca Girona in Spain, just to name a few. As his love partner, you will undoubtedly frequent them often, at the drop of a hat. Don't misunderstand, he also adores letting his hair down, and (extra special if it's long) dining at a local hole-in-the-wall when he feels like it.

He is passionate about travel, and if you go in the style, he is accustomed to, so will you. TPIEWG enjoys going to movies and only sits front-row center at concerts, shows, the theater, operas, and ballets. As it's already been established, he loves fine dining, and everything else that is spectacularly fun, just as long as he can be with you. He is always on the go, and you will be right there with him if you so choose, for he believes you are his other half.

He will be very proud and honored to have you by his side. Don't be fooled, for this man won't possess you. He absolutely wants you to have your own independence, identity, and interests that make you happy. He doesn't want to gobble you up just for himself, as he desires you to shine to your fullest potential. In all your endeavors, he will encourage, support, and always have your back. This is a result of the steadfast confidence and security he possesses from his loving upbringing.

FYI, TPIEWG is obviously the category in which my "*Beloved One*" falls under. (One can hope, right?) Let's be real, this is the dream man every woman and gay guy is looking to catch. He's the fantasy man who'd manifest if Brad Pitt, Chris Hemsworth, Henry Cavill, Chris Pine, Ryan Gosling, Jason Momoa, and Ryan Reynolds combined had a baby.

For the record, good luck finding this one in a bazillion, kabillion, trillion, Hope Diamond of a man. The Perfect-in-Every-Way-Guy is a captivating and enchanting breed. He is rarer than the hunted Elephants in Africa and the Sumatran Rhinoceros. Both of which are endangered species. Still, I sincerely wish you success and good fortune in finding him! While you're at it, look for Cleopatra's tomb, who killed Kennedy, hidden space crafts, aliens, and the Ark of the Covenant.

TWO:
The Normal Everyday Guy... "TNEG"

The Normal Everyday Guy is great at some things and sucks at others. He's either a little pudgy or very skinny and is *almost* good-looking. Yet, you will discover he is abundantly endearing in so many ways. TNEG works hard, but makes an average salary in an unexciting job, better known as, "*The disappearing, but not forgotten,*

American Middle Class." He yearns for your approval. And most of all, hope you'll forever be proud of him. TNEG longs for your praise and needs your encouragement and reassurance. You will always feel that he genuinely appreciates and loves you, but can only show you in a most humble, modest fashion. Still, you'll be pleased by his simple, endearing ways.

TNEG drives a Toyota-esque sports utility and, if it's new, he positively has a car payment. His place of residence is sort of clean, basic, and unassuming. Nevertheless, he feels grateful. You should know his home unquestionably has a mortgage. A loan he dreams of paying off one day before he dies. He sincerely wants to do better, earn more, and climb the ladder of success. With your help, inspiration, and love, he most likely will! There is the possibility you can help transform him into what he truly aspires to be, which is TPIEWG. It could surely happen with your ever-constant support and adoration. His idea of a fancy romantic dinner for 2 is Red Lobster, Carrabba's, Olive Garden, Outback Steak House, Fridays, or even the Melting Pot. Be thankful, at least he won't take you to Hooters. He's far more respectful than that. He goes there with his pals.

I must interject something about the Melting Pot. Men, if we girls wanted to cook dinner, we would have stayed at home! Bring us to a place where we can relax, order a nice meal, and be served without all the gimmicks. Nevertheless, it is a lot of fun for kids! :0)

TNEG is loveable, sweet, kind, and desperately wishes to satisfy you, make you happy, and take care of you completely. He is the type of guy who dances the Macarena and the Chicken Dance because he still thinks it's cool. I promise you won't want to hurt his feelings by telling him, "Honey, that was so totally decades ago!" But he is adorable, and you will happily let it go. To be specific, he is so sweet that he would bring a hug to a gunfight. He wholeheartedly strives to make holidays special and will give you the most well-thought-out and considerate gifts. He delivers these presents to you with all the love in his heart to the best of his financial ability. TNEG doesn't mind fixing things around the house. Sometimes, he will offer to do the laundry, the dishes, or even help you clean up. Ladies, this is your basic *good guy*! He is either shy or a bit too loud. He's loyal, grounded, and can be molded. Typically, this is referred to as *'trained,'* in as much as a man can be trained. Try to ignore his flaws, such as his man boobs or his Cheetah-Pet back hair. You will crush him entirely if you don't! There's a vast pool of these loyal, nice, and caring guys out there. If this is what you are looking for in a man, then girl, go get 'em! With your acceptance and love, he could make you very happy.

THREE:
The Selfish Asshole Man… or "TSAM"

Here, you will find your basic run-of-the-mill guy, The Selfish Asshole Man. In other words, this is the extremely greedy, "I-Me-I," guy, who couldn't care less about you in any real way whatsoever. You'll discover this *thoughtless dick* is cheap, obnoxious, rude, sarcastic, cold, unexciting, self-centered, and unremarkable. *Note that those are his good points.* If you're with him, for the most part, you can count on being treated just ok, or perhaps even worse. You will forever be saying rather reluctantly, "Why am I even with this guy?" Along with, "It figures!"

TSAM is an all-inclusive taker, never a giver, and expects you to make your own way financially and essentially in every other way, but sex. Never mind. He is selfish with sex, too. You can anticipate him taking advantage of your love and devotion. He will use you in any way he can think of, including monetarily. He is a bit of a con artist of sorts. Be very careful if you are with TSAM. Don't let him bulldoze you for his benefit. And be aware, he will most assuredly try. Look for the red flags, for they are impossible to miss in TSAM. They're waving and flapping all around him. It's as obvious as seeing a priest in a strip club, Mark Zuckerberg in a porn film, Paris Hilton in a homeless shelter, or cotton candy being handed out in a dentist's office. As obvious as that, so look for the warning flags.

He drives a used car, whichever one he could rip someone off to buy. His idea of a romantic dinner for two is any joint that's below twenty dollars, where you buy one and get one free. Remember, this man expects you to pay your own way for dinner, even when invited. To add insult to injury, he'll inform you his portion of the bill is the *"get one free"* meal.

He is the paragon of the phrase, *snow job*. TSAM is in no way enjoyable to be with for more than an hour at best. This bully is loud, rude, controlling, argumentative, unpleasant, and extremely uninteresting, which is most likely why he has few friends. He doesn't like to go out much and especially loathes spending money on movies, concerts, dinners, and especially *you!* If you pay, he will go but, only if he wants to. If he doesn't want to go out, and you go with your friends, this will really make him angry. In his world of thinking, if he stays home, so should you.

TSAM is content to stay on his pitted, worn-out cheap couch, with its tacky plaid material, in his underwhelming home or apartment. Nothing pleases him more than getting buzzed alone on cheap beer while wearing his torn t-shirts and shorts. He loves watching reruns of Pawn Stars, Swamp People, Duck Dynasty, shoot-um-up films, porn, eerie films, or other "I am man, hear me roar" television shows. Quaint and charming would not be words used to describe him. He often retaliates with stupid comments like, "Hey, you may think I'm dumb, but you overestimate me." Or the old standby, "Pull my finger," and then he farts. He also thinks it's humorous doing armpit farts for your entertainment pleasure. I must ask, "What's up with men and their endless farting and burping jokes? Why do they think it's so hilarious?" Plus, you'll always catch TSAM touching his balls in public. Ultimately, he's charisma impaired.

In addition, girls watch out. TSAM can typically be a bully who might be physically or mentally abusive. He commonly suffers from severe control issues and a false sense of self-esteem. But if you are a strong-willed, take-charge woman, you might be able to control him. Realize he is nothing more than a browbeating intimidator, a bully, a good ole boy, and a bumpkin. Before rushing in, consider if he's even worth the time and trouble. Ladies, TSAM is the type of guy we've all encountered as often as the number of stars in the sky. And not the lucky stars or the brightest ones either! Listen to me, I don't care how adorable looking he might be. Fair warning, you should still "Run, As Fast as You Can." Fast, as in, "Run, Forest, Run!" Honey, I promise you can do so much better!

Appreciate it's feasible this guy should never be allowed to get his foot in your door or in anything else! He should be in one of your X-Files as an unexplained, hazardous phenomenon. One thing is for certain, *"NO, He Will Never Change!"* Please, oh, please believe me. What do I think of TSAM? Well, let me just say, *"Porky the Pig, Jafar, or Scar have nothing on him!* Too insensitive? Don't judge me, I'm just the messenger! I'm merely telling the truth and saving you years. "And You're Welcome!"

FOUR:

Then, you have The Super Jock Guy... "TSJG"

Now, this Super Jock Guy is out-of-the-box ultra-fun, a casual elit-ist, and the *classically* classic, *"Let's Party Guy!"* He is perpetually smiling, in a good mood, and has a larger-than-life personality. He's extraordinarily entertaining to be around, providing you go with his flow and his idea of fun. I caution you, though, don't ruffle his feathers or provoke him. If you try to control, change, or challenge him, he'll turn 360 degrees on you. He is stereotypically edgy and rugged but cleans up quite nicely. It's pretty easy to detect this cat-egory of men. The *"Mr. Jock, I Presume,"* sort of fellow. TSJG usually played football in high school and college and was the darling stud muffin with all the cheerleaders. He is radically adventurous, game for anything dangerous, whacky, and fun, and cherishes everything to do with his freedom. He most undoubtedly was the president of his frat house in college. I further venture to bet he was the one responsible for coming up with all the fraternity antics and pranks and, perhaps, got kicked out of the house for some of them. Yet, his shrewd, clever-as-a-fox mind always got him back in good graces quickly. He is the life of any party, and positively a down-home guy's-guy. He loves his food, alcohol, and women. So, be careful if you think you are the only one on his roster. He's quite the charmer and very irresistible. You will see and hear him the moment you walk into wherever he is. TSJG is a born leader and super cool! By the way, he knows it too. This jock is popular, mostly because he is a total blast. People want to be with him and be seen hanging out with him. TSJG never misses the chance to attend any sports activities he can be a part of, whether it be playing or spectating. He never fails to catch in person, or on TV, football games, and all the other ball games or sports events. He prefers hanging out with his scads of good buddies at sports bars. He also believes this is a great place to meet fun women, hook up with one, cause hanky-panky, and proudly start a ruckus.

TSJG can be among any of the financial brackets. He might own a grand Harley Davidson Bike, a ten-year-old heap, a Targa Porsche, or perhaps a Range Rover. Whatever he drives, you can be sure it's fun, exciting, and a uniquely awesome-looking ride!

His house is comfortably homey or sexually modern. It'll be filled with oodles of sports memorabilia and athletic paraphernalia. There will indeed be an outrageous sound system, huge televisions, a pool table, and unlimited video games if he has the money. It's all very macho and a true masculine haven for him. BTW, don't mess with his cave, girls. It's his manly-man cave. You're allowed to visit, but not permitted to redecorate.

On the contrary, TSJG is surprisingly capable of commitment and is open to a long-term relationship and marriage. He's even game to have kids if he thinks you are "The One." That's providing you conform to his life of fun and games. Typically, he's a wonderful dad if he takes the time.

His idea of a romantic dinner for two could range from a grungy Key West type of raw bar where you eat with your fingers, to a very sophisticated French Restaurant. What's uniquely captivating about this man is the way he feels entirely comfortable in both establishments.

TSJG enjoys sex anywhere, anytime, and in the zaniest places, just to keep it on the edge. Ergo, he embraces sex and keeps it exciting with an element of nasty. He detests the same ole, same ole, about anything in life, especially his sexual activities. To lure him, think out of the Puritan box.

This pleasure-seeker is comfortable in his skin. He will parachute out of planes, climb to the top of Mount Kilimanjaro, Chogori K2 Savage Mountain, and go down the "Danger, do not enter" ski slopes in Tortin, Verbier, and Switzerland. He won't think twice about kayaking the most dangerous rapids solo or biking up & down Mount Everest if it were at all possible. Ladies, if you're looking for the kind of guy who is fun, thrilling, enthusiastic, and passionate about life, then you for sure want TSJG.

Beware, for you will have to keep on your toes and appear mysterious, intriguing, and forever be willing to go with his free-spirited tide. Don't ever try to cage him. To keep him, you must never let him know all you are thinking. Always have him guessing. Be sly, never whine, or be demanding. That isn't cool for him, and he won't do well with it either! Ultimately, you must be a surreptitious, carefree kind of girl. With TSJG, you'll certainly have fantastical fun, wild adventures, and grand stories together. Girl, if that floats your boat, totally *go for it!*

FIVE:
Lastly, you have, The Eternal Bachelor Guy… "TEBG"

The Eternal Bachelor Guy is predictable to the point of being cliché. He is happy-go-lucky, amusing, and untroubled. He'll never take you, or your relationship with him, seriously. Whether you know it or not, he is dating many other women while you are together. Naturally, he will deny this and keep his secrets under lock and key. Even if you walk in on him and catch him naked, having dirty, outrageous sex with another girl when you confront him, he'll unequivocally totally deny it! *"Babe, I have no idea who she is. Trust me, I don't know how the hell my dick got inside of her!"* His motto to you with other women: "Deny, deny, and deny!"

TEBG is free-spirited and cheerful, for he has no commitments to keep. He has no baggage or drama to unpack or need to do so. The Eternal Bachelor Guy is not always as easy to detect as you might think. He's generally not forthright about his fidelity or his long-term plans. In fact, he doesn't like to make any plans more than a week in advance or, dare I say, two weeks. Be on the alert, for he will commonly cancel those plans he had made anyway for something better that might have come along. He likes to chillax, or whatever else pleases him in his solo Al Pacino, John Cusack, Kevin Spacey, Hugh Grant bachelor world. He is the center of his own alternate, perfect universe, and you will never take his place. I can't tell you how betrayed he felt by his X-hero George Clooney, the sell-out!

"He will never marry you or give you children!" You see, this is the antithesis and the supreme aversion of his world. I will not waste paper by repeating this 20-more-times. We are destroying enough trees as it is!

Don't try to trick him or throw an invisible net over him. For he is far better at deceit than you'll ever be. Take my word for it. You're not in his league. He has spent his entire adult life crafting every personal detail of his bachelorhood. The only thing he is committed to is never being committed to anything or anyone, especially a committed relationship. The last thing he wants to do is settle down. Ever! For him, it's equivalent to being in prison, with a life sentence, and no possibility of parole.

After sex with a new woman, or maybe even a 3-week mini-short-term relationship, his familiar epigram is a notorious *"Wham, bam, and no thanks, Ma'am!"* It's fascinating and ambiguous how this guy is typically capable of being loyal to his long-time friends and family, but that's about it. He prefers hanging out with lots of women, rather than his close mates. However, if his buddies need him, he is right there at a moment's notice.

TEBG never misses the opportunity to 'conquer' a new woman. Frequently referred to as "The flavor of the week" or, as the French might say, "Femme du jour." If I only had a quarter for every girl, the TEBG had sex with I'd be quite wealthy.

TEBG can be among any of the financial brackets depending on his career and status. Remember, he's had the luxury of keeping whatever money he's made, since he doesn't have a wife, children, child support, or alimony payments. He drives anything he wants to and wheels around in a ritzy, impressive, sports car, whether he can afford it or not. Remember, it's all about him. He loves the attention his car brings. Thus, everything in his life, such as clothes, possessions, and his home, is attention-seeking, showy, and ostentatiously selected to his personal taste and desires.

His bachelor pad is outré-sexy and masculine. In furnishing his lair, I think TEBG probably hired the same decorator Caesars Palace in Vegas used in the 70s to decorate their over-the-top, bordello-esque, erotic suites. It has all the essential male gadgets, such as a huge mod bar stocked with liquor, an oversized hot tub, mirrors strategically placed everywhere for his pleasure, a professional massage table, (Aha, whatever), and the best sound system money can buy. There will, of course, be a massive amount of red, black, fur, and leather furniture adorning his pad. There might even be a dancer's pole next to the pool table and a pinball machine for you to bear your talents for him.

His idea of a romantic dinner for two is basically anywhere he won't run into another woman he is also seeing. For this reason, he has an unending supply of destinations where the Maître D's (for a small fortune) all have his back on this detail.

TEBG has many interests and hobbies, for he possesses the

luxury of so much free time to do so. The urgency of *now* is not a part of his joyful universe. If you are searching for short-time kicks, exotic new, and erotic sex (whips, chains, toys, and handcuffs included), or just a quick illustrious rebound, then this is your guy! But, no matter what, "*Don't Give Him Your Heart or Fall in Love with Him.*" Naturally, you think you're different and more special than all the others. You are certain you'll be able to change him, make him see the light, and flip-flop his stance. Honestly, it will never happen, for you will never be more special or important to him than his freedom is. Understand, he'll never be yours!

Take note, if you are naïve enough to bring up any type or sort of commitment, he will commit you to exile in limbo. Very much in the same way, the monarchy sent Prince Edward, Duke of Windsor, formerly King Edward VIII, into exile when he married Wallis Simpson. Here's the thing. She wasn't even pretty! I will never understand why he abdicated the throne for her. The Royal Throne, people, with all its palatial palaces, ornate crowns, and priceless jewels. All I'm saying is that Wallis woman must have been wickedly amazing in every sexual act known to mankind?

To be unmistakably clear, if you even faintly try to capture TEBG, he'll quickly Beetlejuice it the hell out of there, and far away from you.

Single ladies looking for the "Always and Forever," and you are older than thirty, I say pretty much, "Fuck This Guy!" Shine him on. For those of you whom these words offended, well then, I say fiddle-faddle, mumbo-jumbo, and seriously, chill the F#@&*%$* Down!

In closing, I wholeheartedly advise you to look for man One, PIEWG, or man Two, TNEDG. Save yourself, altogether from man Three, TSAM, at all costs.

For those among you seeking a life of spontaneous thrills and adventure, set your sights on guy Four, TSJG. Say, yes, if you love sports, wild fun, screaming men, and keeping it up to *score*. With you, or games!

If you never want a serious, long-term relationship and you're just looking for a sex buddy, TEBG is your man. Or, if you also suffer from "commitment phobia," then run into the arms of the fifth type of guy, The Eternal Bachelor Guy! For this guy's your guaranteed devil-may-care short-term, no drama, respite, and a quickie *'Mr. Right Now'* relationship.

Ladies, I am here to remind you, don't look back to see your poor decisions. The only time you should ever want to look back at your love life is to see how far you've come. If you play your cards right and smart, you will determine that you have come far and in all the right ways. Remember, intelligence is the new sexy. Don't be a fool. Use your brain and choose carefully.

After all, it is your life! Be wise about it...

CHAPTER 19

The Guy with Extreme Peculiarities
The Geek-Nerd... The Alien

BETTER KNOWN AS THE WEIRDO IN HIGH SCHOOL WHO WAS MOST LIKELY TO SUCCEED, BUT STILL? AND... WHAT THE HELL IS HE WEARING?

Miles was a Geek. Miles was a Nerd. "Put down the RPG/MMO-Games, and no one gets hurt." Miles admitted to me on the phone that he was a self-proclaimed Nerd-Geek. I mean, for real, who comes out and discloses this fact before meeting a girl? But I reconsidered because it must not be that bad of a lifestyle when one of the richest men in the world, Bill Gates, once said, "Be nice to nerds. Chances are you'll end up working for one!"

With each phone conversation, I sensed Miles was floating way up in the clouds half the time. He accomplished this without the aid of weed, pills, or alcohol, which the rest of us would need to get us up that high. Part of me thought, "Good for him!" His cosmic mind was frequently wandering, probing distant places, and con-templating complex equations and correlations like when Mariah Carey thinks placing her finger on her ear somehow helps her to reach those high notes. Equations like believing the fairytale that

Republicans and Democrats will one day see eye-to-eye and work together. Contemplating complex correlations and equations like believing Taylor Swift will never, ever, ever stop writing about her love life. But the winner and champion, is how much of what we're told from every rank of the government is true and honest? Or how much is covered up with deception, bribery, lies, and blackmail? All right, now that's done!

I found all of Miles's quirks, gnarly attitude, and peculiarities bewildering. He's the combination platter (number 6 on any Chinese takeout menu), that blends and combines all the Geek-Nerd personalities, which manifested an overly eccentric person. Though perplexed, I found his mind and unconventional manner of thinking intriguing. I had become a mad scientist, needing to know more. Yes, I always bet on the dark horse and the underdog, but does the horse or dog need to be this dark or weird?

Naturally, being a self-proclaimed normal person and journalist (A possible oxymoron there), I did a bit of investigating to see where his head was at before agreeing to meet him in L.A. With this odd fellow I not only had to think out of the box, I, had to throw away the box entirely. Yet, I was still captivated. I guess it's the philanthropic (or foolish) side of me.

To fully appreciate Miles, the Nerd-Geek who I renamed "the *Neek*," I had to understand the throne and rules of his Nerd-Geekdom. I discovered "Geek" came from the word "Geck," originally a Low German word. In the early 1900s, carnivals and circuses had a performer called the geek, or sideshow freaks. The Geek (aka Miles) was to perform bizarre, crazy, revolting acts to entertain the locals. These performances were called "geek shows." Spectacles that are not unlike those performed on any university campus frat house, on any given Friday or Saturday night.

The first documented case of "nerd" was in Dr. Seuss's, "If I Ran the Zoo," in 1950. A year after the book was published, a Newsweek article included the 1st official case of the "nerd," how we refer to it today.

To be fair-minded (which is never any fun), Miles did not sound overly crazy on the phone. However, I did ascertain from our combined phone conversations, he was indeed a classic dork. He seemed socially impaired, awkward, and principally anti-social. I'd bet the ranch Miles was not in the cool group or any group at all in high school. He was undoubtedly the kid people laughed at when he dropped his books. Or, snickered at, for he knew the answer to every math and science question. Miles was that kid who was bullied into letting the cool kids copy off his paper during a test, to have his lunch money stolen, his locker broken into, and a nerd sign put on his back. He obviously was the last to be picked on any sports team, if at all. It was the empathetic teacher who likely came to his aid, placing him on the better team. That's when Miles had to endure the agonizing, *"Oh man, come on! That's not fair,"* outbursts of disgust from the good team and laughter from the shitty one. It's apparent, he was not interested in any mainstream activities. I couldn't tell if the Neek was an anarchist or an anti-anarchist. He was all tech, fantasy, electronics, and spent an inordinate amount of time on his computer and games. I'd bet the same ranch (I don't own) that Steve Jobs and Elon Musk had some or all these traits, too.

I noticed Miles loved using jargon, weird terminology, and obscure references when he spoke. Most of the time, he appeared to be an alien. He acted as if he came from another world, and I'm quite certain he would consider this to be a fantastic compliment. It's my opinion, Miles might be undiagnosed and suffering from Asperger's. When we spoke, he had no qualms about putting duct tape on the nose of his glasses, holding them together until he got around to buying a new pair. If ever. As a staunch fashion sheriff, I found this gravely unacceptable!

From all I had learned and seen in photos, Miles was super cute. Nevertheless, he dressed horribly, was unkempt, and disheveled. He had little experience with women other than those on his X-Box games. This was all I needed to hear. I was sad for him and knew someone needed to lend a helping hand. So, I decided to lend him mine. If nothing else, some basic fashion sense, tips about women, and Lord knows, some real music to listen to. I felt a strong urge to rescue Miles. With my heart filled with compassion, I believed I could make a profound difference in his life.

Fortunately (I thought at the time), I had business meetings in Los Angeles that week. I met Miles three days later in Santa Monica, as his personal Planet Earth Guru. Even before I arrived, I fully recognized there was no love connection feasible with the Neek. He was in no way a hopeful candidate for my affections. This was a nada, nope, negative, but thanks for playing anyway, situation. This rendezvous was nothing more than a goodwill, benevolent assignment. I suppose it's the price I pay for being such a sweetheart, a humanitarian, but more likely, a total idiot!

We met at the True Food Kitchen, a health food restaurant for lunch. When he walked in, I cringed in horror. Shocked, I uttered, "Ah, geez, *no, no, no!*" I panicked, for he literally did have duct tape in the middle of his outdated red glasses. And *'what the fuck'* was he wearing? He was a grown man but resembled a childlike extraterrestrial. (That's an insult to E.T.'s!) I distinguished right away this was an emergency mercy trip. Not to mention a social injustice to fashion. Alarmed, dreading this makeover, I stood frozen. At the very least, he should receive a *fashion fine* for his attire. He was so green, and I'm not speaking environmentally. To his advantage, Miles was adorable, grinning with his outstanding smile and big blue eyes. I concluded under all his messy hair, and lack of style, a chic man could emerge, begging to be let out of the Neek bottle. He was 31 years old, but he acted and dressed like a 12-year-old boy.

I was now on a mission. "Mission Impossible!" Nevertheless, I chose to accept this mission, despite the fact no tape would self-destruct in five seconds, and without being wished the good luck wishes, Dan was given! I was determined to rock this dilemma.

When we first met, I greeted him with a smile and a warm hug. "Hey, Miles, so nice to meet you." To my surprise, he snarled back at me. From there, things quickly went downhill. Readers, I know you will find it hard to believe, but I promise and remind you that this story is 100% true.

"Take your stinking filthy paws off me, you damn dirty ape!"

Then he laughed and said, *"Great Scott! Greetings, programs! Kneel before Zod! Now, Gimme some sugar, baby."*

Sugar baby? Worse yet, Miles was a close talker, and spit when he spoke! All that came out of my mouth was, *"Umm?! What?!* Miles, are you kidding me? Why the hell are you speaking in movie catchphrases?"

"It's a moral imperative. Oooh! Ahhh! It's how it always starts."

"Ok there, movie-quote Neek, cut the shit for real and I'm quoting me!" Sure, I grasped that my response was mean-spirited. But come on, people? You think you could do better? With no time to think, he went on.

"One thing's sure, Inspector Clay is dead, murdered. Somebody's

responsible. Never go in against a Sicilian when death is on the line!"

I realized I was in deeper trouble when he ordered a Big Mac with fries, and a McFlurry, in a health food joint that only served gourmet tofu burgers and baked zucchini wedges. Dumbfounded, because he requested 3 entrees, I sarcastically asked. "Do you think we need a bigger table?"

He countered, *"Yes, captain, we're going to need a bigger boat."*

I disregarded his response, just like I was taught in psychology class during my sophomore year of college. Trying to bring him to reality, I changed the subject. "So, Miles, what are your plans for the holidays?"

"Ha, You Can't Fool Me! There ain't no, Sanity Clause!"

"Dude, are you gaslighting me? If you are, you seriously need to stop! You are really freaking me out!" I quickly learned that dealing with Miles brought a wide spectrum of responsibilities.

"I'm sorry, Miss, I'm afraid I can't do that. Furthermore, don't call me a mindless philosopher, you overweight blob of grease!"

"Miles, do you realize what you're saying? Do you know who I am? Dude, are you playing with me? Is this all a ruse? Am I on a ruse cruise with you? OH, of course! I get it now! Ok, where are the cameras?"

"If we knew what we were doing, it wouldn't be called research!"

Tilting my head in disbelief, I forced a grin, hoping to involve him in a reality-based chat. "Miles, have you ever had a girl-friend before?"

"Yes, Wonder Woman, I have!"

Growing eerier by the second, I asked. "What happened with her?"

"She left me. We had a fight. So, I cut off the heels on every single pair of her shoes! Every pair! Ha, broken cut-off heels were everywhere!"

Furious, I gave him the look of death, thinking, *"You! You Lucifer, Shoe Murderer!"* I hated and detested him so much that I had to fight the urge not to slap the superhero fantasy shit out of him. I could've beaten him like a piñata. My hands were itching to punch him out. He was way over the line, with a deserving large portion of "fuck you, asshole," on the side. This shoe-tale would keep me up for months. I think it was the most horrifying story I've ever heard in my entire life. And I'm a reporter! He was a shoe assassin! Beam him the hell up, Scotty! Wait, I thought? Miles was just like my brother Jeffrey, except with shoes instead of dolls! I was sickened, listening to his story, and desperately trying to control myself from turning into Regan, from the *"Exorcist,"* spewing out green vomit all over him. Being this devastated, all I could think to say was, "Why? Why, why, why would you do something so hideously disturbing? Amigo, you're so frickin' lucky she allowed you to go on living after that event!"

"The answers you seek shall be yours once I claim what is mine! I shouldn't be alive unless it was for a reason. I know what I have to do, and I know it is right. I exist only to protect Krypton. Every action, no matter how violent or cruel, is for the greater good of my people."

"OK, chillax, Thor, Iron Man, and General Zod, wannabe!" I was launched straight into the third dimension of legendary Sci-Fi movie quotes and trivia games. I trust Miles is medically afflicted with "Multiple Movie-Character Personality Syndrome" and "High-Heel Shoe Disorder!"

He then announced to the entire restaurant he was going to the men's room. He stood up hastily, looked at the diners, and affirmed loudly enough for all to hear, *"Some days, you just can't get rid of a bomb!"*

Okey-Dokey. I hoped my ears deceived me, but, yeah, the daft fool said it. He is as *"fresh as a crazy!"* Wait, there's more. He went on.

"No matter what you hear in there, no matter how cruelly I beg you, no matter how terribly I may scream, do not open this door or you will undo everything I have worked for."

He continued, adding, *"If I'm not back in 5 minutes, just wait longer. Kamehameha! Bazinga!"*

It's all true people. You can't make this shit up or would ever want to! Mortified, humiliated, and not prepared to deal with this, my caboose had fallen off its track. I didn't know whether to call a mental asylum, Gamestop, an urgent-care clinic, G4TV, or the game department at Target to find out what the hell he was doing, and what I should do. I wanted to help him, but this predicament was way above my pay grade. Way above.

Dammit, wouldn't you just know it? This was one of the few times I didn't prepare an escape plan. It figures. And it's the number one dating rule, people! As I was searching for an exit strategy, Game-Boy returned greeting me with shiny pearls of wisdom. The pearls I was now clutching.

"Nothing shocks me. I'm a scientist. Well, let's just say, this crumb of apple pie represents the normal amount of psychokinetic energy in the New York area. Based on this morning's reading, it would be a crumb apple pie 35 feet long and weighing approximately 600 pounds."

This time, I didn't fool around or curtail my thoughts. I wasn't going to feather his nest and came straight at him. "Listen, Miles, are you screwing with me? I don't know if you are a freak, a weirdo, an obnoxious jokester, or in dire need of help. Seriously, are you OK? What's going on with all your gobbledygook talk? You weren't this whacky on the phone."

"Girl, I'd love to change the world, but they won't give me the source code. And what's the air-speed velocity of an unladen swallow?"

I waved down the server to ask for some ice water and Miles proudly and forcefully boasted, *"The glass is neither half-full nor half-empty. It's twice as big as it needs to be. Never argue with the data."*

I knew I wasn't losing my mind because our rational, sane, server Debbie looked at me reassuringly, *with a WTF pity smile*, and rolled her eyes in disbelief. "Stop it, Miles!" I demanded, glaring at him. "I mean it, pal! Cut the crap or it's going to get ugly!"

"As you wish."

Debbie chimed in sarcastically. "Hmm. You know, I just realized, this might be the result of Venus and Saturn now being in alignment!"

We both giggled. *Uh-Oh,* that's when the Neek got up, walked clear across the entire restaurant to this dear little old man, his sweet little old wife, and two other tables, and screamed in a panic.

"Okay, you people sit tight. Hold the fort and keep the home fire burning. And if we're not back by dawn, call the president."

Fuming profusely, I ignored him like the bratty OCD child he was. I accepted that I had somehow entered a whole different universe, possibly even a time warp. Because of my reputation, fear of being recognized, and a bevy of other obvious reasons, I had to split immediately. This situation was positively out of my league. Orchestrating a getaway, I picked up my cell to reconfirm a previously scheduled happy hour date with another journalist. I begged her to move up the time we were to meet.

Miles looked at me talking on my phone, pouting like a three-year-old and whispered loudly. *"ET phone home?"*

The well-balanced, rational server, Debbie, overheard and said with an elongated added lilt, "No Waaaaaaayyyy!" She presented me with my bill that I couldn't pay fast enough. A few minutes later, Debbie rushed back with the receipt and some natural vegan mints.

Miles proclaimed with authority. *"Who's gonna turn down Junior Mints? It's chocolate, it's peppermint, and it's delicious!"* He turned to Debbie and blurted out, *"This is your receipt for your husband, and this is my receipt for your receipt. Your soul-sucking days are over, amiga!"*

Debbie clearly had enough and replied wearily and distressed in my direction. "Wow, man, for real? I don't get paid enough to deal with this kind of bullshit. Here's the thing dude, hell no. Like Snap, no!"

With that, I apologized to normal Debbie and gave her a gigantic tip. She declared, "Miles, I think I was wrong before! The moon must be in the fifth house, and Jupiter is most likely now aligned with **your-anus**!"

As Deb left, I was laughing inside over her pretty accurate remark! I collected myself, turned to the Neek, and retorted with disdain.

"Miles, really, it's enough. I'm out of here!"

"Oh, but you haven't finished your food," he said with deep concern. "Engage! The vial contains a nourishing protein complex. And, besides, no matter where you go, there you are."

He just kept going on and on in my face like a Wal-Mart greeter! Concerned, I asked, "Miles, do you have a family to help you? What about parents, brothers, sisters, or cousins? Hostile witnesses? Anyone at all?

"There is no earthly way of knowing which direction we are going. Not knowing where we're rowing, or which way the river's flowing. Is it raining? Is it snowing? Is a hurricane a-blowing? Not a speck of light is showing, so the danger must be growing. Are the fires of hell a-glowing?

"Goodbye, Miles, it was categorically unreal. Neek, you need to hear me, and I say this with all my heart. You, my friend, need some treatment!" Then I brought in some dialogue I predicted he would comprehend using the words of the legendary C-3PO.

"Don't get technical with me. What mission? What are you talking about? I've just about had enough of you. Go that way, you'll be malfunctioning in a day, you near-sighted, scrap pile."

"Don't make me angry," he replied. "You wouldn't like me when I'm angry. Ah-ha, well, I see now. End Of The Line. Ya Ta!"

His insane attitude was further illuminated when he slyly turned to an innocent customer and insinuated cunningly. *"Well, hello, Mister Fancy Pants, I've got news for you, pal. You ain't' leadin' but 2 things right now, Jack and shit. And Jack left town."*

Then, OMG, Miles turned to a huge, tall, redneck sort of guy, all covered in facial hair, tattoos, piercings, gold caps on his teeth, and yelled, *"My name's Inigo Montoya. You killed my father. Prepare to die!"*

After that little ditty, it was impossible (even for me) to hold back my laughter. I was ashamed of myself. But hey, *funny is funny*, even if it was hilarious in a very off-color, outrageous way.

"Ciao, Miles. I hope you get help. You are distinctly a Grey's Anatomy episode and possibly the whole season. Without commercials!"

His behavior was so offensive, everyone cracked up laughing. Unfortunately, I don't think the hairy, tattooed, gold-toothed redneck sort of guy was so happy with it. I'm judging by the bloodcurdling, bursting veins on his neck and the angry fury displayed all over his flushed face.

Hoping to push Miles away nicely, I said, "Although being with you would be like living the dream, I say no, anyway. Bye-bye, Miles."

Upset, he replied like a little boy. *"The world just sucks. It sucks!"*

Bearing in mind his reality, I responded with, "Miles, if it didn't suck, then we'd all fall off! Ciao, Miles, Live long and prosper. Ya Ta!"

Guessing by the look on his face, it appeared my statement made perfect sense to him. It was as though he was starring in his own sitcom and playing all the characters himself! As I slithered out, waving to Debbie and hoping to escape, Miles ran up to me with his last words.

"If you can't take a little bloody nose, maybe you oughta go back home and crawl under your bed. It's not safe out here. It's wondrous, with treasures to satiate desires both subtle and gross, but not for the timid."

Nope… Miles was not done!

"After very careful consideration, sir, I've come to the conclusion that your new defense system sucks."

A girl can hope, but he was still not done yet.

"I'm going to give you a little advice. There's a force in the universe that makes things happen. And all you have to do is get in touch with it. Stop thinking, let things happen, and be the ball. We apologize for the inconvenience!"

By now everyone in the restaurant was earjacking, laughing, and applauding, including server Debbie, of unwavering normal. While Miles relished his 15 minutes of health food restaurant fame, I was mortified and upset. Even after wanting to help him, he put me in a ludicrous situation. *Still,* I imagine Miles was ever so proud of his achievement here today! He brought the restaurant's patrons, "dinner and a show."

Though there are several geek and nerd categories, Miles didn't fit into any of them. Miles was plain textbook insane, an Oscarworthy actor, or an accomplished prankster. With no closure, I'll never know which one was correct. It might have been a good idea to bring a shrink to the party. I thought to myself, walking away, "Mission, very impossible," terminated!

As I escaped in a daze, a lady ran up to me and showed me a photo she had taken on her cell of Miles, talking to me. She asked, laughing.

"Would you like me to text it to you?"

I answered, "You know? That would be a great idea for evidence."

I spent the rest of the afternoon and evening at the Grove having reality-based cocktails with an NBC Journalist. I desperately needed to recuperate for longer than a while. My "Neek Chapter" wasn't quite humorous to me just yet. Although Janet, the NBC Journalist, thought my alien close-encounter was super-di-duper hysterical. She couldn't stop laughing long enough to sip her cocktail. I easily managed to down a few.

To this day, I never found out if I was being hoaxed, punked, or if this online guy was genuinely clinically disturbed. No matter which one, I felt sad for him. This was the strangest, zaniest person *I had ever, or could ever, meet.* Oh, dear God, I hope so. They're out there, people. But, poor little, me didn't know then the magnitude of the crazy yet to come.

The *"Jerry, I swire, I di'int sleep with my girlfriend's four best friends and two cuzins, and gettin um all knocked on up at the same time!"* Kind of crazy people.

The *"Can I have my Jerry beads now, Jerrah?"* Crazies!

I am speaking of the Maury Povich, kind of crazy people. The "You don't know me, you don't know me," people.

The *"I ain't the baby daddy. Even though she tickle my innards. I never had 'sexylations' with that slut, Maury. Ya gots ta believes me, Maury. Look at that child's's's's face. He ain't look nutin' likes me! He gots front teeths and everthin'! She a Ho, Maury, a porcupine!"*

Maury asked, *"Billy-Ray, did you mean concubine?"*

"That what I say, porcubine! It's the same thaang, Maury!"

That's the kind of outrageous people I am referring to. Without bragging, I have faith in my ability to understand and help people with their problems and adapt to life's challenges. Knowing I have a credible approach to these touchy matters, I went all out to help Miles the alien from the planet "Neekzon." Unfortunately, I failed miserably. I came to realize with Miles, the extra-terrestrial from an alternate universe, that in the end, I genuinely didn't have a prayer! Poor lad, his inside voice must be screaming, "Let me the fuck out of here!"

I sure hope he got some help. However, if he was faking it, my gosh, he really needs to start doing standup comedy! All my friends and I would attend, sitting front row center, and screaming Bravo, Miles!

Thank you, online dating, once again, for yet another most interesting mind-fuck encounter of the third or perhaps fourth kind. I chalked this 'strangecumstance' date up to a fiasco of universal proportions. I guess that's how the kooky crumbles! Evidently, this is what happens when you hang out with an alien species.

Horrible Flashback moment...

He cut off the heels of all her shoes! People! Do you hear me? He chopped the heels off!!!! Who does that? What kind of monster does that?????? Shoe, criminals, that's who! His strange, vile, villainous insensitivity boggles my mind! He should have been shot, locked up in a shoe factory prison, or at the very least, committed to an insane asylum for such a wicked act! I don't care how crackers Miles might have been. (Or not.) This action alone proved him to be a legitimate antihero and a heel!

To be honest, if he wasn't messing with me, Miles was completely divorced from reality on so many levels. He was like a "Turducken" of mental illness. Even now, I still believe he was pulling my leg. He was just too good at it. I'm still waiting for his reality show to appear on Netflix called, *"The Lone Alien and Impractical Joker,"* *starring Miles.*

If life is a stage, then where is my best-supporting actor? Romeo! Where on earth are you already, dammit? *Du-Hu-Hude?* You must come and rescue me! You must! My life is becoming a Shit Show!

Focus... Focus...
'Nuff Said, And an Unwavering, Rational, All True, Next!

CHAPTER 20

Bobble Drew
Part 1

A TRUE, REAL-LIFE LOVE AFFAIR AND THE TIME OF MY LIFE!

How can I accurately explain "The Bobble Drew Adventure?" Drew found me online. When he contacted me, I wasn't going to respond since he didn't post a photo along with his profile. This is a solid and paramount deal-breaker for me. Regardless, I broke my unconditional, unwavering rule, because his profile name ended in my lucky number, 33. It's a funny thing about lucky numbers. They never turn out to be lucky in the end. Although intrigued, I couldn't put my finger on why I was? Yet I couldn't resist his bravado style of arrogance and his exceedingly superior confidence. Meanwhile, I was charmed by his humor, which captivated me when I read his profile and self-description. It was written with his keen wit and intelligence. There was something about how he described what he was looking for in a woman that I found fascinating. The fact I wasn't turned off by his flaunting haughtiness and self-importance surprised me. Why I continued talking to him was baffling. I normally feel averse to this sort of person. With Drew, he oddly enough got to me, which attracted me even more. His spirited and egotistical moxie was obnoxiously amusing.

This man knew precisely what he wanted, with no reservations. He was poised and confident, and it didn't amount to a 'hill of beans' what anyone else thought about him. To deflect, I ask, "Has anyone ever seen a hill of beans?" I mean, is there actually a hill of beans out there somewhere? Personally, I have never seen one. Perhaps a coffee bean grower in Kenya or Columbia might have seen this so-called famous hill of beans we all speak of. I really don't understand why we say this. Moreover, why a hill and not a pile, a mound, or a grassy knoll of beans?

Although Drew sounded substantially cocky, something within persuaded me I unquestionably had to respond to him. In retrospect, I would like to strangle that something within me. On second thought, I probably wouldn't. I appreciate it was necessary to experience all the lessons Bobble Drew brought into my life. Store this thought in your mind, as it might come in handy and help you through your own dramas.

Anyway, on our very first phone conversation, I inquired, "Drew, why didn't you post a photo? If your profile name didn't end in the number 33, I never would have opened your email nor responded to it."

He went on to clarify. "Oh, I completely understand your position and I can hardly blame you. But there is a reason for my being so evasive. You see, I am quite well known and enjoy a very celebrated career. Thus, I didn't want to post any photos. I felt it was necessary to keep my online dating private. Being the main topic of my office staff as they chat away in the break room, didn't sit well with me. They'd love this sort of gossip! Not to mention, they'd all want to set me up with their friends, (or themselves) if they knew I was seriously looking for a relationship. The bottom line, my personal life outside of the office is sacred. Consequently, I find it necessary to be discrete. I hope you understand, Mollie!"

"I understand completely. Nevertheless, please send me photos!"

As it turned out, Drew was a great guy, and his ego was entirely justified. He was a bona fide, mega-successful, renowned criminal lawyer in Washington, D.C. And being a D.C. lawyer, he was consumed with work. He also had offices in New York, San Francisco, Los Angeles, and Palm Beach. I understood why he wanted to keep a low dating profile. He represented prominent cases for distinguished billion-dollar corporations and personal criminal cases all over the country. Drew was a world-class, recognizable bigwig. Boy, did he ever know it, too! Magical, how he more than managed to outweigh his tremendous ego with his infinite charm.

Drew had been divorced for about 4 years. He didn't keep in touch with his ex, which was just fine with me and less complicated. What I respected most about him was his undying devotion and all the time he spent with his 3 children. Drew made it clear to me that his kids were his world! They worshiped their dad and were very close to him. I believe the adoration, immense love, and commitment he felt for his children are very special qualities. It is also a monumental accomplishment for such a busy man in today's world to achieve. I admired him greatly.

Alas, for me, I should've paid more attention (right from the beginning) to the screaming communication red flags concerning his poor calling, texting, or any other form of staying-in-touch skills. I warn you, ladies, rapidly going all goo-goo-gaga over a man can easily turn a bright woman into a blind, deaf, foolish, innocent little girl. We all do it, so don't go beating yourself up when you, too, go all goo-goo-gaga over a guy.

Drew was, "Ooooooh, So Very Busy," (and please notice the extra

O's) all the time, which was his steadfast, trustworthy excuse for his lack of communication. Truth be told, he was extremely sought after, had a preposterously overbooked calendar, and was incredibly overworked. He not only kept ridiculous business hours, but he was also on the board of many organizations, charities, universities, and foundations. Drew was constantly booked for speaking engagements and lectures. What's more, he had to fit into his schedule professional lunches, dinners, city council meetings, and openings at many elite gatherings. On top of all that, he kept up with his promise and commitment to spend as much quality time with his children as possible. This included rooting them on with their baseball and soccer games, schoolwork, music, theater, and other such endeavors.

His schedule left me in limbo, feeling like a naïve, silly teenage girl, endlessly staring at the phone, hoping it would ring any moment. It was pitiful, really. Making matters worse, I programmed a special ringtone, so I'd know it was Drew when he'd call or text. I refused to miss his call, even if he caught me in the middle of an important interview with the U.S. President. (And that happened!) My heart pounded, and I jumped each infrequent time I heard his ringtone. I was embarrassed by my love-struck heart and hated myself for behaving this way. I was pathetic and head-over-heels in serious puppy love and infatuation. I was entirely smitten, and we hadn't even met! Desperately trying to be aloof, I realized this was not an advantageous situation to be in, feeling like the underdog.

We spoke on the phone when he randomly had a second to call. Still, it was always fantastic speaking with him. Drew was entertaining, and we got along famously. Both of us are humorous people, so there was a healthy abundance of laughter and joking around. That was one of my favorite things about "us." Oh, how we roared, laughing together. We were becoming a great comedy team. Seriously, though, we should have gone on YouTube, or, even better, had our own podcast. Our bantering was hilarious, and our infrequent chats were lighthearted and great fun.

Then, before I knew it, I quickly discovered the next waving red flag concerning this mysterious man who I hoped to meet. It appeared he got high on legal weed all the time. To be frank, it really didn't bother me that much. Since he was quite used to smoking, he always remained very normal and completely functional. No one would ever detect that he was stoned. It didn't spoil my adoration for him. I wasn't fixated on his getting high, and I never once voiced any concern. Still, it was a sign to be noted.

At last, Drew made all the initial arrangements for us to meet and continued to do so throughout our relationship. Naturally, this was achieved by telling his personal assistant when, where, how, and precisely what to do in anal detail. This wasn't because Drew was lazy. On the contrary! He was always just too "Oooooh, so very busy" to make these trivial things happen. Although I give him credit for all the exciting, marvelous plans and ideas he came up with and for making them possible.

This *meet-cute* was more exciting than being in Time Square on New Year's Eve! Bobble Drew made all the preparations to come out and meet me. He insisted on sending a limo to pick me up at my house. I tried to decline his kind gesture with great appreciation for his thoughtfulness by explaining a limo wasn't necessary. But he maintained his stance.

He clarified, "Honey, I want you to be safe in case we have too much wine. I also want you to feel well taken care of. You shouldn't have to worry about driving when you are coming and going to meet me! I want you to feel relaxed, safe, and carefree."

This impressed me immensely and, of course, turned me on to the point of being giddy! Or what is past giddy? Whatever it is, I was that!

Drew, and I were to meet on January 4th at the Picasso Restaurant, in the actual city that never sleeps. Dazzling Las Vegas, where I call home. I was so excited I could scarcely contain myself. Right on time, the limo driver came knocking at my door, wearing a fancy chauffeur cap and all. Walking towards the super long, movie star-worthy, white stretch limousine, I was hoping my stuck-up, nosey, inconsiderate (for always parking their cars in front of my house), next-door neighbors caught a glimpse of all this. I was dressed like a celebrity on a red carpet, running in my Manolo Blahnik Heels, and my imaginary tiara, as I floated into my story-tale coach. I know it's all so very nauseating, but come on? This was unique. Who sends a limo on a first date? I'm just saying, who does that?

When I arrived at Picasso, my heart was thumping with nerves of enchantment. But this feeling quickly passed as I sat in the restaurant's beautiful lobby, waiting for the now, very late Drew. It felt awkward being gawked at by the staff and other guests. Clearly, my excitement and infatuation were impatiently dwindling down. I became increasingly uncomfortable, lingering alone for over an hour at this extraordinary, refined establishment. I was now self-conscious, feeling as though I were being mistaken for an expensive, upscale hooker. After 2 hours (TWO hours) and being offered huge dollars from men, thinking I was a Vegas prostitute, I was furious. How rude I assumed this was of Drew, keeping me waiting this long without calling, especially for our first meeting. Limo or not! Regrettably, this was a trait I'd soon come to know all too well.

Upset and just before I got up to leave (in an Uber), Drew appeared in all his glorious, glorified, glorylicious, self! His grand entrance sent shivers up (and down) my spine. He was entirely more handsome than his pictures presented him to be. This man was splendidly gorgeous and way too striking and distinguished for his own good. *Or mine!* I was so taken by his stunning presence, I bashfully struck *'that'* pose? You know? The Lady Diana posed look, with my head bent down towards the ground and my eyes looking up at him ever so shyly. He was "Top of the heap," like Sinatra's, New York, New York song describes.

Preposterous as it was, I heard the words in my head, "Mr. Grey will see you now!" Standing before me, he was an endless turn-on with his full head of way too premature salt and pepper hair and his big baby blues. I found Drew completely irresistible, sexy, and exquisite. Just looking at his hair, I was dying to run my fingers through it. He stood before me toned and sophisticated, wearing perfectly fitting Versace from head to toe. So elegant, he made chic and classy fall short. My heart was beating loudly inside my chest. I feared he heard the sounds I was feeling. My anger over his extreme tardiness vanished. As he looked at me sweetly, I thought, you know? I mean? For sure, anyone could be two hours late without calling? Really, what's the big deal? No biggie. It happens!

Through the bewitching haze, I felt myself virtually rising and floating up into the heavens. Realistically, the hazy fog might've been the smoke-filled room of the casino. This polished man was effortlessly doing something inside of me. I liked it, I needed it, and I so badly wanted it!

The first word Drew ever spoke to me in person was, "Wow!"

I girlishly replied, *"Really?"* (Wow! Where did Mollie go?)

He reacted with a smile, put his arms around me, and gave me an enormous bear hug. "Hello." Then he repeated, "Wow, big time!"

I was done! That was it! I was toast! A penalty flag should've been thrown on Drew for a pointless Tackle and a Blitz from my blind side! All the dating books teaching the *"To-Do & Not-To-Dos,"* *and* those movies about dating were now irrelevant. My girlfriends' counsel on the "Must Do & Don't Even Think About Doing Lists, On Dating" foolishly turned into sprinkled dust, floating down all over the fancy restaurant's carpet.

As we walked to our table holding hands, Jon, the Maître D' said, "Right this way, please." He seated us across from one another at a beautiful, private table overlooking the phenomenal Bellagio Fountains.

Being polite, Drew diplomatically asked if he could change our seating arrangements. "Thank you very much for this lovely table, Jon. However, is it possible to rearrange the table settings? I'd like to sit closer and next to this gorgeous woman. I am certain you cannot blame me!"

Jon the Maître D' responded with reserved refinement. "I don't blame you at all, sir. And, as you wish." He swiftly whispered to our head waiter, who immediately came rushing over to us.

"Good evening, my name is Oliver," he announced, beaming cheerfully. "It is my pleasure to rearrange your seating at once! No worries at all, sir!" Feeling myself now gushing profusely, I knew I had to drag my wanting eyes away from this new object of my obscene, sexual desires, and quickly, before he noticed.

At last, we were left alone, and Drew skooched over as close to me as our chairs would allow. He placed my hands in his and smiled. "Mollie, you're spectacular! You are so for me!" From his very first touch, I became timid and starry-eyed. The energy from his warm hands instantly gave me goosebumps. About that, I think they should be called angel flutters, romance touches, or love sprinkles. Whatever they are called, I had them all over my body! I felt a hopeless stab of longing for this man I barely knew. I was sinking deep into his soul as joy ran through my veins.

Drew, and I were physically wrapped up in each other's arms, hands, and legs. As far as we were concerned, we were the only two people in the restaurant. The staff members were refined and professionally experienced enough to give us our privacy and not interrupt too often. It was evident the last thing on our minds was food. Wine? Yes, definitely! Eating? Not so much. We found ourselves intensely in the moment and overpoweringly passionate for one another. Happy and touchy-feely, we had been transported right back to the 8th grade in middle school. Something very special was happening between us. Like soul mate special. Or maybe we were captured in a hot, burning pit of lust.

Somewhere between the fancy appetizer and the elaborate salad (that we barely touched), Drew gazed into my now sparkling eyes and said whole-heartedly, "I think I am in love with you, and I am going to have to marry you!" At first, I laughed, thinking, obviously, he was only kidding. That is, of course, until he declared, "I'm serious, honey! I'm going to marry you and we will have many weddings." With that, he placed the perfect bite of our fancy appetizer and elaborate salad into my mouth, which was already wide open from gasping over his remarks!

I was so into this man I just smiled, chewing the perfect bite, while trying to digest his stunning statements. Entirely hypnotized, I believe I would've married him that night on the spot. I'd marry him with or without an Elvis Minister in "Viva, Las Vegas," and "Aha, I'm All Shook Up!" In my defense and to pardon myself from being unrealistic and absurd to even consider this notion, I had already checked him out thoroughly. I had discovered on paper that Drew had a sterling record, was all he claimed to be, and far more. But in person, "Oh, my heart!"

BTW, if you are curious, the food at Picasso is extraordinary, as I overheard the women talking about it in the ladies' powder room. Judging by the one bite Drew fed me, it really was. Fortunately, or unfortunately, we were too lovey-dovey with each other to waste a moment eating dinner. Of course, we easily managed to share a bottle of wine. Or two? Definitely, two! I learned he was a very experienced wine connoisseur. I adored that about him among a billion other things I discovered that night. With our tummies empty and growling, we went to his hotel room with the promise of only hugging and kissing, as we frantically had to. Honorably, he followed through with this promise along with delicious cuddling and laughter until the limo arrived at 4:00 in the morning to drive me back home. I will say that Drew is hands-down the best kisser and hugger of my entire life. Well, up to date. It was impossible trying to fight my zealous urge to stay overnight with him. I didn't want to leave the warmth and safety of his arms. But I also knew I had to appear a smidge hard to get. Drew was infinitely desirable. Still, I appreciated how this was neither the time nor the place to have sex. If I wanted to gain his respect and mine, the mere thought of sex was months down the road. Months! *Many months!*

On the drive home, I felt pampered, luxuriating in the shiny white stretch limo. I felt like a rich and spoiled character in a sophisticated, hot, steamy romance novel. I was used to limos from my work, but this time seemed different. I hope to never get spoiled enough, not to appreciate basking in a limo. I'm referring to all of you rich, famous, spoiled elitists! Jumping from my Cinderella coach, I thought, "Where are my neighbors?"

Once home, reliving the divinely magical evening, I sensed this just got real! I reflected and questioned how much of it was *"real,"* and how much was, in fact, "fantasy." Was this entire night purely an illusion? For tonight, I didn't care. Cozy in bed, I smiled, still feeling this beautiful man's gentle touch, his tender kisses, and the addicting scent of his cologne, which remained all over my now-awakened body. I never felt more alive or excited. I was savoring the sexy recollections of this night and his cozy warmth. I rarely get the opportunity to savor. It's nice.

The following evening, Drew sent a limo to fetch me once again. OH, GAWD? Did I really say, "fetch?" (Gosh, where the hell did Mollie go?) Understanding more about him, the second night we were to meet, I dressed to the couture "tens!" I had to surpass the now, far too inadequate nines. I wore a very short blue Prada skirt, a white Dior off-the-shoulder cleavage-baring blouse, and my favorite Gucci strappy heels. Though confident that I looked hot in this foolishly expensive ensemble, I was still anxious. My eagerness to be back in his arms was killing me!

When I saw the ultra-magnificent Drew, with his Ashton Kutcher cleft chin, standing there, *on time,* so very fine-looking, and *waiting for me* in the hotel lobby, I blushed with delight. After scrutinizing me intensely, he commented, "Stunning," and then whisked me away rapidly. "We must hurry, baby! I got amazing tickets front row, center for us to see Taylor Swift." I knew all too well, being able to score these tickets to see Taylor (and last minute), that this guy was seriously important and connected.

At the concert, we found ourselves so physically intertwined with each other. So, when Taylor walked off the stage singing with her arm extended to shake our hands; we didn't move a muscle. Poor Swift stood right there before us with an outstretched hand that we ignored, as if she had leprosy. I love her to pieces and all, but I wasn't letting go of Drew, even for her! I didn't imagine this has ever happened to Taylor before. She got it, though! She motioned to her heart, smiled at us, and moved on. We were in a magical rapture listening to hit songs, brilliantly sung by Taylor. Like, "Everything has Changed," and "Love Story!" But were we a love story? Did he really love me, even though he said it? Logically, I knew it wasn't realistic, true, or even possible? But for now, it didn't matter! As the superstar icon sang, time stood still. I took in this splendid moment, pinched myself, and thought. Could this bewitching evening conceivably get any better? Well, that is, until I noticed his strong, *impressive hard-on.*

After the best concert ever, we knew at least for the moment that "Everything has changed," because Taylor Swift sang it directly to us. We then moseyed over to the Palms for dinner, which is one of my favorites. It looked like an amazing dinner that we ordered and scarcely touched. But we were too excited and caught up in our own little euphoria to waste the moment, eating. However, the wine we finished off was a gift from the Gods *and Drew.* We shared a rare bottle of Opus 2006. A small fortune was paid for this unforgettable wine extravagance. Yes, wine me, baby!

Drew repeated his promise with a toast. "I am going to marry you, and we will have many weddings!" Proudly, he began naming some exotic places to celebrate these weddings. I wonder if he noticed the enormous question mark on my face?

I interjected, "You understand many weddings require many gowns and shoes, right?" He laughed profusely, agreeing. No doubt, his laughter was clearly the thousand-dollar bottle of wine, giggling.

Over our untouched, scrumptious-looking steak and lobster dinner, I seriously looked *Bobble Drew* in the eye and asked him for a giant favor.

"Certainly, anything, baby! Just ask me."

"Please, pretty please, promise me no matter what I say, do not let me make love to you tonight!" I explained how important it was for me (us) to wait. "I need your absolute guarantee and your solemn promise!"

He gracefully and respectfully affirmed with a sweet, caring look with his lovely ses yeux bleus. "Honey, I understand entirely, of course! Yes, I Promise! I completely promise! *You have my word, sweetheart!*"

I think it was during my third or fourth orgasm in his hotel suite that I noticed the most breathtaking view of the Las Vegas Strip I had ever seen. He said, gazing at me, "It's beautiful seeing the reflection of the city lights in your exquisite eyes." OK, I get it! It's official. I am now *a slut!* (Loitering 2 hours in the Picasso Restaurant, several men thought so, too?) I also grasped that his "Reflection in your exquisite eyes" comment was such bullshit and too schmaltzy and gooey, even for me. But, Hell, he said it, and I still loved the extravagant romance of it all. So, back off, people!

Without ever leaving his plush hotel suite that evening, I was transported to ecstasy. Talk about the 'Big Bang theory,' Georges Lemaître? I can tell you a whole other theory and a completely different philosophy, through my own, *'Big Bangs!'* I saw endless stars that night, but only one authentic heavenly body, Sir George… **His!**

Drew possessed infinite seductive moves. The man was a sexual ninja! Was this destiny, fate, chance, or kismet? For now, I didn't care. Meanwhile, not to be disrespectful to the beauty of our lovemaking, but there was so much *'Semen'* happening in his hotel bed that night, I thought we were in the middle of a U.S. Navy Base. Just love, sailor fun! We smelled of raw, unadulterated sex. Our neverending, delicious, XXX climactic orgasms left me throbbing with excitement, yet thirsty for more.

And so, I enclosed his plump hardness in my hand as I slid down his body, stroking him wildly with my tongue. OMG, how I adored his lusty sexual moans! Suddenly, I felt the expertise of his tongue on my clit, and he didn't stop until he heard my plateau of pleasure. Delightfully exhausted, my muscles screamed with fatigue, but my heart and desire for him begged for more. He pushed and caressed every one of my sexual and emotional buttons. And some I didn't even know I had! He knew what to do with every inch of me, and I loved what I felt when he did. I even loved his sweat dripping down onto my craving body. I loved how disheveled he looked after our wild sex. I even loved the wet bed sheets, filled with our sexcapade. I felt like a naughty, wicked little hussy. It was fantastic!

I had a *spanking* good time (that too) making love with this man, who I quickly became a slut for. Unexpectedly, though, I sensed our first lovemaking experience uncovered a memory from another life we shared. As insane as Jack Nicholson in "The Shining," I detected everything about Drew, and it all seemed familiar and recognizable. But as I so very much wanted to go out with him again, I kept those thoughts entirely to myself.

Being naked and sharing pillow talk with our bodies interwoven felt too good to be legal and quite felonious. Serene, while lying next to him, my thoughts and feelings equaled one enormous *Taylor Swift song*!

Absorbed in my own world, he caught me off guard and whispered gently, "Honey, I love you so much. I am so completely in love with you."

I went dead silent. I mean, characteristically, those are words I am not usually fond of hearing, twenty-four hours in. Although irrefutably irrational, with this glorious creature, it felt natural, and completely as it should be. I answered him back without hesitation.

"Drew, I'm so in love with you, too!" I smiled, perceiving we were such fools. For the first time in my life, I believed my search was finally over. The love of my life had found me at last. I was euphoric. So why then, did every part of my being cry out to warn me, "Yo, slow the hell down, girl? Relax. Mollie, be careful. Slam on the brakes, don't open your heart so easily!" Yea, like I was going to listen to me, telling me anything to stop me, from going full speed ahead with this stunning man! Putting on the breaks? Seriously, not happening. A steamy love affair was accelerating now, in full throttle.

Suddenly, his whole demeanor changed. He abruptly sat up in bed, apparently alarmed and deeply serious, looking at me with eyes brimming with panic. He placed his hand on my cheek, begging nervously.

"Don't Hurt Me! I Mean It! Don't Hurt Me!"

I replied, "I won't. I never will! Please, Don't Hurt Me Either!" No matter how much I tried denying it, I couldn't refute the overwhelming angst in my gut and my woman's intuition. The second those words left my lips, I knew without a doubt that I was going to be the one who got hurt! Anyway, I didn't care, for I had never known such happiness with a man in my entire life. I hadn't felt this way about anyone before. No one has ever made me feel this whole. Still, I wasn't a total fool. I knew I had to hold back a piece of my heart, so I'd only be 87% devastated later! No way was I giving in to reason. Without any respect for caution, I would entrust my entire heart to him. I wasn't going to play childish games. I needed to love Drew freely, with all my being. Irrational as it might have been, this was a welcomed invasion of love and lust. I was going to have the time of my life with this man, if only, but for a moment in time.

Staring at me adoringly, Drew interrupted my intense battle with myself. He rolled over on top of me, and I felt his renewed hardness firmly digging into my leg. Like a magnet, I happily pushed towards it. I wanted him to possess me completely. It was not a challenge for him, as I had no defense or willpower to control myself whenever I was near him. My body was begging him to enter me again. And just like that, I guided his penis into my awaiting warm wetness. There was a slight scent of our joined passions amidst our sweat and erotic juices. We made love all night in the Vegas hotel. His first broken promise, and on the same night he gave his word it wouldn't happen. I didn't care. That promise was so last night! I guess Drew's enormous penis can explain our insatiable sexual appetite.

From that night, we were caught in a whirlwind of traveling. We took our romance all over the country, sharing sexual ecstasy and a tornado of mischievous and lustful desires. We were jet-setting off to exclusively elite and renowned places. I kept a suitcase packed, as he would call me at a moment's notice to run into a limo and jump on a plane to join him. The yearning, hunger, and passions between us were flaming hot and out of control. No matter how much we made love, it was never enough for us. I heard my continuously beating heart and feelings for him echoing throughout the room wherever we were. Wherever we went, people stared with eyes of envy as they plainly saw our love and affection spilling over. We didn't care who saw us or what they thought!

All of Drew's texts were dreamier than a giant romantic, $20 Hallmark Greeting Card, only better and sexier. The first text I received from him was after our first beautiful trip away together. It read:

"Thank you, thank you, and thank you!!! I Love This Woman!!! I still feel your body against mine, and our lips pressed against each other. Thankfully, we will meet on Thursday. We will hug and kiss and stoke the fires of our love and passion. I long for you whenever we are not together,

but this time apart will be particularly trying. I love you so much that I am diminished without you. I want and need you. Please know that I love you. You're everything to me. I will call you later, just to hear your voice. Eighty-four hours until we will embrace… XXXOOO."

A few days later, Drew came to visit. Sadly, though, for only 16 hours, which was over in the *blink of an eye*. We made the best of it, indulging in a wild, 16-hour sexathon, with very little *blinking*.

We met the following week in Arizona. Drew picked me up in Phoenix, where he jumped out of the car, swooped me up into his arms, gave me a huge voluptuous kiss, then jumped back into the BMW rental. We were off in a flash on our picturesque drive to Sedona. How did he know I'm a total sucker for the "Romantic and showy guy picking up the girl in his arms, Hollywood greeting?" The picturesque drive to Sedona was filled with laughter, singing, and silly-spirited fun. After a few hours, we reached our destination, the Auberge d' Sedona, a posh cabin-styled ranch that Drew knew about. We checked in and then enjoyed a couple's massage in our cabin, he had prearranged. The man thought of everything.

After being pampered, we stepped into our private hot tub on the veranda and made love. Naked in the water, I couldn't help but stare at this fine-looking man, with his adorable face and his teeth that were as shiny and white as freshly fallen snow on Christmas day. I stretched out my waxed long legs and my pedicured toes above the water, rotating my ankles and laughing sensually. He raised his eyebrows, and I could feel a flush running across my face. Holding my naked waist, he kissed me and shouted aloud, "Mollie, you're spectacular, fucking sexy, and I love you!"

"I love you back! Babe, I have such an insatiable desire for you I can't stop wanting your fierce, perfect 7-pack hard body inside me."

Out of nowhere, a furious rainstorm came down in buckets. We loved getting soaking wet in the hot tub, basking in each other's arms. As he stared at my breasts, (like a wolf) I noticed my nipples stood erect as if I were snow skiing in a T-shirt. He picked me up from the water, threw a towel around me, and we continued fucking inside our love nest. Drew poured a bottle of red, lit a fire, and played a mixtape, in that order. We went through two rare bottles of fine wine, laughed, made love, and "love fucked" endlessly. We didn't want to pause for dinner, so we survived munching the 3-jumbo M&M packages I brought and the fudge brownies I baked. There's nothing greater in life than wine, chocolate, wild sex, and being loved. Even better, all at the same time! Heaven is in his arms.

I don't know how Drew always managed, but my "*sexpectations*" were profoundly more than met! My love was 36 years old and could make love continually without stopping. His lovemaking was steamy, passionate, a bit dirty, and intensely erotic. My experienced lover brought me to the abyss of screaming, clenching, and grinding teeth climaxes. (My dentist would be angry with me about that part!)

I loved our "Laugh-Fucking," as Drew eloquently named it. I've never laughed during sex before. It's silly, spicy, liberating fun. I highly recommend it. Our desire for one another had no boundaries. We had to be constantly touching. I craved him and could never seem to get enough of him. I yearned and longed for Drew every moment we were apart.

We enjoyed unbelievable memories in Sedona. With all his thoughtful pre-made plans to tour and show me the beauty and amazing sights in this spiritual little town, we, oddly enough, never left the cabin. I hope one day to see Sedona! I hear it's remarkably lovely and mystical. It didn't matter to us that we forego his plans.

While in Sedona, merely staying in bed, we reached amazing heavenly heights of spirituality and discovered our own personal, divine, transcendent vortex!

When we returned home 3 days later, Drew wrote this:

"I'm still rocking gently at the hips, thinking of your face beneath me, and your legs on my shoulders. I love you so deeply. You are so lovely, and I am so in love with you."

Our next delightful interlude was in Laguna Beach. Bobble Drew arranged for a limo to pick me up and bring me to the airport. I was certain I'd never get over this generous luxury he continually provided.

When I landed, Drew was standing at my gate, eagerly awaiting my arrival. When he saw me, he ran towards me and lovingly picked me up in his arms. I treasured this affectionate tradition I had now grown accustomed to. I breathlessly looked forward to it each time we met.

His personal driver, Quinton, was engaged to drive us to the aristocratic California Beach Montage Hotel in Laguna. After checking in, we both had business calls to make. Regardless, we reconsidered. To hell with everything else, we needed to be 'one' immediately. We jumped onto the bed within seconds of opening the door to our lavish hotel suite, which overlooked the picturesque Pacific Ocean. He tore off my clothes and the rest was history. Reluctantly, we forced ourselves to leave the bed a few hours later to walk along the beach at sunset. Drew picked me up, held me tightly in his buff arms like a baby, and kissed me tenderly. Nothing could be more beautiful than what we experienced together that evening. We danced amidst the crashing waves and joyfully frolicked along the shoreline. How breathtaking it was listening to the romantic forceful roar of the waves while observing the splendid red sun as it began to set across the ocean's horizon. If one didn't believe in God, they surely would have after witnessing the burst of colorful lights from the sunset shining across the sky, hovering over the deep blue sea. It was so divine we were compelled to say a wish and a prayer as she gently disappeared off into the distance. I had never felt more loved, adored, or at peace in my whole life.

That evening, my darling Drew requested room service to arrange a romantic dinner outside on our private patio. The table was elegantly adorned with exotic flowers and candlelight, which overlooked the views of the ocean. As usual (being a foodie) he ordered an abundance of food for us to enjoy and devour. The cool breeze, pounding waves, and the perfect 68 degrees only enhanced an already idyllic evening. Being together was intoxicating. We were silenced by our emotions of love and let our souls speak for us. Drew, and I were cocooned in the heart of paradise, embraced in harmony, serenity, and our electrifying love. Stardust filled our eyes.

Never leaving each other's side, we spent the next 3 days laugh-fucking, talking about our hopes & dreams, and frolicking along Laguna's sandy beaches, searching for seashells as a memento of our time here.

On our last evening in Laguna, he "kinda-sorta," (more kinda, and less, sorta) got a little *"Fifty Shades of Drew!"* He blindfolded me, tied my hands to the bedpost, and had his way with me. 'Me Likey!' Although he didn't need all those shades, for I was his for the taking. Oh, come on, I was a sure thing! Sex that night was smoldering and richly carnal. There was something deliciously naughty about it all. I never desired any man more. And I also realized, I never want to be touched by anyone else ever again. I was hopelessly in love and belonged only to him, evermore. Drew easily, razzle-dazzled me with every color in his big box of *Sexola* Crayons. Loving this hard felt way too vulnerable. "Kinda, Sorta," scary!

When my plane landed back home, Drew arranged for Jon, a limo driver, to be waiting at baggage claim. He held up a gold sign with Mollie Sloan, beautifully written. Inside the limo, I heard the familiar songs of the 'mixtape' my Luv made for us that we enjoyed throughout the weekend. Drew sent it to Jon to play for me and to keep. He didn't miss a trick!

This was the text Drew sent to me while being driven home.

"You are my love through the ages, and I am yours forever. We are one. I cherish our memories of our magical time together. You're my soul mate, you're my gypsy, you're my siren, you're my Venus, you're the woman of my dreams. You're everything to me. You're everything to me! I love you. I love you more than more. I long for your arms wrapped around me and mine around you, kissing deeply and endlessly. Sleep well and visit me in your dreams. I luuuurve you. I'm in major withdrawal mode and it hurts like hell!!"

Our next tryst was in San Francisco. Drew had some heavy-hitter business clients meeting him there for a big case. Luckily, this offered me ample time to explore the art galleries and all the fabulous shopping in this exciting city. I bought 4 pairs of designer shoes I just had to have, and of course, a few outfits. I had no other choice and I blame it on my *F.D.P.S.* illness. ("Fashion Designer Purchase Syndrome.") What else is there for a girl to do with *F.D.P.S.* alone, in love, in San Fran, a shopping paradise?

We stayed at the Mandarin for 4 nights and our suite had the most spectacular panoramic views of the city and its iconic Golden

Gate Bridge. Aside from making love, we ate fancy gourmet dinners at the celebrated North Beach, Lazy Bear, Gary Danko, and San Fran's "in spot," Saison. While we dined, he still always enjoyed preparing the perfect bite for me.

As the trip went on, Drew and I continued to share impassioned, crazy love, walked along the pier, drank bottles of wine, fucked madly, ate a lot, and fell deeper and deeper in love. Leaving each other these days was growing unbearable. Our goodbyes now at airports were agonizing. We had hoped just one more hug, just one more kiss, just one more touch would help get us through until the next time we were together. Of course, it didn't. How could it? That night, my precious man sent me this text.

"I am in a state of awe and bliss. You are my love, like no other that has been or will ever be. The connection of our souls will transcend time apart, just as it always has. Thank you for all that you are and for making me a better person through your kindness and joyful spirit, and for taking the time to be together on this Earth, laughing, loving, and uniting as one. Please let me know that you've arrived safely. I miss you beyond words. I love you. I love you. I love you! Xxxxxoooo! PS I Love You."

Even with this pedigreed gentleman's confessions of undying love, I could not stop feeling the precarious caveat hiding within our love affair. Drew lived in an alternate universe, which made me apprehensive. I sensed the many fears and warnings that he would leave me. I knew it would cause earth-shattering, long-suffering pain, leaving me desperately broken. Or maybe not! I've been wrong before. But this was all too *wonderful* not to take the risk. Thus, I denied the damn caveat and indulged completely.

Our next romantic tête-à-tête was magical because we were so enraptured by our love that it was like a fantasy, mythical, even. It was our Valentine's Day weekend, and I was jittery and quivering with excitement. After we met at the San Francisco Airport, Bobble Drew drove us to the Ventana Ranch, in Big Sur, where we enjoyed 4 fantastical, dreamy days. We settled into our ultra-posh cottage suite sporting a wooden canopy bed.

I wanted to surprise Drew by decorating the room. I asked him to wait out on the veranda. Next, I adorned our rustic love cottage with adorable Valentine's Day ornaments, rose petals, hearts, and placed candy all about. I also positioned several gifts and homemade desserts. When I invited him back into the chalet, he was blown away by all I had done for him and for us. He gave me a bear hug. "Mollie, you're amazing. I can't believe all the time and love you spent making this so special!" Pouring me a goblet of wonderful California wine, Drew asked me to step out onto the balcony over-looking the spectacular view of the ocean, so he could do the same. Precious the way he lined up his many special gifts, impressive flow-ers, exotic sinful designer chocolates, and toys. Ah-Ha, yes, toys!

We made love in the Jacuzzi, gazing at the ocean, and enjoyed the fireplace, flowers, cards, music, and infinite bottles of wine. We ate homemade fudge and chocolate chip cookies, which paired nicely with the wine and candy. Whoops, I forgot to mention my erotic Valentine's Day red satin & lace lingerie. I also wore garters, fury heels, long pink gloves, stockings, pearls, and honey-pussy-powder, which drove my love into an obsession of mischievous desire. What more could any girl want in life?

Sprawled everywhere were unopened Valentine's cards, candles, gifts, passion, romance, laugh-fucking, and each other. This was my utopia. In between volcanic orgasms, we ate, talked, giggled, and joked around so intensely that we burst with unlimited lov-ing vibrations. If laughter and happiness burned calories, Drew and I would become anorexic. After hibernating for over 24 hours of *funtastic* passion, it was apparent we needed to leave our love bubble to venture out and see the awe-inspiring sights of the surrounding cozy seaside villages. As we walked out, we noticed the cute and nosey housekeeping ladies. They were smiling, pointing, and chuckling as they entered our cottage of passion, with all its ornaments of love and romance.

We took day trips and drove around Monterey, Carmel, and Big Sur. We ate at the Nepenthe, the Big Sur Bakery, the Post Ranch for lunch, Point Lobos for the sunset, and, obviously, the Rocky Point for dinner. We also visited McKenna Falls and the Henry Miller Museum. We found ourselves captivated as we gazed at the ocean's hypnotic beauty, and the cliffs and rock formation's stunning visions along the drive.

Back at the ranch, we found our happy place on the premises, other than in each other's arms. We discovered a huge hammock in between two majestic old redwood trees. There we'd lie down and cuddle. As we were swinging in the hammock at sunset one night, I feared this man had stolen my heart forever. In an insecure second, I knew I would never get over losing him. This loss would destroy me. I couldn't handle lingering on this thought too long and swiftly brushed it away.

"What's wrong, baby? Sweetheart, why do you look so lost?"

I deflected. "Nothing, my love. I'm just so happy being with you!"

We stayed in for dinner and enjoyed a delicious room service feast, naked in front of the fireplace. Throughout the evening, we ate, danced, laughed, sang, made sweet love, and we also fucked lovingly. This man possessed some major sexy moves! Expert sex is well in his wheelhouse.

On Valentine's Day evening, Drew presented me with a Tiffany necklace, (I squealed. He had me at the iconic little blue box with a white satin bow) with interlocking rings in yellow, pink, and platinum gold, with diamonds. It was exquisite, like Drew. He also gave me a designer jacket with a matching scarf, extravagant fancy chocolates, and unique flowers.

I gave him a handsome gold lapel pin with his initials, accented with a diamond I had made for him. He had tears in his eyes. "No one has ever given me something this special before!" I was nervous about having it made because he distinctly told me he was not a jewelry guy. Looking at him now with tears of appreciation, I was happy I did it.

When our trip was over and we were forced to separate, I was overcome with mixed emotions. My painful tears felt as if there was a bottomless hole in my heart. When I landed, I saw this text from Drew:

"My heart is full, but my soul is like a scrambled egg without you next to me. I will always, always, always, feel this way. How could I not possibly take care of my greatest treasure: You! Seriously, I love you with all my heart. Please let me know when you arrive home. This is starting to hurt!"

For our next adventure, Drew planned a big birthday surprise for me. He booked us into the rustically elegant San Ysidro Ranch in Santa Barbara. This is where John F. Kennedy and Jacqueline Bouvier Kennedy went on their honeymoon. My incredible man organized and meticulously prepared everything to the last detail, making this an amazing birthday.

He strategically created every little detail down to our names on the cottage door. (A girly gush there, and a huge *Ah*, for sure!)

There were dozens of multi-colored roses set in a pink triangular crystal vase, a large box of exclusive candy, several bottles of wine, and champagne arranged for our arrival. My heavenly gorgeous man had a second gift for me from Tiffany's, in its famous little blue box & white satin bow on the dresser.

Our posh, countryside, all-white, *'Three Little Bears'* cottage had a Country-French cozy canopy bed, dressed in white silk material that this little Goldilocks and her Papa Drew-Bear christened over and over. And, yes, over again! And let me say for the record, it was, *"Juuuuust Right!"*

On my birthday, my love presented me with the celebrated little blue box with the white satin bow. Inside was the most elegant, beautiful Tiffany diamond heart necklace. No doubt Drew had lavishly expensive taste. Indeed, I loved the heart he had picked out for me. Nevertheless, it was *his* heart I loved, needed, and couldn't imagine living without.

Indeed, his gift of love astonishingly softened the blow of being a year older. Well, almost? Ok, not at all, but still, the gift was fabulous.

Clearly, this was the best birthday of my life. It was the best because I was with him. I didn't need all the rest of it to make it so. For I loved this man! But give me a break. Let's be real. I'm glad he did! Geez, a Tiffany diamond heart necklace? Come on, I'm in love, not insane!

After giving me his gift, he gave me another one. Drew locked his long, slim fingers on the elastic of my thong and pulled them down. I could smell the scent of ritzy Parisian soap on his neck as he hugged me. He brusquely tossed me onto the bed as if I were a Raggedy Ann doll. I giggled encouragingly. *"Oh yeah, baby, please go on. Hanky-panky me!"*

Heady waves of horny passion overwhelmed me. Though he

had already undressed me with his eyes, he ordered, "Take off your clothes!"

With an obnoxious guffaw, I replied, "No! Take them off yourself!" Bursting into our typical 'us' laughter, he undressed me quickly and began pounding his penis into me with celebratory glee.

"Happy fucking-birthday, Mollie! I love you!" The glowing red hue of the fireplace attempted to equal our blazing passion. Nonetheless, it failed miserably in comparison to our burning and sizzling lust!

After 4 nights, in the lap of countryside luxury and bliss, being swaddled, loved, and cradled in his protective embrace, leaving his side, and saying goodbye was excruciating. That night, Drew emailed me this:

"I am feeling incredible today. I smiled and thought clearly about business and legal matters during meetings and phone calls, while intermittently flashing back to licking your ears, neck, shoulders, belly, and delicious, sweet raspberry pussy with the wet tip of my tongue, and the sacred moment of smacking the velvety skin of your bottom—deeply fucking you hard, from behind—in a moment of erotic and spiritual perfection. I love you! I love you completely, my angel!"

"My God, is he good or what? The guy should write romance novels!" I admired how he behaved appropriately and elegantly in every situation. And yet, he could still be erotic and nasty when befitting. Drew possessed all the colors of emotion. He always said and did the right thing and was never crass, thoughtless, hurtful, or improper. All that my man had accomplished, he did so with perfection, care, grace, and finesse.

A week later, I visited Drew in his perfect-in-every-way home in D.C. The furnishings were custom-made or imported. Though masculine, it had an inviting, comfortable décor. Everything was state-of-the-art and digitally programmed. Even with my Ph.D., I never did figure out how to open the blinds or turn on the lights, leaving me most of the time sitting in the dark when he was at work. Fearful of looking ignorant, I couldn't admit it to him. Funny, he never asked why I was always in the dark.

While Drew went to work at his office, I did all my work from his home. But, like a good 50s wife, I anxiously waited for him to return home at night. As most of my visits to D.C. were for political assignments, it was a wonderful pleasure to be there for love, rather than dreary politics.

A few nights, we went out to dinner and other evenings we stayed home and just played house. By that, I mean ordering in and fucking all night on his new beige leather bondage sex chair and everyplace else. (*Toys, partners, and batteries not included!*) Feeling safe and unashamed, I even let him take naked photos of me. Now that's quite something! To be candid, I trusted him that much. Yet, I've never, or would ever, do this with anyone else. Or again! Careful here, ladies! This naughty, bad-girl behavior has a way of coming back to haunt you and literally shooting you in the ass! Nevertheless, I'm very proud to admit those photographs of me looked damn spectacular, and I don't regret it. But I know in my gut those photos are hanging in an iCloud compartment somewhere in the sky. Yes, it was worth it! I'm a worldwide porn star now! (Possible accomplishment there.) *Note to self, and as tempting as it is, "Do not add worldwide porn star to resume!" Chill, I hid my face. I'm a newbie porn star. Not stupid!*

His Feng Shui harmonized house had a Steinway Baby Grand Piano that no one knew how to play. It had 6 elaborate, enormous flat-screen televisions that were not connected. See now, that's profoundly senseless and precisely one of the reasons why I love and respected this man. His splendid cherry wood, custom-built closet overflowed with only the best, astronomically expensive designer clothes and shoes. I could smell his cologne's sexy bouquet lingering in his closet. His kitchen was a chef's playground, his pool was a swimmer's dream, and his bedroom was my paradise. It was my favorite room in the house. Here is where Drew gave me all the love, sex, and affection I desired and needed from him.

After our all too brief 5-day visit, on his way to court, Drew dropped me off at the DCA airport to return home, where a limo was awaiting my arrival. Later that day, this was the text he sent to me.

"Heaven on earth kissing your delicious lips… and caressing your exquisite face, looking into your beautiful blue eyes, and glimpsing past lives of loving one another, feeling the pulsing sensation as I thrust into you and you into me, your legs held high, hearing our soft moans escalate as we surrender to one another time and time and time again. I am weakened without you… I love you!"

So, I question, who among us girls could resist him? Exactly, no woman could. Over the next 4 months, we enjoyed and continued our mind-blowing rendezvous. To date, Drew and I made love in Los Angeles, Pacific Palisades, Santa Barbara, San Francisco, Laguna Beach, Beverly Hills, Sedona, Big Sir, New York, Miami, Vegas, Chicago, Dallas, and Washington, D.C. But even though the miles sadly separated us, we were inseparable in our hearts. We were very much in love.

Good Lord, I was completely lovesick. (Where the hell is Mollie?)

Here is yet another sweet, love note from Drew in-between trips…

"Oh, honey, I must thank you! You stole my heart, honey. From the first moment I saw you to the moment we parted, time flowed so quickly and deliciously, leaving me yearning for more. I can't wait to hold you in my arms and feel your kisses and body pressed against mine. (Deep sigh) I will see you soon and speak with you later today. Take care of yourself. You are so precious and beautiful. My heart is full, and I feel you. You make me whole."

"Mush, gush, sigh, and swoon!" Reminder readers, every word is, "The truth, the whole truth, and nothing but the truth, so help me God!"

Every time Bobble Drew and I reunited, he always picked me up in his arms. Then he'd kiss me so passionately that I could literally feel all the love in his heart transferring right into my soul. When Drew held me, I felt held! When he made love to me, I felt loved! When Drew and I laughed, I felt happiness. He never did anything halfway!

During each visit (*no exceptions*), Bobble Drew repeatedly told me, *"We are going to get married and have many weddings all over the world."* Every time we were together, he repeated this promise. One day, he said to me with his eyes overflowing with love, *"Baby, listen. Just go buy the wedding dresses. It's a done deal!"* Only this time, he added a cute little different angle to his promise. *"Doll, it's just a matter of time before placing our flag on top of the mountain!"* To that point, I've always wondered how long, *"A Matter of Time was?"* And, also, what mountain?

As one might expect, I didn't go run out and buy the dresses. Still, I reluctantly and shamefully confess to trying on a few Couture wedding gowns. Fine. Perhaps it was more than a few. I can't resist, Vera! Who can? I even started watching reruns of "Say Yes to The

Dress." The New York and Atlanta series. This is considered two-fold pathetic. Anyway, I was seriously love-struck & foolish. "OMG! Where did Mollie go? Geez!"

When Bobble Drew and I got together, it was all very sensual, spontaneous, and extraordinarily joyous! He was easy to be around. We surely had fun. The *"Feelin' Groovy"* kind of fun! (Gee, so *60s of me.)*

On another escapade, he came to visit me at my house, and we walked to the park by my house blowing bubble wands. We went on the swings and slides. We acted like children! But who was acting? Drew was a phenomenon. Amazing that such a dignified, prestigious man could be so in touch with his playful child within. For dinner, we made extra-long pasta with Bolognese sauce from scratch. We fed each other blindfolded, which was hilarious and immature. However, we wound up wearing most of the pasta. Later, we sat at the kitchen table making each other's private parts with Play-Doh. Yes, we did! His creation was so much better. Mine looked like a mushroom snake. Even more embarrassing, I saved them.

Lying together in my bed, I smiled as I watched him sleep like a little boy. I was completely in love with Drew, every part of him, and everything about him. I was even in love with the *'Oh So Very Busy'* parts and patiently waited for some of his time. I refused to find any fault with him. Gosh, I barely recognized myself. This newly emerging, infatuated girl was somewhat foreign to me and highly unfamiliar. And I wasn't sure if I liked her, either. (Seriously, where's Mollie? Where did Mollie go?)

Perhaps I was sinking into denial and looking through romantic eyes. Still, I chose only acceptance, for Drew made me happy. I was happy all the time. Genuinely happy! It was "The Greatest Love of All!"

After Drew left my house the next day, he wrote:

"Impossible, improbable, inevitable…
We meet, we fall in love, and we journey together as one…
I love my angel! XXXOOO."

Deep gasp, I couldn't be more in love with Bobble Drew.
For the first time, I could see forever, even if I was looking through idealistic eyes!
Being with this man made an indelible stamp on my heart…
Just like a forever tattoo.

But still, I couldn't understand why I was feeling so completely off guard and uneasy. I was blissful and yet frightened at the same time.

Sadly, I didn't understand why?

CHAPTER 21
Bobble Drew
Part 2

YOU BROKE MY HEART!
AGONIZING AND EXCRUCIATING HEARTACHE...
AKA... OUCH, THE PAIN!

CONTINUING THE DREW ADVENTURE...

Everything about our relationship for 4 months was flawless and picture-perfect. But then, the 5th month arrived.

I left on a 4-week correspondents tour to report on several World News events and political assignments. Drew knew about this lengthy tour from the very beginning. He explained, "Baby, of course, that's your job." He acknowledged, "I completely understand. No worries honey, it's fine!"

Except, it wasn't fine. It wasn't fine at all, and I was worried! While on tour, the calls came less frequently, and he didn't call all that often to begin with. When we spoke, he sounded cold and not at all like, 'us.' Further devastating, he canceled several trips where he planned to join me. He seemed distant. Things were rapidly changing for the worse and I couldn't imagine why. I kept going

over in my mind what I could do to stop our relationship from spiraling downward. I worried obsessively, which distracted me from
my work. I couldn't fathom what was happening to us. Being so in
love with Drew and desperately missing him was unsettling and
caused me to behave unprofessionally. When we did rarely speak, he
continuously repeated, "Everything is fine, baby. You're reading it
all wrong. I'm just, *Oh, So Very Busy!*" I had no choice but to accept
his weak, tired answer and be patient. I thought about cutting my
tour short but, thank goodness, I quickly came to my senses. I'm a
journalist with a respectable reputation, and this wasn't an emergency that could justify my stopping the presses. I was certain of
one thing. Bobble Drew was surely not pining away over me and
obviously not disrupting his work with thoughts of us. I let it go.
This *'drama zone'* wasn't a good place to visit at length. Especially
on the phone, having been apart for so long.

This was the most disappointing chapter of my life. At least,
up to now. (Little did I know?) I realized our love was rapidly free-
falling and plummeting downhill. I searched for a parachute to save
us, but it seemed hopeless. Tragically, I was not prepared or close to
being fine with the thought of losing him. My heart was bleeding. I
frantically needed some answers to the "Why, factor?" Also known
as the *"Whaaaat the Fuck Happened, Factor?"* We never fought, so I
was confused, upset, and bewildered that he was ghosting me. Was
our relationship over? Or what?

Someone once said, "Nothing in life is as bad as it seems right
now." Aha! Such BS! Obviously, this person never had to cope with
getting over a great love, with no reason why something perfect
and beautiful ended so abruptly! Had Drew-in-the-box met another
girl? Yet realistically, what we shared was rare and didn't just happen all the time!

Did he fall out of love? But how could that happen so easily? Did he fake it when he said he loved me? If so bravo, and a stunning *Academy Award performance!* I had a birthday. Is that why Bobble Drew vanished?

Six months later (right after my tour ended) I visited Drew in Boston. I felt his detachment at once when he picked me up at the airport and he didn't pick me up in his arms for the first time. *Flag! Flag! Ouch! An icy, aloof, monumental flag there!* Not a good sign, but I let it go. Our first night together and he was too tired to make love? Um, *Ok, like what?* Flag! Flag! Double-red flag. Ouch and a flapping, waving, no-sex flag!

For starters, let me back up a moment to explain why I affectionately call the man "Bobble Drew" and "Drew-in-the-Box." The following day, he gave me a present. No baby blue box with a white satin bow, this time. He gave me a plain, unwrapped, white box. But please, don't misunderstand. There's nothing wrong with a plain, white, unwrapped box. Except, a plain box was never his thing! OK, NBD, no biggie, I thought, at the time. A gift is a gift. All gifts don't have to come from Tiffany's, although, (I might add) a lovely gesture. Anyway, it's the thought that counts. However, this style of giving a gift was so random for him. Regardless, I excitedly ripped open the plain, white box, with no white satin bow. Inside was a ceramic Bobblehead of Drew that he had made of himself. No, you read that correctly. Inside was a ceramic Bobblehead of Drew! As much as I loved him (And I did!) still, what the hell was I going to do with this? *"Ahhhhh?!"* *It* was all I could say to him after opening his gift. Note that the end of my *"Ahhhhh,"* was gasped out loud in a high-pitched voice. I repeated it for effect, not knowing what else to say, trying to fill the awkward silence. *"Ahhh?!"* I knew right then and there I was in trouble. What I didn't know was what I did to get into trouble. This was no longer my paranoid imagination. Like a girl, madly in love, I looked the other way (Far, far, away). So, I put the Bobble Drew on my dresser and smiled each time I passed by it. Though my smile was only a crooked one, it was still a smile. After the trip, my love text me this.

"Shot in my arm when I see you!"

Ouch, disappointing, Ok, and Ahhh? Then came this comment.

"Darling, you melt my heart. Good thing I'm not made of Velveeta. Love you!"

Umm, Ok? Kind of cute? *Ahhh-Ish?* I was officially dumbfounded!

On the next visit to see Bobble Drew, he had another gift for me in a plain, white box with no white satin bow. Understandably, this time I was hesitant and too apprehensive to open it.

"Go ahead, open it," he quipped eagerly! Inside the plain white box was an old-style tin box. With glee, he urged, "Go on and rotate the handle. Go on!" The music that played was the same old-fashioned, scary, Jack-in-the-box, clown music. Only this time, it looked and sounded scarier, like the "Joker" film! Oh, Lord, I hesitate to tell you *love hopefuls* about this, but here goes. This time, bursting out was not a clown-in-the-box, but a *Drew-in-the-Box!* An exact image of Drew popped out. Not to be crass, but if it were a replica of his dick-in-a-box popping out, it could be funny, darling even. I searched inside, hoping to see if he had attached a diamond ring on the *'Drew-thing'* to propose marriage in a fun way. But no, it was just a Drew-in-the-Box! What the hell was I going to do with this? I put the weird box on my dresser. I make a crooked smile each time I passed by it. After the Bobble Drew-in-the-Box trip, this text arrived.

"Thinking of you with waves of warmth and tons of love!"

Then came: "I feel you when I meditate."

Then at last came: "I have your phone cord."

Crash! Total mic-drop, along with my heart that just exploded into a million fragmented pieces! OMG, I lost him. What happened? How did I lose him? Come on, I even faked excitement over those strange, *"What the fuck will I do with these Drew-in-the-Box and Bobblehead gifts?"*

Following the Bobble & Box visits, Drew canceled 4 trips in a row at the very last minute. How could this love affair be over when I was still so hopelessly in love with him? What changed? Let's be honest, I didn't give him some weird "Mollie-Bobble-head" or the "Mollie-in-the-box" crazy presents. I simply went away on assignment. I felt like I was reading a novel with 20 chapters (12 through 32) ripped out of the book. I was dying inside with no resolutions. When I asked him what was going on, he avoided talking about it. "Nothing's going on!" His insensitive silence was screaming at me and hurting my ears. It was unlike him and so painfully callous how he ignored me. Where did Drew go? Still, my pride would not allow me to beg for answers. Having no other choice, I walked away.

And there you have it. After 6 1/2 months of blissful love, total joy, and endless promises of marriage and forever, it was over! I felt like I had been on enormous quantities of *"love heroine"* and now I was forced to go through agonizing withdrawal and detox, cold turkey. Sadly, I knew the instant Drew said, "Don't hurt me," I'd be the one left alone, hurt, and devastated wearing a Vera wedding gown. I thank God, I didn't buy it!

After all our words of undying love and adoration, his guarantees of forever, and the romantic times we spent together, were now over! His bogus, deceitful words pledging, "You are the love of my life," "I can't live without you," and relentlessly touting, "I have to marry you, and we will have many weddings," were all mysteriously broken. After all we shared and experienced, the, I love you more than life itself, soul mate conversations, the lovely gifts, limos, pillow talk, and vows of endless, everlasting love had disappeared. Alas, I didn't know why this happened.

It was like the projector in a movie broke 75% through the film, or a fade-out after watching a movie for 2-hours, leaving the audience with no ending. All the while I was basking in my 7th heaven utopia, with lovely delusions of forever. To him, we were nothing more than a little dalliance.

He became so cold. Cold like a fudge pop from the back of the freezer! To describe the end of this love affair in one song, (thanks to Miley Cyrus) it would be, *"Wrecking Ball,"* with a massive question mark? Sadly, those spot-on lyrics describe exactly what I had gone through in the grand finale of this relationship, and now my personal story of love lost. In a conciliatory approach, I'll forever ask, "Why did we break up?" I don't have the slightest clue! Why couldn't he man up and give me an explanation? I never received the closure I desperately needed! Did he lie? Was he still married? Did he just fall out of love? Oh, and ladies, I'm sure you've all gone through this and felt the same way, too!

Gee, did Greg Behrendt and Liz Tuccillo have it right all along? *"He just wasn't that into me?"*

I guess "All That Glitters Isn't Gold?"

This breakup was earth-shattering. Drew broke my heart,

leaving me distraught. I was sad, reeling in pain and agony for months until I became numb. I really believed the search for my beloved Romeo was over. I learned after this shocking blow, never again to hang my hat on promises given that are only meant as a false sense of security. Learn from me, people! Judge your feelings of love with your mind, not only with your heart. Or you too might be greeted with a big plate of anguish and an in-your-face heart-break! Of course, this all led to major stress eating!

"The Sayers" predict "It takes half the time you dated someone to get over them." FYI, this is ridiculous nonsense! It could take forever.

I wanted to talk it over and express my pain with Drew. I'm sure it would not have mattered. He silently threw us away with no kindness or clarification. The hardest part was I didn't understand why? Which only prolonged my agony and recovery. I trusted all his poetic words of eternal love and commitment. So then why? Dammit, I knew this would happen!

A million times, I wanted to call him up and demand, "What's wrong with you? You can't profess the world's greatest love for a woman and then just walk away without any explanation. Drew, you're heartless." Then I'd make my grand hang-up exit. Grinning and thinking, now that's going to fester! At least in my innocent mind, I assumed it would.

I thought it best to keep my dignity. I never spoke to him again. I could not allow myself to beg, grovel, or call him up crying. What good would it do, anyway? Whatever the reason, I accepted it. Drew's cruel and ambiguous way of ending our perfect liaison left me in dire need of Emergency Dating Life Support. I needed *Courting Survival CPR!* My poor heart was attacked, and I required a love defibrillation or a quadruple love bypass. And stat! I was left saturated in lovesick depression!

Bobble Drew showed a personality to equivocate and make promises he had no intention of fulfilling. And, man, did I ever fall for it! After all his chatter and delicate dance of seduction and denial, "And just like that, I was *alone again!*" I sat solo that night listening to the pouring rain and recognized, **"Girl, *You Got Maled!*"** I wondered if I'd ever get over the dick-in-the-box who slaughtered and destroyed my heart. I learned emotional abuse is truly the worst form of abuse. *Big teardrops.*

I wanted to hate him, but I couldn't, and I never would. Getting over him and finding a way to stop loving him was an uphill battle. (And let me tell you, it's not easy climbing in high heels!) Unfortunately for me, there was something about him that sticks! In the illustrious, soulful words of Bob Marley, *"The truth is, everyone, is going to hurt you. You just have to find the ones worth suffering for!"* And *"The biggest coward is a man who awakens a woman's love with no intention of loving her."* True, Bob!

Regardless, this beautiful affair, which I fondly call a *"Love-ette,"* is best described as one of the most unforgettable and exciting chapters of my life. Sensibly, I came to understand it wasn't healthy to linger very long in unrequited love. I had to get over him. Moreover, I realized all this sorrow would cause premature frown lines and wrinkles. I say to hell with that ghastly outcome. Thus, it was imperative to regain my confidence and my unique *'je ne sais quoi.'* I did everything in my power to march on. And, thanks Miley Cyrus, your song, "Flowers" helped me to do just that!

The Big Takeaway...
I opened my heart and soul, and they were crushed.
But, Guess What? I Had the Time of My Life!

Drew was a great love who remains forever in my heart.
Regrets are a waste of time.
They are the past paralyzing your present.

Still, though, I will sadly never understand why...

Oh, and by the way Drew,
I want my naked photographs back!

OMG... IT'S NOT OVER YET!

Wait, Hold On! There's More!

DON'T WORRY!
The continuation of Mollie Sloan's
nonstop search for love is in bookstores,
Right Now!

So, fear not, all you devoted seekers of love.
There is much, much more to come in...
You Got Maled!

Volume 2!

You cannot even begin to believe or imagine what is going to happen to our romantic, love-seeking girl, Mollie Sloan, in her ongoing search for, "The One!"

"You Got Maled!" was merely a dress rehearsal. A caravan of men, and all the wild and crazy, head-shaking predicaments in store for Mollie will keep you giggling and feeling dreamy, enchanted, sexual, shocked, and on the edge of your seat. You will not be able to turn the pages fast enough. Without a doubt, book one will look like a fairytale compared to all the insanity in, *"You Got Maled! Volume 2!"*

You can look forward to reading about a sea of men, nonstop dramas, hysterically funny stories, galas, fashion, lots of travel, and close friendships. You'll also enjoy endless, ridiculous dating situations you will surely relate to and most likely have endured yourself!

Such new and exciting dating experiences in Mollie's future include:

The Rock Star (Rocket-Man) who is more famous than Elton John. Justin, The Beverly Hills Plastic Surgeon. Plus, Nikolai the Russian. And let's not forget Cameron, the high school drama teacher trapped in the 60's. You will read about lots of random playas, as well as the Pool of Bad Men, just to name a few. Furthermore, you'll meet some really, lovely men too.

Of course, Mollie and her adorable, spirited, and feisty friends will all be back to play their part in Volume 2. You can count on Mollie continuing to share her endless hilarious tales of dating in her own language and style. She holds back nothing. And I mean nothing! So, hold on to your hats. Remember, she is a reporter who never buries the lead.

Fear not, readers. Mollie Sloan will be there holding your hand every step as she continues to guide, support, comfort, and pave a smoother road to help in your search for "The One!" Our energetic journalist, as always, offers her advice, knowledge, and directions to follow reassuring "You Are Not Alone" and warning you to pay attention to all red flags!

Gosh, who knows? Will our lovely *Mollie Sloan* find "The One" and enjoy her own, Happily, Ever After?

READ ON...

You Got Maled!

Volume 2!

Wait, Hold On!

There's *SO* Much More!

Epilogue

P.S. IT'S COMEDY PEOPLE!

In Summation...

If I offended any race, creed, color, sexual preference, religion, or anyone else by my usage of bad or sexual language, music or film preference, political views, opinions on people, men, handicapped situations, illness, or any other position which I might have upset or insulted any of you...

"It's Comedy, People!?!!?!"

All joking aside and to be perfectly honest, please understand... Everything said in this book that might have appeared to be mean or politically incorrect, was only meant to be humorous, amusing, comforting, and basically intended for the purpose of entertainment and fun. So please, don't be put off or offended.

Laughter is better than crying.

P.S.S. Those of you who went online and found your love quickly and easily, appreciate you were blessed, and your stars were very lucky ones!

About the Author

Robin Roth is an accomplished professional singer, comedian, and entertainer. This consummate performer has been described as "The Singer Extraordinaire with a Comedic Flair." She has performed her versatile one-woman show, "The Ultimate Entertainer" to sold-out crowds around the world. Robin can also be seen in her many acting performances and roles on commercials, television, stage, and in movies.

Ms. Roth has also enjoyed an illustrious, successful career in journalism. As a distinguished reporter, photographer, and writer, she has interviewed and photographed just about everybody who is anybody. Furthermore, she is a notable photographer for some of the biggest photo agencies.

Robin writes and shoots for prominent magazines and major Cable News Networks. She has photographed and interviewed six presidents as well as other prominent political figures, and famous A-list stars. These include… Actors, singing artists, bands, all-star athletes & teams, business figures, and well-known personalities and celebrities of the world.

Robin Roth is also a very proud and loving mother of two girls.

Look For Robin's Other Books...
"You Got Maled!" VOLUME 2
and
"Heart to Bump Conversations"
They Are NOW in stores everywhere!

You can also, CHECK OUT ROBIN'S TWO WEBSITES:
Robinrothreporter.com
Robinrothentertainer.net